Advances in Human Factors/Ergonomics, 13

# Designing User Interfaces for International Use

**Advances in Human Factors/Ergonomics**

Series Editor: Gavriel Salvendy, Purdue University, West Lafayette, IN 47907, U.S.A.

---

Advances in Human Factors/Ergonomics, 13

# Designing User Interfaces for International Use

Edited by

**Jakob Nielsen**
Technical University of Denmark, Lyngby, Denmark

ELSEVIER

Amsterdam–Oxford–New York–Tokyo 1990

ELSEVIER SCIENCE PUBLISHERS B.V.
Sara Burgerhartstraat 25
P.O. Box 211, 1000 AE Amsterdam, The Netherlands

*Distributors for the United States and Canada:*

ELSEVIER SCIENCE PUBLISHING COMPANY INC.
655 Avenue of the Americas
New York, NY 10010, U.S.A.

ISBN 0-444-88428-9 (Vol. 13)



Printed in The Netherlands

# Preface

International user interfaces are those which are intended for use in more than one country. Designing international user interfaces may or may not involve translation, but it should certainly involve consideration of the special needs of other countries and cultures. Increasing technological sophistication in many countries of the world and the resulting larger world trade implies greater need to pay attention to international aspects of user interfaces. Many American companies are approaching a situation where half their sales are outside the U.S., and companies in smaller countries often have a much larger proportion of their sales outside their own country. Viewed from the vendor perspective, this means that software sales will increasingly depend on the international usability of products and not just the domestic usability. And seen from a user perspective, we will end up having more than half the of the world's software users using interfaces which were originally designed in a foreign country. Usability for this large number of users will depend upon having increased awareness of the issues in designing user interfaces for international use.

Increased importance of the non-U.S. markets can be expected from German reunification and the emergence of market economies in Eastern Europe. As the European Community aims to establish the so-called Single Market by the end of 1992, international software will become even more important in that part of the world with the growth of cross-frontier trade and with more companies going multi-national. It is important to realize, however, that the Single Market will not be a "single" market in the sense that all Europeans can be treated the same after 1992. The language differences will not go away and the cultural differences between the regions will also remain. So "1992" will actually increase the need to pay attention to the issues discussed in this book.

There are lots of issues in the design of user interfaces for international use. The book starts with a discussion of some of the general issues by del Galdo. Ossner then goes into more detail with the specific issues concerning the use of icons. This is followed by a chapter by Nielsen on usability testing of international interfaces with examples from tests of the initial (poor) Danish translation of the Macintosh.

The next several chapters present case studies. First, del Galdo describes the usability testing of three manuals from Digital. Sprung then draws upon his consulting experience in the United States with its trend to isolationist attitudes in some designs. Peterson describes the efforts started by one American company to redesign its user interface for the international market, and Baird gives a case study of a hypertext system.

With respect to practical computer support for international user interfaces, Taylor first gives a detailed example of the use of Hewlett-Packard's Native Language Support System. Nielsen then follows with a chapter showing that also a small company programming administrative applications in Cobol may use a technological approach to help solve the internalization issue.

As if it wasn't hard enough to design user interfaces for use in Europe, there are a further set of problems connected with user interfaces for Asia. They are discussed by Sukaviriya and Moran in a general chapter about the wide spectrum of countries, cultures, languages and character styles in Asia. Zobel-Pocock follows up with a case study of converting UNIX System V for Japan.

The reader should note that the author of the chapter *International User Interface for INFOFLEX* and the editor of the book (and author of the chapter *Usability Testing of International Interfaces*) are two different people, even though both are named Jakob Nielsen. Jakob Peter Nielsen (author of the chapter *International User Interface for INFOFLEX*) is with Data Reforming while Jakob Nielsen (editor and author of the chapter *Usability Testing of International Interfaces*) is with the Technical University of Denmark.

The fact that two authors can have the same name is yet another example of the problems in international user interfaces. The population in many countries have a large variation in their family names and the practice has therefore developed of referring to people by their initials and family name only. In Denmark, however, a very large proportion of the population share a few, traditional, family names. The three most popular names (Jensen, Nielsen, and Hansen) account for approximately 25% of the Danes.

Because of this phenomenon, initials plus family name is not sufficient to specify a person in Denmark. For example, there are six staff members named "J. Nielsen" at the Technical University of Denmark and several letters and fax messages from abroad have been routed to the wrong person because they did not include the full first name.

An additional example showing the clash of cultures in the naming situation occurred once with a letter I received from France. The French often use "M." as a form of address (as an abbreviation of *Monsieur*) and the letter was therefore addressed to `M. Nielsen`. Because so many Danes are named Nielsen, there happened to be a person named Mogens Nielsen on the faculty and our mail room naturally routed the letter to him. Luckily his field is very far from user interface design so he immediately understood that the letter could not have been intended for him and passed it on to me.

This naming problem can have an impact on the design of computer systems since it means that systems sold in Denmark should be able to write the full name of people in the address field on envelopes etc. Some simplistic designs from other countries may have an "initials-only" assumption hardwired into them at a level where no traditional translation can change them.

There are an endless number of problems like that. It is impossible for this book to enumerate them all but it can stress the need for flexibility and for being open in observing the needs of other countries and cultures. We *do* give basic advice, including a set of general guidelines to follow, technical information about how to store the user interface separate from the code to facilitate translation without recompilation, and the advice to conduct usability tests of translated interfaces.

*Jakob Nielsen*
Copenhagen, February 1990

# Contributors

**Patricia Baird**
Strathclyde Business School
Department of Information Science
26 Richmond Street
Glasgow, G1 1XH
United Kingdom

**Elisa del Galdo**
Digital Equipment Co. Ltd.
Worton Grange Industrial Estate
Imperial Way
Reading RG2 0TU
United Kingdom

**Lucy Moran**
The George Washington University
Department of Electrical Engineering
and Computer Science
Washington, DC 20052
USA

**Jakob Nielsen**
Technical University of Denmark
Department of Computer Science
DK-2800 Lyngby Copenhagen
Denmark

**Jakob Peter Nielsen**
Data Reforming
Linnésgade 12
DK-1361 Copenhagen K
Denmark

**Jakob Ossner**
Pedagogical Institute of Heidelberg
Keplerstraße 87
D-6900 Heidelberg
West Germany

**Matthew C. Peterson**
Affiliation when writing the chapter:
Sigma Design Inc.
Current affiliation:
Eidolon Enterprises
PO Box 20451
Englewood, CO 80156
USA

**Robert C. Sprung**
Harvard Translations
17 Arlington Street
Boston, MA 02116
USA

**Piyawadee 'Noi' Sukaviriya**
The George Washington University
Department of Electrical Engineering
and Computer Science
Washington, DC 20052
USA

**Dave Taylor**
Intuitive Systems
201 Ada Street, Suite 41
Mountain View, CA 94043
USA

**Rosalie Zobel-Pocock**
Commission of the European
Communities
Directorate-General XIII
Rue de la Loi 200
B-1049 Bruxelles
Belgium

# Table of Contents

*Designing User Interfaces for International Use*, edited by J. Nielsen
Elsevier, 1990



# INTERNATIONALIZATION AND TRANSLATION

## Some Guidelines for the Design of Human – Computer Interfaces

**Elisa del Galdo**

Digital Equipment Corporation, Reading, United Kingdom

### 1.0 INTRODUCTION

When designing a software product for an international market, the designer must consider both the form of the system and its function. The form of the system is its user interface and the manner in which the user must interact with the system. The function or functions of the system are the capabilities of the system. The capabilities discussed in this Chapter refer only to those that are included to enable the system to be international within European, British, and North American markets unless stated otherwise.

In order for a software product to be translated, the necessary capabilities of the system may include, handling of multinational character sets, various collating sequences, ability to display international date and time formats, and presenting text for right to left or vertical languages. An international product does not necessarily have to be translated, but its interface must take into account the varieties of text and data display, local conventions, and cultural differences for graphic representation of icons and symbols in order to be acceptable for an international market. This Chapter mainly addresses the affect that internationlization has on the form of the user interface or software applications and designing interfaces that facilitate their own translation.

Many English language products are not produced with problems of translation in mind or the effect that differences in culture and language have on the usability of software interfaces. Making an interface suitable for international users or 'international' requires incorporating the ability to vary the representation of text and data to conform to conventions of language and locality. Producing products that are suitable for translation, in addition to being suitable for an international audience, requires that allowances for modification to the user interface text,
on-line graphics, and technical components be designed into the underlying mechanisms of the product from its conception.

Very often the task of translating a product's interface or making the interface suitable for international markets is not taken into consideration until after the product has been finalized in its original language version. By not taking these issues of translation and local conventions into consideration early in the design stage of the product, much time and money can be wasted. To effectively and efficiently make a product international these issues must be considered from the time of the products conception. The design of the product must include requirements and product testing must be performed with users from various cultures.

## 2.0 Cultural Differences and Local Conventions

The format and presentation of many classes of common data and text vary from country to country, not just by language. This means that, although Belgium, France, and Switzerland use the French language, their local conventions may differ significantly. In addition, in countries such as Switzerland where three different languages are spoken (French, German, and Italian) depending on the geographic region, local conventions and language differ within a single country. When designing formats for data and text, the same format should be used for both the input of the information and its display. If the format must change, due to local conventions, it should change for both the input of information and its display. In general, do not make formats dependent upon other features of your application or dependent upon each other. There are some cases were there may be a dependency between formats, for example, currency and numeric format both use a separator for units of thousands and a decimal. For consistency, the thousands and decimal separators for these components (currency and numeric format) should be identical. A selection of components affected by culture, language, and local conventions is detailed in the following sections.

## 2.1 Character Sets

There are many different character sets in existence. Normally a character set covers only one language or group of languages. For example, Semitic languages, such as Arabic and Hebrew, and languages which are based on the Latin alphabet, such as, French, Spanish, and Italian. In addition, most European languages contain a variety of characters with diacriticals (a sign used to indicate that a letter has particular sound), such as 'å, à, ö, ì, or ç'. When designing your application, you should allow for the display and input of all character sets of the countries in which you wish to market your applications.

## 2.2 Collating Sequences

Whenever printable characters need to be sorted with respect to other printable characters, to produce an alphabetic or alphanumeric list, they are sorted according to a collating sequence. Printable characters include letters, numbers, punctuation characters, characters with diacriticals, and other symbols such as asterisks (*) and ampersands (&). The collating sequence defines the value and position of each character relative to other characters.

Many applications make frequent use of collating sequences to produce alphanumeric lists. For example, a directory listing of file names, an address or telephone directory, or the output from a sort utility. If your application contains sorting functions, it must be flexible enough to accommodate individual country specific collating sequences.

Figure 1 displays three different collating sequences, English German and Swedish, which are composed of various sets of characters sorted differently. In addition to containing different characters in different sequences, characters identical to the German and Swedish sequences are not sorted using the same rules. In the German collating sequence, letters with umlauts, a diacritical, (ä,ö, ü) are collated as the same letters without umlauts (a, o, u). In contrast, the Swedish collating sequence sorts the 'ü' the same as a 'y' and places other characters with diacriticals at the end of the sequence.

There are many different rules associated with each country collating sequence as to how characters are sorted, the sorting of diacriticals, and the sorting of proper nouns. Two character strings, such as ll in Spanish are treated as a single character, some characters with diacriticals, such as å, can be treated as a single character or as two letters (aa) depending on how it is pronounced. In German some characters are treated as equals, when sorting proper nouns ä=ae, ö=oe, and ü=ue. This is useful for a German telephone directory when trying to locate names such as, Mueller which could also be spelled as Müller, but is pronounced the same.

Country Collating Sequences

| English | German | Swedish |
|---|---|---|
| aA | aAäÄ | aA |
| bB | bB | bB |
| cC | cC | cC |
| dD | dD | dD |
| eE | eE | eE |
| fF | fF | fF |
| gG | gG | gG |
| hH | hH | hH |
| iI | iI | iI |
| jJ | jJ | jJ |
| kK | kK | kK |
| lL | lL | lL |
| mM | mM | mM |
| nN | nN | nM |
| oO | oOöÖ | oO |
| pP | pP | pP |
| qQ | qQ | qQ |
| rR | rR | rR |
| sS | sS | sS |
| tT | ß | tT |
| uU | tT | uU |
| vV | uUüÜ | vV |
| wW | vV | wW |
| xX | wW | xX |
| yY | xX | yY ü Ü |
| zZ | yY | zZ |
| | zZ | åÅ |
| | | äÄ |
| | | öÖ |

Figure 1 Country Collating Sequences

## 2.3 Numeric Formats

Depending on language and local convention, the format in which numbers are presented will vary and can cause confusion. In Europe, frequently the character period (.) is used as a separator for units of thousands and a character similar to a common (,) is used as a decimal point, as opposed to North America and the United Kingdom which use the reverse convention. For separating units of thousands, allow for the use of a comma, period, space and apostrophe. Also allow for the use of no separator. For separating decimal fractions, allow a period, a comma, and a center dot. If the user has the ability to interactively select separators, safeguards should be included in your application to prevent the selection of identical characters for thousands and decimal separators. For indicating positive and negative values, allow the plus (+) and minus (-) signs to appear before or after the number and in any combination. Also allow for the indication of a negative number by enclosing it in parentheses.

## 2.4 Date Format

When displaying the date in either numeric or alphanumeric characters it is necessary to allow for three sequences of date; month-day-year, day-month-year, year-month-day. Input and output displays should always be identical in sequence. If an application will have an audience of more than one nationality, for example information kiosks in airports or trains stations, use only alphanumeric characters for the display of month to avoid confusion caused by the various conventions of date formats. Separators for day, month, and year should allow for a hyphen, comma, period, space, backslash, or no separator. Separators between each component of the date should be variable. Lengths of month names and abbreviations will vary from language to language.

## 2.5 Currency Format

Currency formats differ among countries. To account for country and language differences allow for the following conventions.

- o The use of a comma, period, colon, or currency symbol as a decimal separator.
- o The choice of thousands separators as described in the section Numeric Formats.
- o The currency symbol to be placed before or after the numerical value and to be used as a decimal separator.
- o One space or no space between the currency symbol and the numeric amount.

The currency symbol can be up to four characters long, and varies within and among countries.

## 2.6 Time Format

Applications that display time should allow both 12 and 24 hour clock notation. For time format, the hour, minutes, and seconds components must always appear in that order. Allow the use of a colon, period, space and no separator as valid separators. A 'no separator' option should only be valid when a 24 hour clock notation is in use and when only hours and minutes are displayed.

The display of time zone for international and translated applications must use either the full name of the time zone on a notation of time indicating the variation from the Greenwich Meridian or Greenwich Mean Time (GMT). Local time vary throughout the world by as much as -12 hours (west of the Meridian) and by as much as +13 hours (east of the Meridian). The more popular alphabetic codes such as, PST, EST, and CET should not be used.

## 2.7 Telephones Numbers

The format for telephone number varies from country to country. Telephone numbers can be between 5 and 21 digits in length, and they often include special characters to separate different components. Also, numbers are sometimes displayed differently according to whether they are for international or national use. The space, hyphen, period, comma, square brackets, parentheses, and plus sign are all valid separators. For national numbers, any separator can occur, so it is advisable to design for arbitrary formats.

## 3.0 Design of Software Interface

The following section gives details of the more graphic aspects of the user interface that can affect or be affected by translation or the suitability of a product for internal markets. The recommendations presented can be applied to products that are intended for translation and those that are intended for an international audience without translation.

## 3.1 Icons and Symbols

The terms symbols and icons are sometimes used interchangeably in the computer software industry. The differences between icons and symbols is not the medium they are presented on or with, (i.e. icons are usually seen on-line, and symbols are usually associated with signs or labels on hardware) but the message that they are meant to convey to a user. An icon is an image or a likeness of a person, place or thing. For example, an icon of a pen and paper can be used to represent a word processing system. A symbol is used more commonly to suggest something, and is often a more abstract representation. For example a 'do not enter' symbol (as red circle with a white horizontal bar across the middle) is a fairly abstract representation. With the more frequent use of icons and symbols, and the introduction of direct manipulation interfaces, the definition of the two becomes more and more overlapped. Throughout this section, most recommendations apply to the design of both icons and symbols. The recommendations presented are not intended to constrain or duplicate the artistic knowledge required to produce suitable icons or symbols.

When designing or selecting existing icons, the culture of the user population for your product must be considered. Care must be taken to design an icon or symbol that adequately represents an object or function internationally. Culture is inherent, even in the design of a seemingly universal icons. For example, sending and receiving mail is a fairly international activity, but representing a system that provides this activity with an icon of a mailbox turns out to be inappropriate. The icon of a mailbox is not suitable because the appearance and shape of a mailbox or letterbox varies greatly from country to country. A more appropriate icon for this type of activity would be the representation of an envelope, which is familiar internationally.

The use of icons which are designed to be language and culture independent can increase the usability of an application across international markets. To facilitate this, icons should not contain any text or culture specific graphics. When designing icons or symbols, check international standards to ensure that your designs do not conflict with local conventions or existing icons. If designs are based on a local convention, for example, adaptations of a road sign to create an icon for a software interface, ensure that conventions from the source country will carry across to an international market.

An example of a case where a local convention can not be used in another market is, the use of a cocktail glass icon in a calendar application to signify after-work appointments. This icon would not be appropriate in countries where alcohol is not associated with social activities. Another example of an unsuitable symbol that has two different meanings depending on culture, is the use of a black cat as a symbol for luck. In the United States a black cat is often associated with bad luck, but in the United Kingdom, a black cat is considered good luck.

A set of guidelines for the design of icons and symbols for an international market follows.

- Designs of icons and symbols should be simple.

- The icon or symbol should be repesentative or symbolize the necessary action, or object.

- Always check international standards for symbols and icons to ensure that you use exisiting internationally recognized icons, and to ensure that you do not give a different or inconsistent meaning to a similar or existing icon.

- Avoid using text with icons. Text within an icons will be difficult to translate on a one to one basis from the original language to another language (i.e. the same amount of words or letters). Therefore, translations that will fit in the same amount of allocated space may be very difficult to achieve. The advantage of designing icons with text is that it can increase the usability of the icon. The advantage to having (usability) and not having (ease of translation) text within or accompanying an icon may shift depending on the intended market for the product. If the text is scientific notation, in a language common to a profession, or greatly increases the usability of the system, the advantages of not having text may be outweighed by the advantages of including text with the icons.

- Design the icon or symbol with the entire intended market for the product in mind.

- Testing should cover suitability for all intended markets.

- Do not use culture specific icons, such as mailboxes.

## 3.2 The Use of Colour

The perception of colour is universal across international borders. However, be aware that colours have different connotations in different countries. For example, in North America a blue ribbon signifies the best or first in a given class, and a red ribbon signifies second. In the United Kingdom it is the opposite, a red ribbon signifies first and a blue ribbon signifies second. A teaching application for young children which uses a scheme of awarding coloured ribbons for performance, would have to be adapted for different markets. And as suggested previously, using symbols, which in this case are ribbons, may not span all cultures.

In addition to the symbolism of particular colours being different in various cultures, preferences for colours or combinations of colours may differ. The most visible examples of colour preferences varying based on market, is the alteration of packaging of consumer products from one culture to another. Products targeted for a female market in the Far East tend to use subtle or pastel colours on their packaging, as opposed to North America which tends to use brighter colours (Lamacraft, 1988).

## 3.3 Screen Text

By the introduction of direct manipulation interfaces the use of screen text has been reduced, but it has not been eliminated. There is a decrease in the use of screen text aids in the translation process of an interface, simply because there is less text to translate. The following is a set of general guidelines concerning the construction of text for the user interface that, if adhered to will facilitate its translation.

- o Avoid using acronyms and abbreviations. Acronyms and abbreviations are difficult to translate for several reasons. When translated, an acronym may no longer be as effective or as concise as in its original language. The acronym in its original language may have negative associations in a different language. Abbreviations that are not translated for users whose native tongue is not of the original language may not readily recognize or understand the abbreviation. Abbreviations of words, if being used to save space, may not decrease to the same number of letters in other languages or there may not be an abbreviation available. In addition both acronyms and abbreviations may cause confusion for the translator.

- o Do not use an over-friendly writing style in which the author addresses the reader in the first person or in a childish manner.

The over-friendly writing style can sometimes be considered to be condescending and irritating to other than English speaking countries. For example, the following instructions are in the over-friendly style.

> "Now that you have completed the installation of your new printer, you can perform a test to give you confidence with its use. Be sure to follow the sequence of tasks carefully."

The over-friendly style also has a tendency to become verbose. A decrease in word count, in addition to lessening the necessary amount of translation, can increase the clarity of the instructions. For example, a more concise way to express the previous instructions is,

> "After the installation is completed, perform the print test to ensure the printer is functioning and has been installed correctly."

- o Do not use culturally specific examples. Examples that include national games such as baseball (North American) or plays on words are not suitable for international markets. In addition, they are difficult to translate because the translator for each country must re-create the example so it is suitable for their particular language and culture.

- o Avoid references to national, racial, religious, sexist sterotypes and individuals of alternative lifestyles.

- o Avoid stringing three or more nouns together. Relationships between nouns become very explicit in other languages besides English and it is difficult to determine what terms are modifying on another. The use of prepositions, such as, at, in, by, and on, can help to clarify the relationship between nouns. For example, the noun string 'cable adapter number table' is confusing and unnecessarily verbose. An alternative construction is, 'table of cable adaptor numbers'. By using the second version, it is clear which nouns are used as modifiers.

- o Limit text in length where possible. Text translated from English into any other language may expand up to fifty percent.

- o Do not store separate sections of a message for assembly at time of output. The grammatical structure of languages differ. This must be allowed for at time of translation. Store the message as one entire sentence or construct the message such that the variable is not included directly in the message.

- o Avoid using complex terminology, or country specific computer jargon.

- o Always use consistent terminology throughout the interface and its documentation. Always use terms consistently to describe concepts, items or actions throughout the interface. If more than one term is used where only one is intended or needed, a wrong translation can occur. Translators may also assume that two translations are needed instead of one.

- o Avoid using a telegraphic style of writing. A telegraphic style of writing is when a terse style of writing is used. This is often found in on-line messages. Words such as, 'and', 'the' and 'is' are left out. It is easy for a translator to misinterpret or incorrectly translate messages or other screen text written in this style. Examples of the telegraphic style are messages such as 'insufficient privilege', and 'address unreachable'. These messages would be much clearer if they were rephrased as 'privilege is insufficient' and 'the address is unreachable'.

### 3.4 Menu Accelerators and their Documentation

This section concerns mostly menus and menu item accelerators for windowing or direct manipulation systems, frequently referred to as pulldown, pop-up or sub-menus. Although, some of the recommendations will carry over the other interface types. It is important to recognize that almost every country in Europe including the United Kingdom uses a different keyboard than those used in North America. These local or country keyboards have many different character positions, excluded characters, or additional characters. This can lead to problems when producing an international product or a product to be translated.

Mnemonic accelerators can cause problems when producing a product for international markets. Because mnemonics are based on the first letter or first few letters of the command or menu item name, it is necessary to translate the accelerators on the interface and in the accompanying documentation. In order for a translator to keep that mnemonic pattern of accelerators, it may be necessary to constrain the translation of a menu item or command in order to have menu item accelerators that do not overlap. If the mnemonic accelerators are not translated, as a measure of the convenience, then there is no longer a pattern to aid the user in remembering accelerator assignments.

An example of a problem that may arise is, the case where a person is using two different applications simultaneously through a windowing environment and one application is in English and the other is in French (i.e. there are several countries that are bilingual, such as Canada and Belgium). If both applications have a 'File' pulldown menu which includes the commands, Save and Exit (Sauver and Sortie in French). The mnemonic accelerators for these command in English would be '*S' for Save and '*E' for Exit. If the accelerator for Exit in the French application was '*S' (for Sortie), there would be a confusing overlap. An additional problem arises due to both commands in the French language beginning with the letter 'S'. The user may end up using four different accelerators for two commands or the same accelerator for two different commands.

Positional assignment of accelerators do not have to be translated in on-line and hardcopy documentation if their location on the keyboard is indicated, not on the keycap character. On several windowing products that include an Edit menu, the positional accelerators for the commands Cut, Copy, and Paste are *X, *C, *V (US keyboards) respectively. What is intended by the use of the character X, C, and V is that the accelerators for each command be positioned next to each other in the lower left-hand corner of the keyboard. Although the characters on the key caps will be different depending on the keyboard, the position of the accelerators will always be the same.

In order to not require translation, positional keys or accelerators should be documented by using a graphic illustration of the keyboard without any markings on the keycaps. If when representing the assignments of these accelerators, the on-line or hardcopy documentation refers only to their position on the keyboard (using a reference tag), the need for translation of the relevant characters for each country keyboard is unnecessary. On the other hand, the application must account for the fact that what is displayed on the on-line menu must be altered depending upon which keyboard is being used.

## 4.0 Summary

As presented in this chapter, when setting out to design a user interface for translation or introduction into an international market there are several aspects of the product's design that must be taken into consideration. The most important of the recommendations presented in this chapter is, to include the user interface requirements for an international or translatable product in the design of the product. This process will help to identify system capabilities necessary to make the product suitable for an international market. The user interface designer and the technical writer must also take into account possible tradeoffs between usability and the ease of translation. Finally, the use of interactive design methods, standard interface design guidelines, and good writing practices will not only help to create a quality product, but can also greatly facilitate the translation of the product and increase it acceptability for an international market.

## REFERENCES

Lamacraft, J. (1988). Graphics in 1992, Pack up your troubles. Design, 477, 36-38.

*Designing User Interfaces for International Use*, edited by J. Nielsen
Elsevier, 1990


# TRANSNATIONAL SYMBOLS

## The Rule of Pictograms and Models in the Learning Process

**Jakob Ossner**
Pedagogical Institute of Heidelberg, West Germany

### 1. THE PROBLEMS INVOLVED

In a developed society, learning is inseparably likely linked to the use of symbols. As a rule these are in the form of written records of knowledge or experience gained which are transferred to the learners by a teacher (or by a teacher as the author of a book used by other teachers as intermediaries). Depending on the situation, the teacher can adapt the learning medium to the learners' special requirements. The teacher functions as an informer, insofar as this is required above and beyond the learning medium, and as a kind of co-thinking and thus adaptable vademecum through the learning medium. This situation changes if the teacher ist replaced by a medium. In this case the learning media must be designed more explicitly, and their signpost functions, which are otherwise taken over by the teacher, must be reflected directly and integrated into the medium. Logically, however, the difference at the symbollevel between the item to be learnt (actual subject content) and the signpost to the item to be learnt (control function) should be retained. Here so-called iconic signs as used nowadays in complex environments especially in the transport sector (airports, stations etc.) or in hospitals are particularly useful.

The idea of iconic signs can be justified by a second consideration that results from a new project of the EC called DELTA (=Development of European Learning through Technological Advance). The idea of this project, a Europe-wide combined learning system depends heavily on transnational presentation possibilities. This means methods of presentation that do not have to be adapted to specific national or cultural backgrounds. Generally speaking, iconic signs rank as transnational signs. Graphics or animated films can be considered as complex systems of transnational signs which, as they do not reproduce reality photographically, can abstract themselves from individual cultural backgrounds. This will always mean a strong orientation towards the typical features of objects and their structures which is thus isolated from the particular context.

This paper intends to investigate:

- the nature of the iconic sign against the background of a general theory of signs. Particular emphasis is here to be placed on the transnational character of these signs. Within the terms of the theory of signs this means that the arbitrariness and conventionality of iconic signs must be discussed.
- The theoretical discussion will lead to a designation of iconic signs, particularly of pictograms, exemplified by common examples.

The same discussion will have to be held for complex signs, for which I shall be using terms taken from model theory.

- The background to the discussion of the two first points is provided by the question of the learnability of transnational signs.

This question must be extended by the explicit discussion of the role of non-arbitrary signs in the learning process. Here it is particularly important to determine the systematic position of iconic signs and models in the learning process.

- This question must once more be extended to deal with the question regarding the role of the iconic signs and models in CBT. Alongside questions of monitor design, the planes at which iconic signs and models can be used must be investigated: the device plane, the orientation plane in the field of learning processes, the content plane of the item to be learnt.

## 2. GENERAL THEORY OF SIGNS

### 2.1 THE DIMENSIONS OF THE SIGN

The concept *sign* is used ambiguously. Firstly, for a concrete object (an ink blot, a sound wave etc.), in which case the shape of the sign, the representamen, is meant. Secondly, as a two-stage relationship between expression and content (1) or as a three-stage relationship between representamen, the represented contend and the representing interpreter. What follows is based on this latter scientific, three-dimensional concept of signs developed by Peirce (2).

### 2.2 ICONIC, INDEXICAL AND SYMBOLIC SIGNS

In its relation to an object, a sign is either iconic, indexical or symbolic in nature.

As a *symbolic* sign it is associated with a content by convention. The relationship between representamen and content is arbitrary. In this sense all words of a phonographic document (see below) are symbolic (3).

*Indexical* is the term used by Peirce for those signs which, while indicating the represented content without any similarity, still exhibit a temporal or spatial relationship between representamen and content. Smoke, for instance, indicates fire. Alongside this direct relationship there is also an indirect one, such as in the case of the so-called indexical pronouns.

In what follows I shall be employing the term in a slightly different way, distinguishing between indexical signs with a natural meaning (4) (smoke as a sign for fire) and those with a symbolic meaning (as in the case of the pronouns).

Finally, iconic signs are related to the contents which they represent by their similarity, which means that elements of the content - anything from the concrete form to the abstract structure - will be found in the representamen. In this sense the concept *natural meaning* may also be applied here.

In contrast to symbolic signs, iconic signs are important in what follows. Indexical signs may be lumped together with iconic or symbolic signs depending whether they have natural or non-natural meanings.

An example to clarify matters. The backs of diskette sleeves often contain hints on correct handling of the diskettes along the lines of the following:

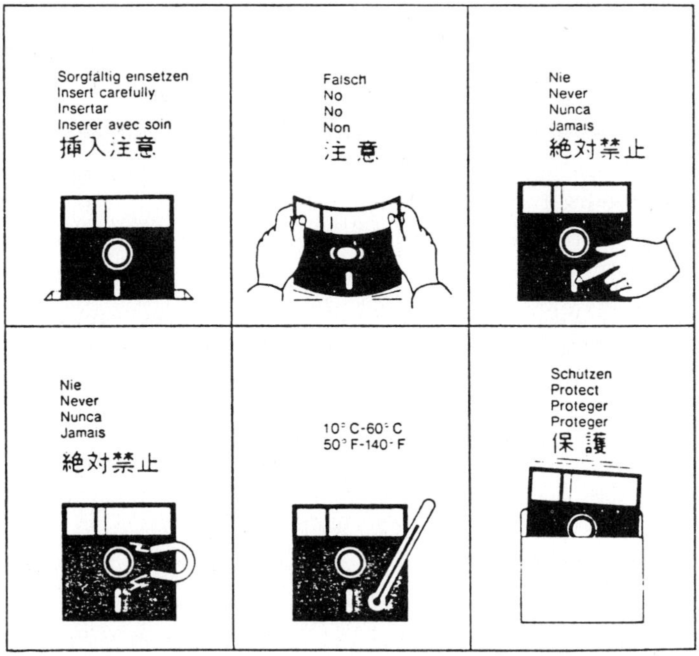

This is a mixture of symbolic and iconic signs. The instructions in the various languages are symbolic. The representation of the diskettes, of the process of bending, the finger pointing to the read/write opening, (5) the horseshoe magnet together with the jagged lines representing the effects of magnetism, the thermometer and, finally, the sleeve into which the diskette has been half inserted are iconic. The iconic signs employed are not used indexically here but have, without exception, the character of requests.

### 2.2.1 Phonographics versus logographics

Iconic signs can never be elements of a phonographic script, as their elements never exhibit similarities with the object represented. Iconic signs are elements of a logographic (ideographic) (6) system. The difference between a phonographic and a logographic system consists mainly in the fact that the elements of the former are meaningless in themselves, only fulfilling their task of representation when they are syntactically arranged in a conventional order. The units of a logographic system (called *radicals* in Chinese ideography) simultaneously represent meanings and are thus meaningful themselves.

Even if there are also iconic signs in a logographic system, this does not mean that all logographs are iconic signs. Logographs should not be identified as iconic signs, for it is perfectly possible to imagine logographic signs which simultaneously represent contents without having a relationship of similarity toward the object represented. This is, for instance, the case with modern Chinese ideograms.

In order to have a means of distinguishing between concepts, the term *logograph* will be used to express the aspect of simultaneity, the term *pictograph* to express that of similarity.

### 2.2.2 Arbitrariness, conventionality and transnationality

Symbolic representamens are arbitrary and conventional. By *arbitrariness* we understand that the representamen is not similar to the content represented. There is thus no similarity between the expression *tree* and the content the tree itself.

By *conventionality* we mean that a community of senders uses one particular representamen (7). The English word *tree* thus translates into German as *Baum*, into Latin as *arbor* etc..

So iconic signs are never arbitrary, but they are generally conventional. "It is not the object itself that is similar to the icon but only culturally acquired contents, 'codified expectation systems' that construct the similiarities which the viewer perceives in the icon. Analogy and similarity are not naturally perceivable facts but are determined by culture and have to be learnt." (8)

Familiar examples will be found in the field of sign language. In our culture complex we wave someone toward us by opening and closing a hand held at breast height with the palm upwards. We send someone away by performing the same gesture with palm downwards. In China, however, this latter gesture signifies "Come here".

One more example. In the Federal Republic of Germany and other countries, you can see the following sign, that means *you may telephone from here*.

But in particular cases it also means that a special kind of telephone can be hired at the place indicated by the sign without one's being able to telephone. This shows that not only the individual sign in isolation but also the context in which the sign is used has to be considered.

Even if iconic signs are generally conventional, this circumstance is, however, alleviated by the feature of similarity. The iconic sign generally reflects the sector in which what it signifies is to be found, or the object's structure, though it cannot always express exactly what is meant by the sign in the particular sector. The sign of a telephone at least has something to do with telephoning, even if the sign alone does not say what this connection exactly is. So when we talk of conventionality in the case of both types of signs, something different is meant each time. In the one case, convention rules the relationship between representamen and sign content with reference to a linguistic community that is often identical with a national community. Symbolic signs are thus national-language signs. In the case of iconic signs, convention regulates what the eye focusses on. Iconic signs are, within certain limitations transnational as convention does not affect the relationship between representamen and sign content. Representamen and sign content share a certain similarity. Transnationality, however, has twofold limitations: firstly, the object or circumstance depicted may not itself be conventional and, secondly, it must be posssible to assume that people are actually familiar with the content depicted or with its shape (9).

In order to stress this once again: transnationality does not mean that the full meaning of iconic signs is immediately understood at first glance, but only that the field of what is meant is understood. Focussing on exactly what is meant must be learnt or deduced.

## 2.3 THE LEARNABILITY OF SIGNS

Applied to those who use signs, what has so far been said means that iconic signs, because of their similarity with the object implied, can be more directly understood via the impression they make on the senses than symbolic signs.

But their directness is limited, as it is not possible to create entirely unconventional signs.

As iconic signs are conventional they also have to be learnt. Their learnability is, however, simplified from the learner's point of view by the obviousness that stems from the similarity. From the sender's point of view, iconic signs are, on the other hand, hard to learn, as they presuppose a specific knowledge of the content and its structure as well as the capacity to abstract from all attributes in such a way that they can be represented without losing their obviousness. But even from the recipient's point of view, the advantage reaches its limitations when the number of iconic signs that have to be learnt) exceeds a certain number.

The use of iconic signs becomes engrained via the frequency with wich signs are used in the same contexts. This means that iconic signs are prescribed for the recipient, who uses them receptively but not productively.

With phonographs, on the other hand, one always has to learn a few individual units (e.g. 26 symbols as letters of the alphabet) together with a few rules for combining them, both, however, at the price of obviousness. Here it hardly matters whether one is a sender or recipient once one has mastered the signs and the rules for producing them.

## 2.4 SUMMARY

In summary, the following characteristics can be listed for the two types, iconic signs and symbols, discussed here:

| Characteristics | Iconic Sign | Symbol |
|---|---|---|
| Arbitrariness | no | yes |
| Conventionality | yes | yes |
| Transnationality | yes | no |
| Distribution | Traffic signs etc. | Many nation. languages |
| Clarity | Very good | Poor, as they can only be shown in succession |
| Learnability (Recipient) | Easy if few, otherwise difficult | Difficult as represent-aments, easy from the number involved |
| Learnability | Very difficult even if familiar | as above |

# 3. NON-ARBITRARY SIGNS

## 3.1 CONCEPTUAL DISTINCTIONS

Kapitzki (10 )makes the following distinctions among iconic signs:

- Iconogram, "an iconic sign which, as the representation of an image, illustrates characteristics which both sign and object referred to have in common. A photo, for example, is an iconic sign of the object of reference *Landscape*."
- Pictogram, "an iconic sign which represents complex states of affairs not in words or sounds but in visual complexes of meaning, e.g. how to use an escalator."
- Cartogram, "a cartographic presentation with complexes of function (statistics etc.) and iconic contents, e.g. a map or the plan of a house."
- Diagram, "a visual sign which is partly an iconic representation, but more a complex of function illustrating function sequences or situations that can be qualified."

## 3.2 PICTOGRAMS

Pictograms are the best known iconic signs. Today they have become an indispensible means of communication. "The acceleration of this development since the beginning of our century indicates that, for certain communication situations, national languages and their written or typographical transfer are increasingly being replaced by symbols. This is certainly true wherever language barriers have to be overcome. This applied first of all to international road traffic, but in the meantime local and even national self-sufficiency has, in the wake of the explosion of industrial developments, given way to communication on all sides, to a multilateral interdependence of the nations on each other." (11)

Nowadays pictograms are used in the leisure-activity sector (12), in the fields of travel and transport, gastronomy and hotels, sport, hospitals and department stores, and in the public sector in general. Pictograms are used both in guides to evening classes (13) and in school textbooks (14).

By contrast to iconograms, cartograms and diagrams, pictograms are always indexically declarative, with signpost function ("You may telphone from here"), or indexically imperative ("Do this exercise in writing").

One of the biggest problems in the introduction of pictograms is their design. No ad-hoc signs should be introduced. Scientific investigation based on one of the following well-tried methods of inquiry should, rather, precede any decision (15):

- Production method: subjects are asked to draw prescribed concepts. A statistical evaluation shows which elements of the symbol are of significance for the user.
- Recognition method: subjects reconstruct the meaning of presribed signs.
- Selection test: from a number of alternatives, subjects select the most suitable pictogram to express a certain meaning.

According to the findings quoted by Aicher / Krampen, the results of the various methods appear to be related to the semantic features (16) inherent in a content/proposition without, however, determining them. Thus, for example, the production method represents the term *letter box* by "a rectangular box with slot and letter" (17). In the case of *car hire*, the selection test preferred "a female hand holding out a key with the car shown from the side" - a sign expressing the semantic components of renting, of the person renting, of the object being rented and the method of renting - to "side view of car with car key above it", which lacks the component of the person handing over the car. For *restaurant* the selection test preferred a knife and fork crossed to "knife and fork beside one another at the side of a circle (plate)". While this shows that the plate is a redundant feature, it also demonstrates that the crossing of the knife and fork is not predictable from the semantic features alone.

If these observations are combined with considerations of conventionality, we will see that the semantic features control the similarity, while the design and arrangement of the contents of the semantic features, for example, follow aesthetic considerations and are thus controlled conventionally. Thus to the conventional factor of reception is added one of production.

## 3.3 COMPLEX REPRESENTAMENS: MODELS

Pictograms generally represent one proposition that could be stated logographically in an indexical sentence (an ellipsis), for example: *You may telephone from here, No smoking, Not drinking water* etc. .

If more than one proposition is to be put across, more comprehensive models must be employed (18).

### 3.3.1 Defining models

Stachowiak (19) defines the term "model" with the help of three basic characteristics:

- The depiction characteristic: "Models are always models of something, i.e. depictions; representations of natural or artificial orginals, which themselves may be models."

- The abbreviative characteristic: "Models do not generally include all attributes of the originals they represent, only those which seem relevant to the creators and/or users of the models in question."
- The pragmatic characteristic: "Models are not attributed per se to their originals. They fulfil their function as replacements a) for certain subjects who recognize and/or act, making use of the model, b) within certain intervals of time and are c) limited to certain intellectual or actual operations."

The relationship between original and model is characterized by

- Preterition: attributes of the original - of a structural and/or material nature - are passed over insofar as they are outside the scope of the interest being pursued (cf. above: abbreviative and pragmatic characteristics).
- Abundance: the opposite process: the model exhibits attributes that cannot be found in the original. "Such characteristics do not fulfil any function of depicting the original. The represent mere 'technical vehicles' for constructing models in that their selection - if any choice were offered - is generally made out of considerations of economy, production or economical presentation and explanation."
- Contrast: "Attributes or classes of attribute exhibited by the original model are particularly emphasized and contrasted with the original's other attributes."

The above definitions show that models can be considered as complex iconic signs.

3.3.2 Examples of models: graphic art and films

Typical examples of models in the sense used here come from the world of graphic art and films. In all of them the relationship between what is represented (the original) and the presentation (representamen) can be described with the concepts of preterition, abundance and contrast. The difference between films and graphic art is, mainly, in the temporal extension and the opportunities related to this. While graphic art is a simultaneous presentation of a picture, however complex, films have a temporal dimension, so that entire action sequences, for instance, can be shown.

The function of graphic drawings or films is, if they are employed instrumentally, the illustration and explanation of texts. In the former case the content structure of the text is repeated in a visual medium. In the latter case the visual medium goes beyond what has already been presented in the test. A typical example would be graphically presented summaries of texts that reflect the abstract structure of relationships.

3.3.3 The transnationality of complex signs

The similarity between graphics and films as representamens and the reality portrayed may be fairly close or less close. The closer the two get to becoming iconograms, i.e. the smaller their classes of preterition and abundance, the less transnational in characer they become. From the point of view transnationality it is required that the preterition consists in the neglection of national attributes. This will generally result in an emphasis on structural attributes.

In this graphical context, cartograms or diagrams which neglect the material contents in favour of structural contents are of interest. In the case of graphic drawings, all national attributes must be neglected.

The logical consequence of this consideration with regard to films is the choice of animated cartoons, where the preterition of national attributes (physiognomy, colour of hair, clothing etc.) can be achieved to the maximum extent.

With graphics and cartoons one must remember that they are rarely presented in their pure forms, i.e. without language. This is most likely in the case of purely illustrative drawings accompanying a text, but these are often provided with captions, so that the portion of the text that they illustrate is quoted.

3.3.4 The learnability of models

Graphics and films as complex iconic signs are also conventional (20). But insofar as they are graphics accompanying a text or sound films, the focus of attention can, by means of the accompanying text, be concentrated on the contents or structures that are of importance in the given context. So the degree of conventionality is low, insofar as the considerations regarding transnationality are observed. And this, in turn, means that learnability in this case is, by and large, unproblematic.

This would be different in the case of graphic and film material isolated from textual contexts. Here the learnability would be considerably restricted by the complexity of the sign and the related intensifying effect of possible focuses of attention.

Complex iconic signs such as graphics and cartoon films can not unreservedly be compared with pictograms within the learning process. This will have to be considered later on in this paper.

# 4. NON-ARBITRARY SIGNS IN THE LEARNING PROCESS

## 4.1 THE ORGANIZATION OF THE LEARNING PROCESS

### 4.1.1 Organizational aids

Ausubel distinguishes between reception and discovery learning. This distinction more or less covers that between guided and unguided learning: "In reception learning (root or meaningful) the entire content of what is to be learned is presented to the learner in final form. He is only required to internalize the material [...] that is presented to him so that it is available and reproducible at some future date. The essential feature of discovery learning [...], on the other hand, is that the principal content of what is to be learned is not given but must be independently discovered by the learner before he can internalize it." (21)

In the context to be discussed here, reception learning is thus of interest. In connection with this type of learning, Ausubel introduces the concept of organizers. "These [...] organizers provide relevant ideational scaffolding, enhance the discriminability of the new learning material from previously learned related ideas, and otherwise effect integrative reconciliation at a level of abstraction, generality and inclusiveness which is much higher than that of the learning material itself." (22) Organizers are more suitable for learning factual material than for learning abstract material (23).

This concept of receptive learning with the help of organizers operates without the factor of motivation in the learning process. Ausubel believes that his concept can dispense with this factor (24). This would appear to be a reasonable and realistic assumption for CBT-projects for adults nowadays, so that Ausubel's concept is particularly suited to such projects, in contrast to other concepts such as that of Bruner (25), who insists more on discovery learning, or of Jörger (26), who places more emphasis on the role of motivation as an initiator of the learning process.

### 4.1.2 The fact-learning process

Presentation of the organization is followed by the task of coming to grips with the actual subject. Here, too, the learning material has to be organized in such a way sensible learning is possible. Indeed, the value of the preceding organizers "depends, in part, quite plainly on how well the learning material itself is organized." (27)

In the case of media-controlled learning, i.e. learning that is not guided by a teacher who can react situatively to the answers given by pupils, the organization of the content is a particularly important point. How and when can the learner get at the contents that will help him make progress? In the main this will depend on the learner's answers with relation to a particular problem posed. The question then is what information is to be given for which answer, whether the information given is of a factual nature or whether it is aimed at the organisation of learning. In the latter case the learner would be referred to preceding learning steps, to the special nature of the task etc.. The precondition here is an intelligent system that can give intelligent responses - i.e. responses adapted to te specific situation - to learners' answers.

4.1.3 Exercises

Learning in any form whatsoever cannot do without phases of practice. What has been learnt has to be automated and consolidated. Exercises of the most varied levels, especially transfer exercises, must be offered. Here, too, the aspect of effective learning poses the question as to which exercises and tasks are most suitable. In order to be able to answer this question we need an idea of which types of exercise can be associated with which level of acquisition. The level of acquisition itself can, in turn, only be determined by the learners' answers.

## 4.2 THE SYSTEMATIC PLACE OF PICTOGRAMS AND MODELS

The thesis to be defended here is that pictograms and models are particularly suited to the organization of the learning content. In addition it will have to be shown that models can, in addition, represent the learning content visually.

4.2.1 Pictograms as organizers

Pictograms have a capacity for coding which is exhausted once a declarative or imperative indexical proposition has been represented. They cannot therefore represent more complex interrelationships. As such they are not organizers in the sense meant by Ausubel and described above.

In his considerations, Ausubel assumes normal schoolroom teaching with a teacher. So he is only concerned with the organization of the learning content, not the organization of the learning process. But as mentioned at the beginning of this paper, teaching that is not guided by a teacher requires transparent organization of the entire learning process, a signpost system, so that the learner can determine his own individual position at any point of time in the learning process. He should known what learning stage he has reached and be shown, if he wishes, what the next teaching steps will be and how much he has learned already. He should be given the opportunities which the learning material offers. (It is, for example, interesting for the learner to know whether, at the stage in the learning process that he has currently reached, a visualization, an exercise, additional bibliographical details, cross-references to other subjects etc. are offered). This information can be given by pictograms with a declarative indexical function. Furthermore, imperative indexical pictograms can give orders to find information, do exercises etc..

Thus pictograms have a role to play wherever a signpost is required within the overall organization of learning. This could be formulated the other way round: if one considers the learning process as an organizable structure, pictograms as signposts have a genuine place in this organization.

### 4.2.2 Models as organizers

The role of organizers in the sense already discussed can be taken over by graphic models. Here, however, it will not be possible to do without verbality completely. The transnational graphic portion clarifies the necessary structural contexts of the new learning material and its links with the consolidated knowledge of the learner without, understandably, being able to offer any organizational help with regard to the content. An example of a structural graphic organizer will be found in Appendix 4 (28).

On a less abstract level, an organizer could, of course, be provided by a cartoon film in which the individual learning fields are successively generated in accordance with their learning context and/or their subject context. Here a whole series of variants are conceivable. The basic problem remains: such organizers are never entirely free of language and can thus never be designed for transnational use.

### 4.2.3 The function of visualization in the learning process

The presentation so far has been related to the organization of learning. In what follows we shall be dealing with the visualization of learning contents.

In a pedagogical context all forms of visual depiction at the learning content level are referred to as visualization (29).

As functions of pictures in general, Issing/Haack quote as examples: "Pictures can motivate pupils to learn, can provide structural frameworks in the sense of advanced organizers that guide the learner's attention, present new information, give concrete form to abstract concepts, stimulate comparisons, give examples, simplify, enable conclusions to be drawn by analogy, summarize, go over the material again and offer test questions." (30) In a more systematic manner Michael speaks of visualization as

- an aid to motivation
- an aid to recognition
- an aid to reproduction (31).

The emphasis here is clearly on helping. "The extent of visualization can not be determined objectively but only in relation to the learning task and the individual viewer. A graphic presentation can be understood by the learner if it corresponds to the inner image of the object which the learner already has or can accept. Since bad visualization is a hindrance to learning rather than a help, visualization should be dispensed with if there is any doubt as to its effectiveness." (32)

As the authors clearly show by discussing various psychological approaches, this statement should not be understood as arguing in favour of a particularly high degree of similarity in the representamens. On the contrary, the image to which the visualization corresponds is a function of the learning process and of the learner in each instance. Investigations undertaken by Dwyer (33) unmistakably refuted the realism hypothesis "the greater the similarity, the more useful it is". Even if the subjects of the experiments clearly preferred realistic depictions, learning success is often greater in the case of more abstract symbols. This result is, however, more applicable to guided learning and less to learning where the learner himself can set the pace. Here greater similarity is indeed an advantage. The reason is assumed to be the fact that, in externally controlled learning, "attention (is) drawn to minor details, so that the learner no longer had sufficient time to take in important visualization details. Learners setting their own pace, on the other hand, were able to take sufficient time to assimilate many of the visually presented details" (34). This means that the degree of similarity depends on the forced learning pace and the objects to which the learner's attention is directed (35).

Here, of course, what has already been said concerning organizers also applies here: models which visualize learning contents cannot always dispense with language. If they are, as is the case with pictures, the aspects of transnationality and learning theory decree that graphically accentuated illustrations abstracted from national peculiarities schould be preferred to naturalistic pictures. The degree of abstraction will be determined by the prescribed or assumed learning speed.

## 5. PICTOGRAMS AND MODELS IN CBT

### 5.1 THE ERGONOMY OF THE MONITOR SCREEN

"The design of friendly, robust man-machine interfaces is of paramount importance as computers become widely available to non-expert users." (36) Acceptance of the use of computers is heavily dependent on the ergonomic design of the user interface.

The development of the *Xerox Star* was a decisive step (37). In order to simplify the operation of this office computer, an analogy of a secretary's desktop surface was transferred to the monitor screen. "The office objects such as document files, filing cabinet, paper and wastepaper basket were visualized by pictograms." (38)

This development of a multimedia, two-dimensional user surface with the possibility of overlapping, enlargeable and reducible windows is represented today e.g. by *Xerox Ventura Publisher.*

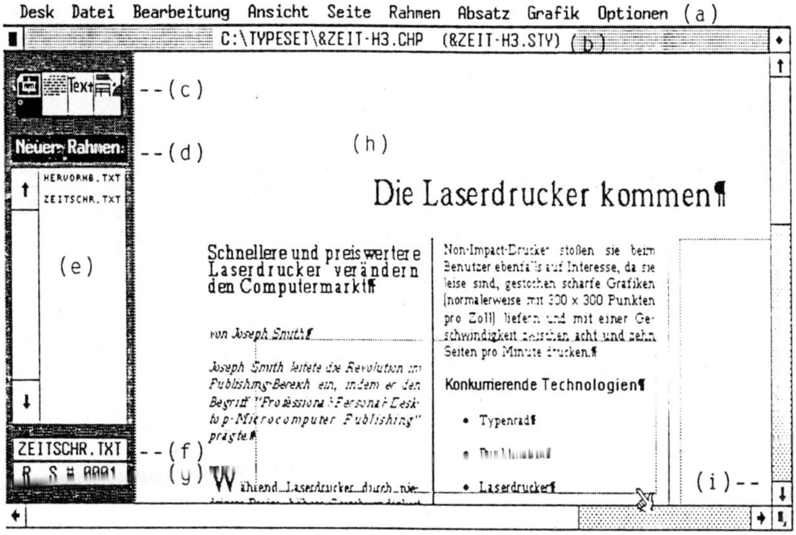


The basic element is a display divided into three parts with a menu across the top of the screen (a). Below this the file currently being used, plus its layout, is displayed (b). Down the left-hand half of the screen, four pictograms (39) represent the four basic processing modes: framing, paragraph, text-processing and graphic modes (c), and the current mode is displayed verbally below it (d). The space below contains, on the right, the menu relating to the selected mode, and on the left there is a scroll field for this menu (e). Below this is the name of the file currently in the frame (f), and below this again is the page number and the indication of whether it is a left-hand or right-hand page (g). The large space is reserved for text-processing (h), while to the right of this space and below it are scroll zones for the text to be processed (i). By clicking into one of the commands on the menu, a processing window is opened which, depending on its position, spreads out over the basic display, and every subsequent command either opens another window or executes a command that restores the screen to basic display mode.

The pictogram process is used not only in the design of the display but also in the processing mode. Thus a pencil,

replacing the mouse indicator, represents the drawing mode for lines and boxes in the graphics mode, the formating of a paragraph is represented by the following pictogram  and so on.

It is, however, doubtful whether this is more than just a gimmick, as these are redundant features. The mode activated in the left-hand column indicates what can be done: in the frame mode, frames can be opened; in the graphic mode lines can be drawn, so that this duplication is unnecessary. One could, of course, argue that every mode represented by a pictogram has its own pictogram package, but this only means that a lot of pictograms are introduced unnecessarily, which contradicts the idea of a pictogram as illustrated above.

*Windows* by Microsoft works in a similar way to *Ventura Publisher* as far as the pictograms are concerned. For the 13 application programs of the 1.03 version, 13 different pictograms are optionally available. Optional means that the pictograms going with the application programs have to be called up. They are not immediately available with the programs. An application program permanently and verbally displayed on a strip at the top of the monitor can be concentrated as a pictogram and stored in the pictogram strip in the bottom segment of the screen that can be switched on and off. From there it can be called up at any time by picking out the pictogram with the mouse and drawing it into the main working field on the screen. The special advantage here is that several programs can be active simultaneously, so that they are immediately available.

Pictograms are employed particularly widely in the paint program. The user is offered no less that 22 different modes here, all of which can be clicked on with the mouse and drawn into the working field. Here all modes are represented by pictograms that are permanently present in a picture strip of their own.

To summarize it can be said that pictograms are presented in a pictogram strip that may be

- permanent (Ventura Publisher, paint program of Windows)
- displayed (Windwos) and/or
- called up (Windows).

Functionally they are used as indexical signs. They represent:
- processing modes. By clicking onto a pictogram the processing mode is called up;
- user programs. A userprogram can be stored as a pictogram and be restarted by drawing the pictogram into the working space.

There are, however, no representations of the state of processing, of work done or work still to do, no displays of alternative processing possibilities, no displays for hardware operation.

Determined not least by the special nature of the programs presented, there are no imperative applications. These are, if present at all, indirect in the case of Windows, when one has to draw a pictogram into the working field in order to start it. The pictogram does, however, not represent this imperative application: the user himself has to be aware of the imperative.

In general, developments are heading in the direction of increased variety, so that, on the one hand, the user does not have to change his habits overmuch and, on the other, there are more variants offered for dealing with any given task. Balzert (40) gives the following survey of developments past and future:

"Generations of User Surfaces

| Characteristics | 1st Generation | 2nd Generation | 3rd Generation |
|---|---|---|---|
| General | monomedial,one dimensional user surface | multimedial, two dimensional user surface | polymedial, multi-dimensional, intelligent user surface |
| Input media | punched card, extended typewriter keyboard (cursor keys, function keys, ten-key block | extended typewriter keyboard | in addition: each key has its own LCD display (context-dependent inscriptions) |
| - Pointer | | mouse | "static" mouse |
| - New possibilities | | | horizontal screen with touch foil; hand written input with and without recognition, voice recognotion; video input |

| Characteristics | 1st Generation | 2nd Generation | 3rd Generation |
|---|---|---|---|
| Output media | telex; symbol-displaying mono chrome displays | high resolution graphics screens; no flat graphics screens | in addition: colour; large flat graphics screens |
| Screen size | approx. 1/3 A4 (24-25 lines with 80 characters) | 1/3 A4, single A4, double A4 | > double A4? |
| - Screen: type of info display | negative(green, amber on black) | positive (black on white) | colour |
| - New possibilities | | | speech output; sound; movies |
| Dialogue form | command language, menu and mask systems | direct manipulation, menu and mask systems | in addition: natural and spoken language |
| Screen layout | one-dimensional: line-oriented;"split-screen" still rare | two-dimensional: over-lapping window technology; pictograms desk top | two-and-a-half & three dimensional presentation (otherwise as 2nd generation) |
| Dialoging | non-unified, in some cases analog functions to same funtion keys | unification via generic operations and desk top operation | user-adaptable or user-adaptive polymedial dialoging and dia logue design based on knowledge bases |
| User target group | expert operators | in addition: computer beginners | individuals |
| Help system and tutorial systems | rudimentary: on line-user manual | passive help systems, adapted to situation | passive and act. help systems and tutorial systems; general user-support,information and advice systems" |

This development is not uninteresting in the context to be discussed here, as a high degree of flexibility in the learning process and in the individual organization of learning will be possible, so that learning which is not guided by a teacher will not be dictated by the media in his stead. Only in this way can non-guided learning become self-determined learning in the field of the organization of learning (41).

## 5.2. NON-ARBITRARY SIGNS ON THE VARIOUS PLANE OF CBT

### 5.2.1 A scenario

Let us assume that a user has purchased a program package for a further education measure. The package contains a learning program consisting of

- diskettes
- video
- audio
- print material (42)

whereby a variation and varied number of media will be used depending on the type of material to be learned.

The structure of a learning sequence might then look as follows:

Firstly the user will, on calling up a sequence, be given an overview of how the contents are structured. The overview may be presented as a static graphic or as a moving sequence of pictures (film), depending among other things on the complexity of the subject to be dealt with. The principal concepts of the sequence will be listed here. This information only deals with the structure of the contents. Further information relating to the media to be used, for instance, should, for reasons of learning theory, not be given here. The learner should, as will be mentioned later, perhaps have the opportunity of choosing the media path for himself. So at this first orientation stage, familiarity with the structure of the contents is important as the basis for later decisions, whereas no knowledge of the media possibilities from which he can choose is required yet.

The graphic overview is the first thing to be shown at the start of each learning sequence. The contents fields must be selected and can, if for instance the learnig sequence was interrupted, be called up individually.

The user begins to work through the learning sequence. If he does not select a definite learning field from the graphic survey, he will be offered the first contents field. The learning field selected will be presented, again in graphic form, but this time the media possibilities will be presented, again in graphic form, but this time the media possibilities will be given as well as the structure of the contents. Three possibilities for media selection are conceivable:

- The learner can choose from various media. This assumes that the learning material is presented to the same degree in the various media.
- One medium is in the foreground, e.g. video film.
- The learning material is only available in one medium.

In the two latter instances, the media to be used would be represented by imperative pictograms.

Video cassettes/Video disks can be called up directly from the program. With prints, the corresponding page number is displayed. The learner can thus organize his workplace in such a way that he can follow the commands given by the pictograms.

In the first example the learner selects the medium that appeals to him more, depending on his type of learning (visual rather than verbal, or vice versa).

The learner then makes a second selection, deciding whether he wants to have the learning material in the basic version, or to be offered all the sidelights and cross-references (ideal for a first encounter with the material), or even to be shown the further possibilities associated with these sidelights and cross-references. The prerequisite for this is that the learning material should be highly organized for the learner and thus easily comprehensible:

- with foreground information that is displayed and background information that can be called up. The points where background information can be brought in are marked, though not always visibly;
- with an internal cross-referencing system within the subject matter;
- with exercises evaluated according to their degree of difficulty.

Accordingly, the learner has the following possibilities:

- the screen is entirely free for the learning material (basic version),
- the screen also displays a pictographic strip which shows
  - whether the learning material is linked up internally (cross-references to other sections of the learning program) or externally (bibliographic references), and
  - whether background information going further into the subject is available
- the screen permanently displays all help and references.

Finally the learner selects the point of time at which he wishes to do the exercises, either at the end of a learning sequence, after individual learning steps or at freely selected points. Here, too, a pictographic selection strip is available.

Only if the learner decides on the basic version do the programs for backround information and cross-references remain unactivated. Otherwise they should be active, so that the information contained in these programs can be displayed at once in windows. This could be done by clicking onto the corresponding pictogram or drawing the pictogram into the main working area. The learner should always be able to decide on the size of the window.

The help program is always active.

Thus the precondidtions for getting to work on the material contained in the learning field are fulfilled.

Only in rare cases will the learning material be presented on the screen. More often, the computer will be used as a control unit (for calling up addresses on the video tape, background information, exercises etc.). In all these cases the graphic overview of the learning field will be presented on the screen, while the point reached on the video will be displayed by marking the fields worked through (43) an emphasizing the field currently reached. If the pictographic strip is displayed, it shows whether background information is available, refers to other subject fields and other learning sequences.

The learner always has the possibility of calling up a help function if he has trouble understanding. As the learner previously had the opportunity to decide whether the screen should be completely free or whether the strip of pictograms should also be displayed, the help function is not called up via a pictogram but via F1 or Alt-?, for instance. Help may be available at very different levels, ranging from information about the hardware and the explanation of expressions right up to the explanation of a train of thought by means of summary or rearrangement. The explanation levels are themselves displayed pictographically. So if a learner calls for help he is first given a pictographic selection strip from which to choose. Information can be encapsulated. Return to the learning material is either automatic or manual (44).

The solutions to exercises are evaluated and, if the answers are wrong, corresponding help is given (45). Here, too, the learner should again have the possibility of changing the presentation (verbal/visual). He should be offered a corresponding selection function pictographically (see above).

Thus the following pictograms would be required:

- various pictograms for the various media
- three pictograms for dealing with the pictograms strip
- three different pictograms for setting tasks
- two pictograms for cross-references
  - one for cross-references to the learning program
  - one for external cross-references (these pictograms must also give a verbal indication of the place where the reference will be found.)
- a pictogram offering the possibility of calling up background information

- three pictograms for help
  - on the hardware plane
  - for partial help with regard to the contents (help for unknown expressions)
  - for overall help (explanations of the sequence of argumentation)

The number of pictograms is thus below 20, whereby, for example, the pictograms for the various media possess an extremely high degree of similarity, so that learning the pictograms poses no problems.

Alongside their use within the learning fields, graphics and animated cartoons would be employed as cognitive organizers.

This results in the following overview of the various screens:

*Calling up learning sequence*

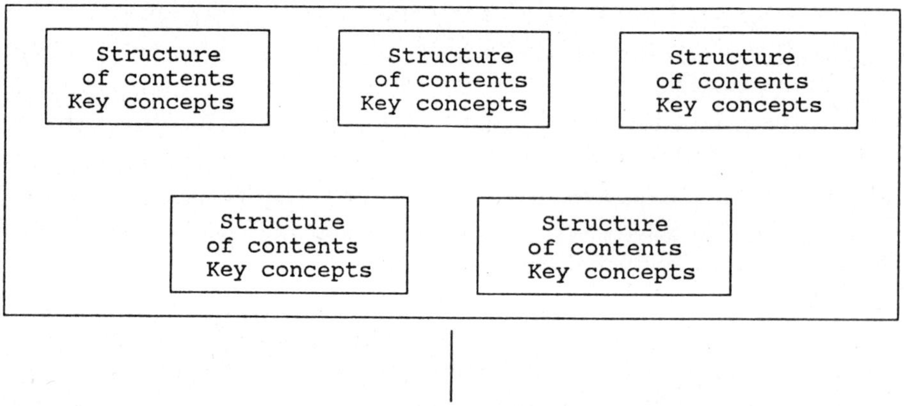


*Selecting content fields*

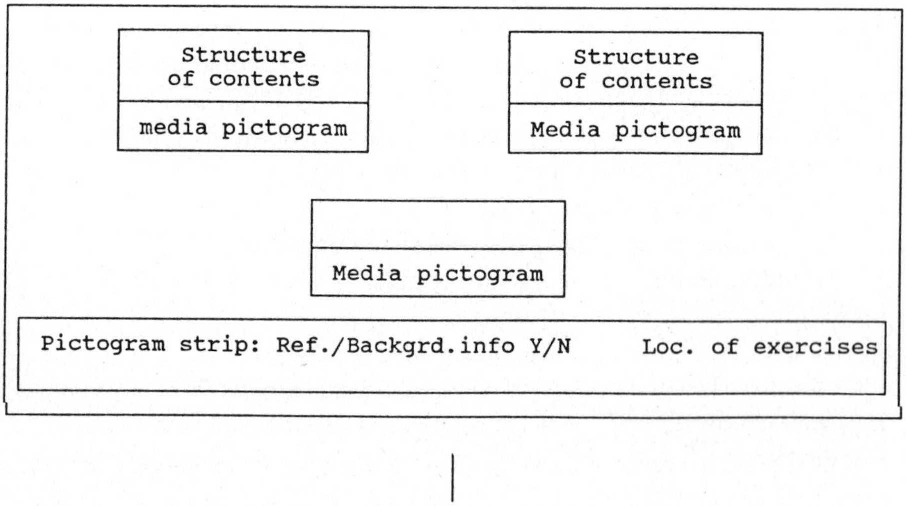

*Possibly: Selection of medium, pictogram strip, exercises*

```
Marked field                    Emphasized field
already worked through          currently being worked on

Help pictogram     Ref. pictogram     Backgr.inf. pictogram
```

The prerequisite for such a system is a motivated learner who can make confident decisions. It is obvious that the less motivated the learner is, the fewer the choices that he can be offered, as these would only encourage him to play around and experiment. Motivation, however, cannot be generated by the medium itself.

## REFERENCES

1 As in F. de Saussure's classical theory of signs: F. de Saussure, 1949. Cours de linguistique générale, 4th ed. Paris.

2 cf. Peirce, C.S., 1931-58. Collected Papers, ed. Hartshore, C. / Weiss, P. / Burks A.W., Cambridge, Mass.: Harvard University Press.

3 Note that this concept of a *symbol* goes far beyond the word's everyday meaning. In everyday language, symbols are pictures with a theoretical significance, a cross as a symbol of Christianity, for instance.

4 Concerning this term, cf. Grice, H.P., 1957. Meaning: Philosophical Review 66, pp. 377-388.

5 The right-hand picture in the upper row could, without the text that goes with it, also be understood indexicaly as depiciting an indicating finger, an interpretation which could lead to incorrect handling with serious consequences. This shows that the interplay between the various systems of signs is, in this case, not unproblematic.

6 For a differentiated distinction, cf. Chao, Yuen Ren, 1968. Language and Symbolic Systems, Cambridge, Mass.: Harvard University Press.

7 For a precise definition of convention, cf. Lewis, D., 1969. Convention, Cambridge, Mass.: Harvard University Press, p. 76: "A regularity R in the behavior of members of a population P when they are agents in a recurrent situation S is a convention if and only if it is true that, and it is common knowledge in P that, in any instance of S among members of P,
(1) everyone conforms to R;
(2) everyone expects everyone else to conform to R;
(3) everyone has approximately the same preferences regarding all possible combinations of actions;

(4) everyone prefers that everyone conform to R on condition that at least all but one conform to R;
(5) everyone would prefer that everyone conform to R' on condition that at least all but one conform to R'."

8 Cf. Eco, Umberto, 1976. A Theory of Semiotics, London: Macmillan.
The aspect of conventionality has been pointed out by anthropologists in particular, for instance: Mead, M.: Communication among all people everywhere. In: Natural History, 1968, 7, 56-63.

9 Malay aborigines might possibly take the telephone symbol for a fruit, as they are not familiar with telephones.

10 Kapitzki, Herbert, 1980. Programmiertes Gestalten. Grundlagen für das Visualisieren mit Zeichen. Karlsruhe: Verlag Dieter Gitzel, p. 18.

11 Aicher, Otl / Krampen, Martin, 1977. Zeichensysteme der visuellen Kommunikation. Handbuch für Designer, Architekten, Planer, Organisatoren, Stuttgart: Verlangsanstalt Alexander Koch.

12 Cf. Appendix 1, which includes various pictogram designs for the various sectors. The collection is taken from: Aicher, Otl / Krampen, Martin, 1977, pp 121-150.

13 Cf. Appendix 2.

14 Cf. Appendix 3.

15 Cf. Aicher / Krampen, 1977. pp. 112-119, where the various methods of inquiry are presented.

16 On the theory of the semantic features, cf. Katz, J.J. / Fodor, J.A., 1964. The structure of a semantic theory. In: Fodor, J.A. / Katz. J.J. (eds). The structure of language, Englewood Cliffs, pp. 479-518.
In mention this linguistic approach here as it makes it possible to theoretically investigate the typical features that have to be incorporated into a pictographic representation.

17 Aicher / Krampen, p. 114.

18 Considered theoretically within the framework of a general theory of models, pictograms can also be considered as models. The distincition made here between pictograms as iconic signs mirroring one single proposition, and models mirroring complex states of affairs is of a heuristic nature.

19 Stachowiak, H., 1973. Allgemeine Modelltheorie, Vienna (etc.): Springer.

20 Cf. Eco, Umberto, 1972. Einführung in die Semiotik, Munich: Fink, p. 254.

21 Ausubel, D., 1963. The psychology of meaningful verbal learning, New York: Grune & Stratton, p. 16.

22 op. cit., p. 214

23 Cf. op. cit p. 215; also: Ausubel, D., 1968. Educational psychology: A cognitive view, New York: Holt, Rinehardt and Winston, Chapter 4.

24 Cf. Ausubel, D., 1968. Chapter 10.

25 Cf. Bruner, J., 1961. The process of education, Cambridge, Mass.: Harvard University Press

26 Jörger, K., 1975. Lernprozesse bei Kindern, Stuttgart: Klett

27 Ausubel, 1968. p. 161.

28 The example is taken from: Grimm, H. / Engelkamp, J., 1981. Sprachpsychologie, Berlin: E. Schmidt, p. 52.

29 Cf. Issing, L. / Haack, J., 1985. Bildverarbeitung und Bildrepräsentation im dialogischen Lernen. In: Mandl, H. / Fischer, P.M. (eds).: Lernen im Dialog mit dem Computer, Munich (etc.): Urban & Schwarzenberg, pp. 106-117. Michael, B., 1983. Darbieten und Veranschaulichen, Bad Heilbrunn: J. Klinkhardt.

30 Op. cit., p. 107.

31 Op. cit.

32 Issing/Haack, op. cit., p. 113.

33 Dwyer, F.J., 1978. Strategies for improving visual learning, State College, PA: Learning Services, quoted from Issing/Haack, p. 108 f.

34 Issing/Haack, 1985. p. 108.

35 Let us just recall in this context the concept of attentiveness put forward by Galperin, P.J., 1972. Zum Problem der Aufmerksamkeit. In: Lompscher, J. (ed.): Probleme der Ausbildung geistiger Handlungen. Neuere Untersuchungen zur Anwendung der Lerntheorie Galperins, Berlin: Volk und Wissen. Here the content of attentiveness is seen as a controlling action, while the form of attentiveness is conceived as the idealized, abbreviated, automated exercise of this action. It is, however, true that "not all control stems from attentiveness, and not all attentiveness exercises control. With the help of control, the activity and its consequences are just evaluated. Attentiveness, however, improves the activity and thus also the results." (p. 18 f.). Important in our context is the following: "The question now arises: How can attentiveness be explained until a concrete impression of the object has been formed? The following may serve as an explanation: If this attentiveness is spontaneous, the first impressions will be used as a yardstick for those that follow. If the attentiveness is arbitrary, schemata which previous experience has formed are used." (op. cit., footnote).

36 Carbonell, J.G., 1983. User modelling and natural language interface design. In: H. Balzert (ed.): Software-Ergonomie. Conference I/1983 of the German Chapter of the ACM held on 28th and 29th April 1983 in Nuremberg, Stuttgart: Teubner, p. 21.

37 For the following, cf. Balzert, H., 1983. Benutzeroberflächen. In: H. Balzert (1983), pp. 34-42.

38 Op. cit., p. 35.

39 In computer literature, handbooks etc., the scientific term *pictogram* is not used, being replaced by the colloquial term *icon*. These are, in fact, pictograms.

40 Balzert, 1983, pp. 41-42.

41 Cf. Delta. Initial Studies, ed. by The Commission of the European Communities. Directorate General XIII: Telecommunications, Information industries and Innovation, Brussels and Luxemburg 1987, ch. IV: Learner Environment, p. 161.

42 Op. cit.

43 A field will be considered completed when the exercises associated with it have been successfully worked through.

44 Every user program nowadays offers these help function facilities.

45 Cf. e.g. the KAVIS (= Knowledge Acquisition Video Instruction System) Project of the DIFF (=Deutsches Institut für Fernstudien an der Universität Tübingen), where material of this type already exists for biology.

# APPENDIX 1: COMMON PICTOGRAMS

1. General: *Stairs*

2. Leisure: *No smoking*

*Restaurant*

3. Travel: *Left-luggage office*

4. Sport: *Hockey*

5. Health: *Lung Dep./Dermatology/Dental Dep./Paedriatric Dep./ Psychiatry*

## APPENDIX 2: PICTOGRAMS AS SIGNS FOR ADULT EDUCATION CENTRE GUIDES

*Growing old*

*Health*

*Mathematics, Natural Sciences*

*Housekeeping*

*Languages*

*Professional Training and Law*

*Philosophy, Psychology*

*Regional Studies and Geography*

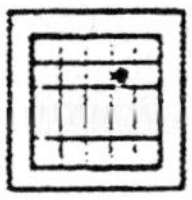

*History, Contemporary Events*

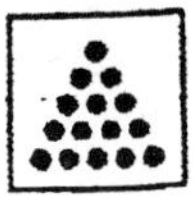

*Art and Creativity*

(These pictograms are rather negative examples as their degree of similarity is very low. They are therefore not used in some adult education centre guides. -Personal information from Dr. Krüger, Upper Enztal Adult Education Centre.)

## APPENDIX 3: PICTOGRAMS IN SCHOOL BOOKS

*Look it up in the Dictionary!*

*This work should be carried out in writing*

(Pictograms are seldom used in school books. This is due to the fact that the teacher is leading through the course and that learning at school is orally intensive.)

## APPENDIX 4: EXAMPLE FOR THE GRAPHICAL ORGANISATION OF A LEARNING FIELD

(The following diagram, which presents the main concepts and connections between learning fields, opens the chapter *Biology and Language* in: Grimm, H. / Engelkamp, J., 1981. Sprachpsychologie. Handbuch und Lexikon der Psycholinguistik, Berlin, E. Schmidt, p. 52.)

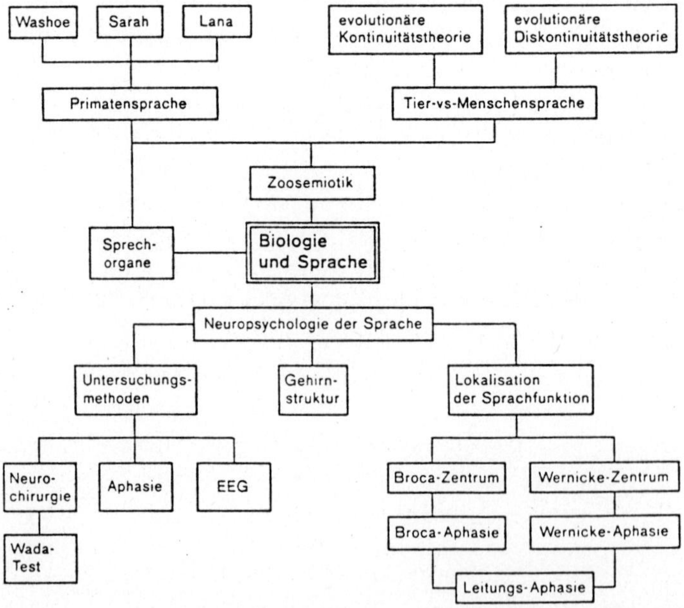

*Designing User Interfaces for International Use*, edited by J. Nielsen
Elsevier, 1990


# USABILITY TESTING OF INTERNATIONAL INTERFACES

**Jakob Nielsen**

Technical University of Denmark, Lyngby, Denmark

The basic argument of this chapter is that an interface which is used in another country than the one where it was designed, is a *new* interface. One cannot trust the original usability work on the user interface to necessarily have produced a design which will be equally usable around the world. This again means that it is necessary to conduct usability analyses and tests also for the international versions of the interface.

Sometimes cultural conditions may have a fundamental impact on the very structure of user interfaces which are not just a matter of translations. As an example, consider LYRE which is a French hypertext system for teaching poetry. LYRE allows the students to see the poem from various "viewpoints", each highlighting certain parts of the poem as hypertext anchors to relevant annotations and allowing the student to add new annotations. LYRE does not, however, allow the student to add *new* viewpoints since that capability is reserved for the teacher. The premise is that students should work within the framework set up by the teacher and not construct completely new ways to analyze the poem. This is obviously socially acceptable in the Southern European tradition in France, and indeed an alternative design might well have been deemed socially *un*acceptable in that country because it would have undermined the teacher's authority. On the other hand, many people in e.g. Denmark where Scandinavian attitudes are more prevalent, would view the current design of LYRE as socially unacceptable because it limits the students' potential for independent discovery. Obviously, designing such a hypertext system to fit both cultures would require more than just changing a few words in a menu.

Even in cases where the basic structure of the interface is acceptable also in other countries, one cannot be certain that the various elements of the interface will be usable in all countries. Obviously, the language of the original interface may not always be understood in other countries and a translation will have to be made.

However, translating the text strings and icons in the software is not enough—one has to translate the **total user interface** including manuals. In Microsoft *Word* version 1 for the Macintosh, the way to include page numbers in running headings was to type a special code. This code was rather obscure, and certainly not immediately obvious, so all users had to look it up in the manual where the code is explained as containing the word "page" (since the original English manual was sold with the Danish version of the program). Every *Word* user I have interviewed has proceeded to fall into the trap of following the instruction from the manual to the letter. But this does not work as the translator of the program also translated this special code to use the Danish word side instead of "page".

Translating the total interface for a single program should always be possible. But in a small country as Denmark only the more popular programs are translated, while more specialized programs are used in their original versions. This means that users will have to transfer back and forth between two different versions of the same menus, thus diminishing the potential advantage of the consistent user interface architecture on computers like the Macintosh.

As an example, one medium-experienced user had been using exclusively an English version of the desktop publishing program *Ready–Set–Go*. He then transferred to using a Danish program and suddenly found himself in the position otherwise characteristic for novice users. He wanted to save his work, and he already knew of the existence of a "save" command from the English *Ready–Set–Go*, but even so he was simply unable to find the command in the Danish menus and finally had to give up and ask for help. The Danish translation of the save command is arkiver ("archive") which matches the desktop metaphor very well and is easy to remember the *second* time one has to use it. But initially this user had trouble making the transfer of skill from the English term to the Danish one.

If users have to transfer between different languages, it is probably best not to translate the control-key assignments since inconsistency in control/function-keys is one of user interface problem users hate most . Perhaps because of this problem, the Danish translation of e.g. *MacDraw 1* retained the English control-keys such as R for right-justify and L for left-justify (instead of H for højre and V for venstre), thereby destroying their mnemonic value.

The problem with having manuals and software in different languages might be solved by only translating those programs where one can also translate the manual. But it is more or less impossible to solve the problem with the coexistence of programs in different languages.

In some cases, problems are simply due to poor translations not following human factors principles. One example comes from our studies of the Danish translation of *MacPaint* vers. 1. One of the menus in MacPaint is called "Goodies" which may be acceptable as the name of a menu in English. The Danish word used in the translation, godter, is indeed a proper translation of "goodies" but has another set of connotations (mostly having to do with candy), leading many of our test subjects to misunderstand it.

Another example comes from *MacDraw* where the word "ruler" has been translated by lineal which mostly has the connotation among technical draftsmen of something used to draw straight lines (a straightedge) rather than something with which to measure things. The word målestok ("yardstick") ought to have been used instead to capture the meaning of the *MacDraw* rulers. This translation does not give rise to problems in the interactive context but lowers the usability of the program for a class of specialist users who will be bothered by the misapplication of their argot. General users will probably not care about the difference between various drawing tools, however. The reason for this usability problem is probably that the translator failed to follow the principle to "know the user" with respect to the technical draftsmen who would constitute one of the important categories of users. Just "knowing" the general population is not enough.

These examples show how a carefully crafted user interface may be debased by a poor translation. In the future it should be just as commonplace to conduct human factors testing and iterative development of a translation of a user interface as to test the original version during its development. We know that "details matter" in user interfaces – and the details may very well change during a translation. Therefore it is not enough that the details have been polished in the original version. One also has to conduct usability tests of the translation.

Furthermore, translating a user interface is not the same as translating a book. The translator has to be aware of the usability principles for constructing good dialogues in an interactive and dynamic context. And the general lessons from usability engineering does apply to the extent that one can never do a sufficiently good job on a user interface design without subjecting it to some form for usability testing with real users.

*MacDraw* may be used with or without a special drawing grid. The English version uses the commands "Turn Grid On" and "Turn Grid Off" to switch between the two drawing modes. The Danish version, however, uses the commands Med net ("use grid") and Uden net ("without grid"), respectively. Several test subjects have been observed to have problems with these commands: Novice users do not realize that these two commands toggle the same option, because they look sufficiently different for a user quickly scanning the menu where only one of the commands is displayed at any given time. The English version starts with the same two words for both commands, thus improving the likelihood that a novice user will recognize them when scanning the menu. Also, the English versions have more active connotations, implying in what *direction* the drawing mode will change if a command is selected. The Danish versions are more passive, which in our experiments led some users to think that the command displayed in the menu was indicating the *current* drawing state rather than being the name of the *opposite* drawing state (which one can change to).

Each of the translated menu items was perfectly adequate when seen by itself. But when used as part of a dynamic interaction, several users erroneously reversed their meaning. Even experienced users sometimes made this mistake. This example shows the need for attention to the principles of dialogue design even during a translation. It also shows the need for empirical testing with real users.

In addition to our general tests of various translated user interfaces, we conducted a major empirical test of the initial Danish translation of the Macintosh system user interface. The test was intended to probe the usability of the translated interface for novice users. The method was simply to sit people with no prior computer experience down in front of a Macintosh with the *MacPaint* program (probably the simplest of the Macintosh applications) and give them some easy tasks to solve with the computer. While they did so, they were asked to think aloud, thus providing information about their understanding of the various interface elements and their strategies in handling the dialogue.

One of the more interesting results from this study concerns the standard dialog box for saving files. This box has buttons which save the file or cancel the command as well as buttons used to change the diskette on which the file will be saved. One of those buttons is marked "eject" in the English version and is used to have the computer remove the current diskette from the drive to make room for another. The Danish translation of the eject-button was aflever which means "hand over". Considering the action of the button, this translation was fairly reasonable seen in isolation.

As noted above, dialogue elements cannot be seen in isolation, however, since they form part of a dynamic interactive context. In this case, the user had the task in mind to store away the file and therefore interpreted the aflever button as one used to "hand over" the file from the computer to the disk. In other words, the user thought that the eject button was the save button. This problem would never occur in the English version of the interface since one would not want to "eject" a file. The very word implies some kind of physical movement.

As a result of this research, Apple Denmark has now changed the translation of the eject button to skub ud , meaning "push out". With this new translation there is no doubt that the "direction" of the action resulting from the command will be *from* the computer rather than *to* the computer as might be the case for "hand over".

The second example from the empirical test of the Danish translation of the Macintosh is the generic command undo which is one of the most important commands in this system. The difficulty here is not with the dynamic interpretation of words as part of the dialogue but with the connotations of a single word. The translation of "undo" in the initial release of the Danish Macintosh system was glem which means "forget". A very large proportion of the users in our studies either failed to understand the meaning of this word in the context of a computer system or were simply afraid to issue the command.

I am happy to report that Apple Denmark took the advice we gave them as a result of our tests and changed the translation of undo in recent releases of Macintosh software. Now the word fortryd is used instead. It means something like "regret" and captures the meaning of undo much better. Even the new translation is not perfect, but it is probably optimal since it is really impossible to translate "undo" exactly without inventing a new word. This was illustrated quite well by an experience I had recently while visiting Japan where I was shown a lot of Japanese user interfaces. Among them was a menu-based system (not the Macintosh) where all the other commands were listed in Kanji, but the **undo** command was in English. I asked about this and was told that they had not been able to come up with a good translation of the concept, so they were perfectly happy with having that one word in European characters.

We also found lots of minor difficulties with the translated Macintosh interface which were not absolutely necessary to correct. These problems mostly show that the perfect interface is difficult indeed to achieve since there are so many small aspects of an interface. As an example, the **quit** command had been translated by the Danish word slut. This word means something like "the end" and is a perfectly reasonable translation. It is hard to recommend a significantly better word. Our experiments showed, however, that some novice users were scared by the word since they felt that it might be *too* much of a termination of their session with the Macintosh. They only wanted to shift from one application to another, not to shut down the computer.

This problem was due to the very slight change in connotations from the English word quit to the Danish word slut. The Danish word is ever so slightly "stronger" and is therefore interpreted slightly differently. We should note that the quit/slut problem was only observed with naive novice users. This translation was no problem for more confident new users and it also no problem for experienced users.

To conclude, it is highly recommended to treat an international version of a user interface as a new interface and take advantage of established usability engineering techniques to ensure its usability. Two steps are especially important:

- Use translators with knowledge of HCI principles for dialogue design.
- Test the interface with real users from the target population.

Obviously it should not be necessary to invest major resources in this usability engineering process. Presumably a lot of effort has gone into the usability engineering of the original interface, and it should be possible to benefit from this work even for the international version. This is true even though it would be impossible in principle to develop the "perfect" interface for a one country on the basis of an interface from another country. To be 100% like a locally developed product, you probably *have* to be a locally developed product and start from scratch on the interface design. This is not feasible in most cases, and it is not even desirable.

The search for the perfect interface is like the search for the Holy Grail: It will consume a lot of time and effort which is better spent on more productive efforts. One must not sacrifice the search for a *good* interface, however. Just a small usability engineering effort will change a mediocre international interface to a good one. It is extremely important not to give up on doing usability work on international user interfaces just because one knows that there are enough resources available for a complete redesign.

Run a few thinking aloud studies of your first cut at a translation: You will be surprised at the number of user difficulties which will be uncovered even by just two or three test subjects. Then iteratively redesign your translation and test again. This simple process is quite cheap and can be used in all cases.

*Designing User Interfaces for International Use*, edited by J. Nielsen
Elsevier, 1990



# A EUROPEAN EVALUATION OF THREE DOCUMENT FORMATS FOR HARDWARE INSTALLATION GUIDES

**Elisa del Galdo**

Digital Equipment Corporation, Reading. United Kingdom

## ABSTRACT

Formats of computer hardware documentation can cause difficulties for translation and increase the cost of production. Documentation produced for hardware usually includes illustrations, it is the arrangements of the artwork and text that can cause problems during translation. In particular, formats that use text labels within artwork make the physical translation of the documentation difficult. The difficulty is caused by the expansion of text upon translation. To account for the expansion of text, labels and artwork must be manipulated or require manual cutting and pasting. This process can greatly increase translation cost and can affect time to market for the entire product, simply by increasing the amount of time for translation. This study was designed to investigate the effect of three different hardware installation guide formats on user performance and user preference. The installation guides used for testing were for the Digital LN03 Laser Printer™. Participants in the study included speakers of English (UK), French, German, and Dutch. The subjective and objective data collected was used to develop a set of recommendations. The recommendations include guidelines for original writers, graphic artists, translators, the layout of guides, and the process by which they are produced. The factor that is found to have the most influence on the usability of the installation guides is the quality of the original documentation. The collection of recommendations produced reflects this finding.

# INTRODUCTION

## Background

There are several aspects or issues involved in the translation of documents for foreign markets. Some of those issues involve the actual accuracy of the translation and the use of translators that are native speakers. These translators would speak the original language of the text as a second language. This would also include using translators who are familiar with current usages of existing words and phrases and those words and phrases recently developed for the computer industry. Another example of a translation issue is how and when the documentation will be produced, either parallel to the original language version or after it is completed. This can greatly effect the time to market of the translated document.

This study deals with the problems involved with physically translating the documentation on the hardcopy page. When a hardcopy document also includes artwork or illustrations, the translation of the artwork labels can also cause problems. When translated into European languages, English text may expand up to 50% in length. This expansion of text must be compensated for on artwork by manipulating the labels and artwork. However, even if the problems with text expansion were alleviated, labels for different language versions of the documentation would still require to be cut and pasted manually. This process greatly increases cost and time of translation and can therefore effect time to market for the product.

A possible answer to these translation problems is to have translators equipped with state-of-the-art technology that allows text and artwork to be held electronically in two superimposed layers. Although this technology is widely available in the US, it is not yet abundant in Europe, mostly due to the cost. In the absence of state-of-the-art equipment, attempts have been made to develop a documentation format to alleviate physical translation problems. This study was designed to evaluate the suitability of these documentation formats.

Hardware Documentation Design

To address the problems of physically translating hardware documentation, three different documentation formats were tested, Format A, Format B, and Format C. Two of the formats, B and C, were developed to address the problems described above. Format A is the standard format currently used for English language documents. Format B is a variation of A and was designed to specifically address the problem of translating text labels on artwork. Format C was designed also to address the problem of translating text labels. In addition, Format C uses very few words and an increased number of illustrations to convey the necessary tasks. A decreased number of words, if the documentation is usable, would decrease the cost and time for translation of the document. Each documentation format is described in more detail below.

Format A: Format A consists of a combination of artwork and text such that the user relies equally on the test and artwork to provide the necessary information to complete that task. Figure 1 is a representational sample of the Format A style. Artwork labels are placed directly on the illustrations. This is a standard format that has been used to produce hardware documentation and installation guides. Approximately every page has one piece of artwork with text either above, below, or in both areas. The text also contains 'notes' and 'cautions' signified by a title 'note' or 'caution' and using a smaller font size.

Format B: Format B contains text identical to Format A. In contrast to Format A, for Format B callouts are used to label the artwork. Figure 2 is a representational sample of the Format B style. Callouts are single alphanumeric characters used to label the artwork and a corresponding character tag and text label are positioned with the text that accompanies the illustration. The use of letter tags to label artwork facilitates the translation of the document. Text on artwork no longer has to be manipulated to account for expansion of text upon translation and no manual paste-up of artwork labels is required.

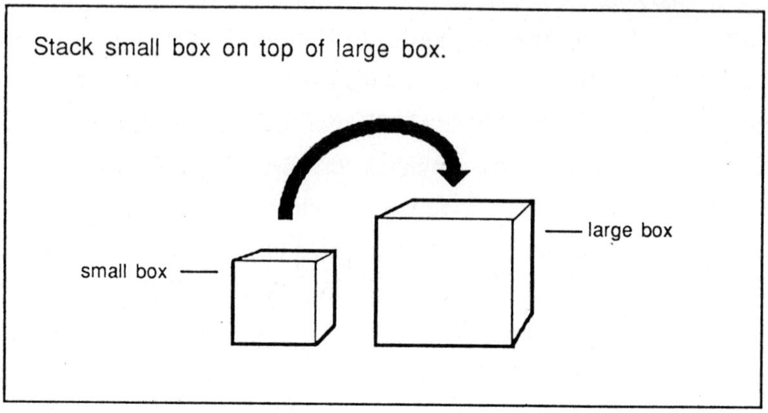


Figure 1. Example of Format A Documentation Style.

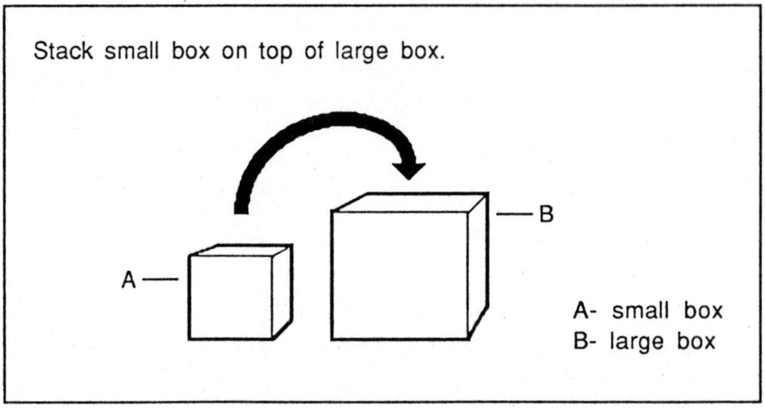


Figure 2. Example of Format B Documentation Style.

Format C: Format C uses mostly illustrations to convey to the user the tasks necessary to install the hardware. Figure 3 is a representational sample of the Format C style. Format C minimises the use of text by using mostly illustrations with 'captioned directives' along with each illustration. The artwork in this format is different from that used in Format A and B,. This artwork was produced by enhancing and manipulating illustrations from Formats A and B. The illustrations use numbered callouts which correspond to the directives. Format C contained the same 'notes' and 'cautions' as A and B, but also used symbols in the margin to denote a 'note' or 'caution' (see figure 4). Besides the use of the callouts easing the translation, mostly illustrations and little text decreases the time for translation simple by there being less text to translate.

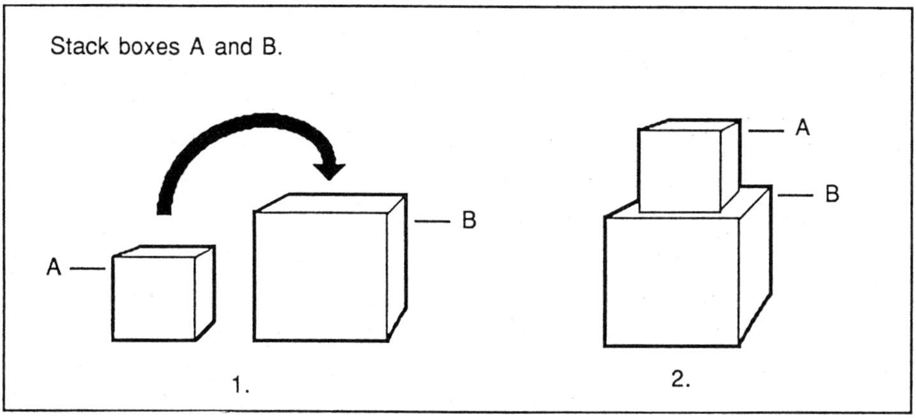


Figure 3. Example of Format C Documentation Style.

Figure 4. Symbols contained in Format C.

## PURPOSE

The purpose of this study was to determine if variations in hardware documentation, some of which were developed specifically to ease the present translation processes, affect the performance of, or are preferred by European users (German, Dutch, French, and English speakers). An additional objective of this study was to identify which problems are unique to a particular format and which are common to all three formats examined, and to develop recommendations for writers, graphic artists, and translators to alleviate these problems in future versions of hardware documentation.

## METHOD

This evaluation consisted of an examination and a comparison of three different formats of the Digital LN03 Laser Printer™ Installation Guide. These are Format A, Format B and Format C. For this study, only information for installing the printer was investigated or available to participants.

### Experimental Design

The study used a two-factor, between subjects design to determine significant variations in performance or subjective preference among Europeans, based on their use of one of the three documentation formats to install the printer.

### Participants

A total of 45 participants took part in the study. All participants had no previous experience in the installation of a Digital LN03 Laser Printer™. Participants included 12 native speakers each of, Dutch, German, and English and 9 French speakers. French speaking participants included French, Belgian and Swiss nationals. German speaking participants were from Germany and Austria. All Dutch participants were from Holland, and the English participants were from the United Kingdom.

Participants consisted of 33 males and 12 females, ranging in degree of technical background and level of experience in installing computer related hardware. Those individuals that were considered to have a technical background, were educated or employed in a technical (computer) field involving the development or maintenance of hardware or software. The non-technical participants were individuals whose professions ranged from being a physician to writers, but were all interested or involved in using computers and printers in their work. The distribution of participants based on background and experience was 22 technical with experience, 9 non-technical without experience, and 3 non-technical with experience.

### Apparatus

The experiment used a Digital LN03 Laser Printer™ and three variations of its installation guide. The printer was at no time connected to a network. Additional equipment included a video monitor, a U-matic video recorder, a video camera, and microphone to video and audio record participant sessions.

### Documentation

The three different documentation formats were produced and evaluated in English, German, French and Dutch. The documentation tested in each format consisted of one chapter detailing the tasks required to install and bring the printer on-line.

### Experimental Procedure

Participants were tested on an individual basis and no time constraints were introduced. Before testing began, each subject was asked to sign a video release and a consent form. Both forms were presented to the participant in their local language. Each participant was given a brief verbal description of the objectives of the study before beginning.

Each participant was video and audio taped from the time they received the documentation and asked to proceed until they had completed the installation or requested to discontinue the task.

Participants were provided with one of the three versions of the installation guide in their local language, and requested to install the printer as if it had been delivered to their office. To avoid injury, before the experimental session began, the shipping cartons were emptied and their contents placed on a table adjacent to the main body of the printer which had been placed on a separate table.

Participants were encouraged to comment and express their opinions while performing the installation task. The experimenter did not avoid answering questions from participants, but did avoid giving assistance directly related to the installation of the printer.

A debriefing period followed each test session. First, a short Usability Questionnaire (see figure 5) in the participants local language was administered. The usability questionnaire was created by altering a questionnaire developed by Brooke (1986) to fit this particular test application of installation guides. some questions were re-worded and others deleted. The questionnaire is based on a 5-point scale, 5 being the highest or the most positive response, 1 being the lowest, and 3 being a neutral score.

Finally, participants were encouraged to give detailed impressions of the documentation and point out areas in the installation guide where they had difficulty using or understanding the documentation. The majority of participants gave comments in English, although some were able to give comments in their local language when an experimenter fluent in the participant's local language was present.

## RESULTS

### Usability Questionnaires

The scores for the Usability Questionnaires were totalled and averaged within each cell. A Friedman two-way analysis of variance by ranks was used to test significant differences in preferences across documentation format and language. The Friedman analysis showed, when collapsed across documentation format, no significant differences in rating based on language. The Friedman analysis, when collapsed across languages, (Table 1), did show a significant difference in preference of documentation format over all languages at $p=.042$.

Based on the results of this questionnaire, Format B of the installation guide was found to be the most usable by participants. No information was collected as to the reason for each participants preference, except that information provided by the content of the questions contained in the Usability Questionnaire (figure 5).

Hardware Documentation - Usability Questionnaire

English

| | Strongly disagree | | | | Strongly agree |
|---|---|---|---|---|---|
| 1. I think that I would like to use this type of documentation frequently | 1 | 2 | 3 | 4 | 5 |
| 2. I found the documentation unnecessarily complex | 1 | 2 | 3 | 4 | 5 |
| 3. I thought the documentation was easy to use | 1 | 2 | 3 | 4 | 5 |
| 4. I think that I would need the support of a technical person to be able to install this system | 1 | 2 | 3 | 4 | 5 |
| 5. I thought that there was too much inconsistency in the documentation | 1 | 2 | 3 | 4 | 5 |
| 6. I found the documentation very cumbersome to use | 1 | 2 | 3 | 4 | 5 |
| 7. I felt very confident using this type of documentation | 1 | 2 | 3 | 4 | 5 |

Figure 5. Usabiltiy Questionnaire.

TABLE 1

Friedman Two-Way Analysis.

| Language | Documentation Format Conditions B | A | C | | B | A | C |
|---|---|---|---|---|---|---|---|
| French | 4.24 | 3.33 | 4.1 | → | 3 | 1 | 2 |
| German | 5.52 | 5.05 | 3.19 | → | 3 | 2 | 1 |
| English | 5.57 | 4.86 | 4.38 | → | 3 | 2 | 1 |
| Dutch | 6.05 | 5.0 | 4.2 | → | 3 | 2 | 1 |
| | | | | Rj | 12 | 7 | 5 |
| | Xr^2=6.5 | | df=2 | p=.042 | | | |

Participant Comments

In addition to questionnaire data, participant comments were collected during each test session and debriefing period. These comments were organized into categories based on the component or attribute of the documentation that led to problems during the installation. The majority of comments for all three formats, during both the test session and the debriefing period, were negative. The experimenters did not specifically solicit positive comments.

The categories for comments include Problems with Text, Problems with Artwork, Incorrect Translation, Poor Layout of Artwork and/or Text, Problems with Hardware Design, and Problems with Symbols (only Format C used symbols within the text). Each category is described in more detail below:

- Problems with Text: Includes text that is ambiguous, unclear, complicated, or has typographical errors.

- Problems with Artwork: Illustrations which display poor perspective, poor labelling, poor orientation, and poor artistry.

- Incorrect Translation: Wrong choice of words, inaccurate, unnatural, or inconsistent translation, incorrect translation of entire concepts, wrong information added upon translation.

- Poor Layout of Artwork and Text: Artwork and corresponding text physically separated, sequence of artwork incorrect, poor positioning for notes and cautions.

- Problems with Hardware Design: Problems due to the design of the printer, its components, displays and controls.

- Problems with Symbols: Problems with recognition, misinterpretation, and dislike of symbols used in the documentation.

Table 2 displays the distribution of comments within each documentation format. Format categories were collapsed across language. No significant differences were found within the distribution of comments. No significant differences were found between the number of text-related and artwork-related comments within or across documentation formats.

TABLE 2
Distribution of Comments by Documentation Format.

| | Documentation Format | | |
|---|---|---|---|
| Comment Category | A | B | C |
| Problems with Text | 32 | 27 | 45 |
| Problems with Artwork | 20 | 26 | 42 |
| Incorrect Translations | 8 | 19 | 1 |
| Poor Layout | 9 | 24 | 21 |
| Problems with Hardware Design | 3 | 2 | 4 |
| Problems with Symbols | -- | -- | 6* |

* Only Format C contained symbols.

Problem Frequency

Problem frequency experienced by each participant during the installation was determined by dividing the installation into ten sub-tasks (figure 6) and categorizing each problem observed by the experimenter into one of the sub-tasks. Each sub-task was further broken down into specific actions required for correct installation. Actions which were not performed, were performed incorrectly or caused damage to the equipment were classified as problems.

1. Inventory
   - *identify components*
   - *expose OPC to light*
2. Output Tray
   - *orient tray*
   - *locate slots*
   - *install tray flush to printer*
3. Paper Tray
   - *remove tape -paper tray*
   - *remove tape -drive arm*
   - *install tray*
   - *identify drive arm*
   - *locate drive arm*
4. Development Drawer
   - *locate drawer*
   - *open drawer*
   - *remove drawer*
5. Toner Cartridges (2)
   - *identify cartridge*
   - *shake cartridge*
   - *remove tape*
   - *orient cartridge*
   - *place cartridge in hopper*
   - *close cover*
   - *remove tape*
   - *remove cartridge*
   - *shake cartridge*
   - *remove tape*
   - *orient cartirdge*
   - *place cartridge in hopper*
   - *close cover*
   - *remove tape*
6. Organic Photo Conductor Cartridge
   - *unpack*
   - *remove green spacers*
   - *remove tape*
   - *remove paper*
   - *identify green handles*
   - *orient OPC*
   - *install i n slots*
   - *close drawer*
   - *touch surface*
   - *expose to light*
7. Add Paper
   - *open cover*
   - *add paper*
   - *check limit*
   - *check size guide*
   - *close cover*
   - *sheck paper size switch*
8. Power On
   - *locate power switch*
   - *check poswer switch setting*
   - *plug to machine*
   - *plug to socket*
   - *turn on*
9. Panel Indicators
   - *identify indicators*
10. Test Sheet
   - *locate test button*
   - *print test sheet*

Figure 6. Installation Subtasks.

Table 3 displays the distribution of problems in each documentation format, collapsed across languages and broken down by sub-tasks.

TABLE 3
Problem Frequency within Documentation Formats.

| | Documentation Format | | |
|---|---|---|---|
| Problem Area | A | B | C |
| Inventory | 5 | 4 | 10 |
| Output Tray | 7 | 3 | 9 |
| Paper Tray | 9 | 10 | 16 |
| Development Drawer | 9 | 7 | 7 |
| Toner Cartridges | 40 | 29 | 75 |
| OPC | 19 | 16 | 26 |
| Paper Tray | 9 | 3 | 10 |
| Power On | 6 | 8 | 7 |
| Panel Indicators | 3 | 3 | 7 |
| Test Buttons | 0 | 1 | 2 |
| Totals | 107 | 85 | 169 |

Only 9 French speakers were available as participants, three participants for each French cell. Therefore, the fourth value in each French cell was estimated by averaging the other three collected values. Table 4, Problem Frequency Data, illustrates the breakdown by documentation format and language.

A analysis of variance (ANOVA) for problem frequency showed significant differences in the number of problems observed for language (df=3) at p=.05 and for documentation format (df=2) at p=.001. One hundred and seven problems were observed for the Format A, 85 for the Format B, and 169 for Format C. Further analysis was conducted using a Newman-Keuls Test. This analysis showed no performance difference between Format A and Format B. The difference among formats is due to Format C being worse than the other two formats.

An additional analysis of variance showed no effect of documentation format on the time for participants to complete the installation of the printer.

TABLE 4
Problem Frequency Data.

| Language | Documentation Format A | B | C | Totals |
|---|---|---|---|---|
| Dutch | 2 | 8 | 10 | |
| | 6 | 3 | 6 | |
| | 9 | 5 | 9 | |
| | 6 | 8 | 11 | |
| | 23 | 24 | 36 | 83 |
| French | 6 | 4 | 12 | |
| | 8 | 5 | 6 | |
| | 6 | 4 | 10 | |
| | 7* | 4* | 9* | |
| | 27 | 17 | 37 | 81 |
| German | 9 | 3 | 9 | |
| | 5 | 8 | 13 | |
| | 11 | 3 | 15 | |
| | 7 | 4 | 22 | |
| | 32 | 18 | 59 | 109 |
| English | 8 | 8 | 11 | |
| | 7 | 7 | 11 | |
| | 12 | 8 | 16 | |
| | 5 | 7 | 8 | |
| | 32 | 30 | 46 | 178 |
| Totals | 114 | 89 | 178 | 832 |

* Estimated scores.

## DISCUSSION OF QUANTITATIVE RESULTS

The main purpose of the study was to determine if the use of alternative documentation formats to ease the translation process, would affect the usability of the installation guide, and if there were differences in preference and performance among European users.

Analysis showed that there were no significant differences in performance between Format A and B, but that the difference was due to Format C being worse than the other two.

It was found in a previous study, (del Galdo and Baranski) that Format C was appropriate for an installation guide for a terminal. The installation of the terminal is clearly a much simpler task as compared to the installation of the printer. Upon comparison of the results from both studies, it was determined that Format C is not appropriate for a complex installation task, such as the LN03 Printer. It appears though, that a textless format is appropriate for hardware documentation, where that hardware and associated tasks are simple and easy to illustrate.

Analysis of the questionnaire data showed a subjective preference for the usability of Format B. It is difficult to determine the exact cause of participants' preference for Format B, but the comments collected may give an indication of what was NOT a factor in Format B being preferred. Format B received 24 negative comments concerning poor layout (i.e. format), where Format A only received 9 negative comments in this category. In addition, Format B received a greater number of comments than Format A concerning incorrect translations, Format B received 19 and Format A received 8.

The perceived differences in translations are difficult to explain because the translation for Format A and B were identical. The only possible explanation for this result is that Format B had some influence on the participants' ability to recognize this type of problem. As a result of the comments collected for Format A and B, it is likely that the reason for participants preference for Format B was not due to its layout or the quality of its translation, but to some other attribute. From these results, it can not be concluded that Format B is better or worse than Format A.

The quantitative data collected did not indicate that Format B is better or worse than Format A, or much information as to what was wrong with the design of each format. The richest data available was the comments collected during and after test sessions, and experimenter observation of participants. From this information, a set of recommendations for the improvement of documentation quality and translatability could be developed that cover all aspects of producing hardware documentation, excluding its publication.

## RECOMMENDATIONS

Although there were differences found between all three formats, there were many problems observed and expressed by participants that are common to all three formats. Most of these common problems were related to the quality of the documentation. Due to the fact that the quality of the documentation, regardless of the format, was not considered to be adequate, further work was done to determine a set of recommendations for the development of quality hardware documentation.

The information resulting from the study suggests, that for all formats, there are some general recommendations that can be made about the style and production of the documentation that should increase the quality and usability of the end product for European users. Because many of the recommendations for the design of hardware installation guides appear to be universal for all three formats investigated, our recommendations apply to all three, unless specifically stated otherwise.

The recommendations are organized into five specific categories:

- Text. These recommendations concern the development of text and its presentation.

- Artwork. These recommendations deal with the development of artwork.

- Layout. These recommendations deal with the interaction between, or combination of artwork and text.

- Translation. These recommendations address problems that can occur on translation.

- Process. These recommendations concern the development and translation processes.

Text Recommendations

- Always ensure information is accurate. This is one of the most important recommendations that can be made. The term 'information' includes descriptions of items, processes, tasks, and movements which the user must clearly understand in order to install the equipment correctly.

- Never use two different words for the same object, component, or actions. Names for objects should be as simple as possible and always be kept consistent throughout the document and any related documents.

- When using abbreviations or acronyms, for example the use of OPC for Organic Photoprocessing Cartridge, always use the full name the first time it is mentioned in the document, followed by the abbreviations in brackets.

- Writers and translators should be careful to correct all typographical errors and inadvertently misspelled words. Users appear to be very aware of these and find that it reflects poorly on the quality of the document.

- If during installation the hardware makes particular noises, describe these in the documentation and use them as audio cues if appropriate.

- Use different fonts, point sizes, symbols or borders to draw attention to notices, warnings or important steps in the installation. Depending on how borders are produced, using them may cause problems upon translation. The text within borders will expand and may hinder the translation process. When using symbols, be sure to check if your symbols are acceptable for the European market.

- Do not refer to hardware, or any of its components, in the documentation without labelling them in the artwork or first describing them fully in the text.

- Always use accurate terminology (technical and non-technical). For example, if you refer to a cartridge covering as a *foil* , be sure that it actually will be foil and not plastic or some other material.

- Give quantitative information for actions to be taken if it will help the reader. For example, "*Pull tape out approximately 3 inches* ".

- Give qualitative information for actions to be taken. For example, "*Press firmly to install cartridge*". This type of information should be used sparingly. When qualitative information is used extensively it can be confusing for users.

- Writers should not mix within a sentence or paragraph procedural information with general information about the hardware. For example, when documenting display panels and their indicators, be sure to do this before describing tasks to be performed using the panel.

Artwork Recommendations

- As with text, it is very important that the artwork or illustrations should be accurate, and uncomplicated. Artwork should be produced by a professional who is familiar with the hardware and with the tasks involved in its installation.

- The perspective of illustrations is very important for usability. Illustrations should be drawn from the perspective from which the user sees the hardware. The illustration must be recognizable from the angle from which the user is viewing the hardware when installing it correctly. In addition, users should be able to position themselves correctly by referring to the artwork. For example, if the user will be looking down into a cavity to install a component, the artwork should illustrate what the user will see when looking down into the cavity.

- Illustrations of part or parts of a large piece of hardware or a single large component should show enough of the total piece of hardware to enable users to recognize the part within the whole.

- Orientation of a component is important for usability. Illustrate how the component should be held by referencing handles (if available) and positioning of hands. Always make it clear which is the top, bottom, back, front, left side, right side etc., by using physical cues on the hardware and its components.

- The direction in which components are to be lifted, closed, opened, pushed, and so on, should be clearly illustrated with arrows. Arrows displaying the necessary movement should be included in the artwork illustrating the installation of the component.

- Use physical cues on the hardware and its components whenever possible to help the user with orientation. For example, draw attention to text on components, colored areas or obvious characteristics of a component or the hardware.

- The relative size of objects shown in illustrations should be the same as for the actual objects. For example, when including an illustration of hardware inventory, all objects in the illustration should be scaled down by the same degree.

- When using blow-ups of a part of an illustration, it should be made clear what part of the hardware is being detailed. The use of expanding arrows may be helpful.

- When showing display panels, identify all indicators in the artwork and explain their meaning clearly in the accompanying text.

Layout Recommendations

- Always keep a piece of artwork and the text which it describes in close proximity and on the same page if possible.

- Keep procedural steps limited to one action and represented vertically in sequence. Present tasks in a list format, do not place them scattered on the page. Only use a cyclical representation when the task is a cycle and can be represented on a single page or across facing pages.

- Limit the number of actions or tasks that are illustrated on one piece of artwork. Too many actions on one illustration will confuse users or cause them to leave out steps.

- If you are using callouts within the artwork to label areas, parts of the hardware, or actions, link up artwork and text by placing the corresponding callouts within the task instructions. For example, an illustration of the printer has a view of a drive arm labelled 'A'. Instructions to check the position of the drive arm should incorporate the drive arm label. For example, "*Check that the drive arm (A) is in the down position....*".

- When using symbols that will occur periodically throughout the text, (for example, to signify a note or a caution) explain or define those symbols at the beginning of the document.

- Simple operations or tasks need very little text, but artwork must be clear. Leave out unnecessary text for simple tasks. Safety and warning labels should always be written in full.

- Cautions and notes should be placed before the action to which they refer and preferably on the same page.

- If an action which only involves a few steps is to be repeated, repeat the text and artwork describing the action. If an action involving a lot of steps is to be repeated, do not repeat the text and artwork, but instead refer the user back to the beginning of the process in the document. Always explain to the user first, in either case, that the process is to be repeated and why.

- Do not use lettered callouts if the hardware that is being documented contains components that are labelled with letters. For example, a disk drive with two drives may refer to the drives as drive A and drive B. Use numbers or symbols as callouts to avoid confusion.

Translation Recommendations

- All general points on original writing apply to translation.

- Translation must be correct and concise. For example, the use the word belt in the original version of the documentation is meant as a mechanical belt. When the work 'belt' was translated, the word for a trouser belt was used. This may have resulted from the translator not having access to the hardware when doing the translation.

- Translators should not add any extraneous information to the documentation without consulting with the individuals responsible for producing the original document.

Process Recommendations

- Writers, artists, and a human factors specialist should collaborate on the development of the document in order to determine the most effective format.

- Translators, writers, and artists must be very familiar with the hardware and the processes involved in its installation. Writing, illustrating or translation cannot be done properly if the individuals involved are not familiar with the product they are documenting or illustrating. Individuals involved with the development of the guide should have access to the hardware and have performed the installation themselves.

- Editors should be familiar with the hardware and the installation process before reviewing the translated versions of the installation guide.

- Installation guides should be tested before the final version of the document is produced. Testing of a few user (4-8), may give some very useful information which can be used to refine the documentation.

# CONCLUSION

It was found that all three formats could be improved upon and the majority of comments and problems did not relate to the documentation format, but its quality. Many of the quality problems noted, besides affecting usability, also hinder the translation process. If the original documentation is not perceived to be of high quality, translators may change or add text to the document. If good writing and graphic design practices are not followed in the production of the original document, it is likely the quality of the translated version will be negatively affected. In addition, poor quality original language documentation increases the time for translation because translators must spend extra time to clarify text and related artwork.

It can be concluded from the results of this study that the suitability of a documentation format is governed or constrained by the complexity of operations required to install the hardware, and the quality of the hardware design. For simple installations, such as installing a terminal, that require straightforward tasks, of operating switches (on/off), and plugging in connectors, a format that uses most illustrations is appropriate. But these illustrations must be tested an validated to ensure their usability.

For more complicated hardware installations, it is necessary to use both text and artwork to illustrate the installation tasks. A textless version with tags on the artwork would also decrease the amount of translation needed. Unfortunately the textless format did not prove to be an effective format for an installation guide for this particular piece of hardware.

In addition to format, the process by which the installation guide is produced, also affects the usability of the documentation. Writers, artists and translators all must have access to the hardware, its packaging and all of its components before they begin to produce their component of the documentation. Writers, translators and artists, must be familiar with the look of the hardware, how it operates, the tasks involved in installation and the perspective at which the user will see the hardware in order to develop effective installation guides. The original documentation should be tested with users and subsequent translations should be reviewed by editors to ensure the quality of the final product.

Additional research would be necessary to determine any dependence or interaction between the design of the hardware and the documentation format. Further analysis could also be performed on time data to determine the distribution of participants time between reading the documentation and performing the task.

The present methods used to translate the documentation constrain translators' ability to manipulate text on artwork. It appears that the use of callouts (Format B) did not have a negative effect on the usability of the documentation when used by a European population. This format can alleviate much of the difficulty of manipulating the artwork and text during translation. Individuals involved in the design and development of hardware installation guides should be aware that there is a difference between the format of a document and the quality of a document. It is the format provided by B that was found to be suitable, not the documents general overall quality.

In the future the integration of new technology, graphics products that layer text on top of graphics, should be able to alleviate most problems with translating text within artwork. Until this 'layering' technology is widely available in the European community, the use of various documentation formats are effective for translation purposes. The usability of these various formats should also be investigated for US, Middle Eastern, and Far Eastern users. Eventually, the problems with physically translating the documentation can be overcome by the development of new technology and the introduction and use of some of the current graphic layering tools. Unfortunately, the use of these newer techniques can not compensate for a poor quality original document. In order to produce a translated document of high quality, the original language version must be of high quality.

## ACKNOWLEDGEMENTS

Several individuals deserve recognition for their contributions and assistance during this project. Maria Choules, Maggie Baranski, Janice Kite, and Jeanita Snowdon for their assistance before, during and after the study and Betsy Comstock for contributing her technical expertise and advice.

## REFERENCES

Brooke, J.B. (1986). Usability Engineering in Office Product Development. In M.D. Harrison and A.F. Monk (Eds.), People and Computers: Designing for Usability (pp. 249-259). Cambridge, England: Cambridge University Press.

del Galdo, E.M. and Baranski, M. (1988). A Study of the International Format VTX20 Terminal Installation Guide: Report of the Findings, February 1988. Digital Equipment Internal Technical Report, International Engineering Development, Reading, UK.

# TWO FACES OF AMERICA: POLYGLOT AND TONGUE-TIED

**Robert C. Sprung**

HarvardTranslations, Boston, MA, U.S.A.

US attempts to export high-tech products read like a Jekyll-and-Hyde story. American firms have been leaders in developing new technology for product internationalization and localization; yet Americans themselves are sadly deficient in the linguistic and cultural skills necessary for doing business internationally. This article surveys both sides of the issue.

America, the great melting pot, is notoriously monolingual. Of those graduating from public high school today, fewer than four percent have two years of foreign-language study. According to a 1973 survey—things have not improved much in the meantime—only five percent of those graduating to become teachers had taken courses introducing them to the culture of another country or to international politics.[1]

Americans traditionally harbor the same aversion to foreign languages as they do to dentists and tax collectors. The humanistically minded have done their best to promote foreign-language study—with very limited success. Their most powerful argument to date was the aesthetic and cultural benefit conferred by encountering a new language. Foreign-language study, we were told, would broaden our minds and bring us closer to our fellow men on the other side of the globe. Some stressed the practical use of language study: studying Spanish, for example, would allow us to communicate with our neighbors to the south and with Hispanic immigrants in the big cities. Such arguments fell on the deaf ears of local school boards, who had tight budgets and short horizons.

But a new sound is in the air—the tinkling of coins flowing into the coffers of American companies doing business abroad. Like the early explorers returned from the New World, US companies have peered into foreign markets and have brought back fantastic reports. Take the case of Digital Equipment Corporation. DEC's stock tumbled a full 10 percent of its value recently, due to lower-than-expected sales. Meanwhile, DEC's foreign sales were up 28 percent and, led by especially strong European activity, they now account for over half of the company's total sales.

Another surprise: the boom in exports is by no means limited to the IBMs and AT&Ts. James Howell, Chief Economist for the Bank of Boston, concludes in a recent study of the high-tech industries that young companies are competing as successfully as large ones in foreign markets.[2] Small US companies are exporting successfully practically from birth, Howell observes. A panel discussion organized recently by the International Business Center in Boston featured talks by representatives of small high-tech companies which had only recently begun exporting to Europe. Logicraft, a $10-million company based in New Hampshire which manufactures 386Ware, a multi-user DOS server, has seen its European sales jump from zero to 25 percent of total sales in less than four years. Bedford, Massachusetts-based Progress Software, manufacturer of a relational database language and program, derives almost 40 percent of its sales from Europe, and this small company began exporting only in 1985. The consensus among the experts: if a company's product can compete successfully in the US, there is generally no reason it should not compete successfully abroad. Yet many smaller US high-tech firms are just now waking up to foreign demand for their products, and most of them are ill-prepared to deal internationally due to linguistic and cultural barriers.

*Made in America*, MIT's recent study on America's declining productivity, offers these sobering words for those who doubted that foreign-language study had any concrete pay-off:

> Many Americans pay scant attention to life beyond the nation's borders. The educational system, from kindergarten through graduate and professional schools, has reinforced this inward-looking bias and has failed to open windows onto the world. The principal economic rivals to the United States, on the other hand, have long understood that operating in a foreign society requires mastery of the language as a prerequisite, together with significant exposure to different cultures.[3]

What has all this to do with international user-interface design? Everything. It first impacts the talent which produces internationalized or localized products, including everyone from translators to copy writers and graphic artists. While the demand for translation in America has skyrocketed as a result of the export boom, qualified translation talent has remained in frighteningly low supply. A mere half-dozen undergraduates major in German each year at Harvard, for example, compared with a figure at least ten times as at the current Catch-22: only a handful of Americans opt for a career in translation each year; meanwhile, the profession of translator does not command the respect due it from the general public (causing fewer to choose it). The American Translators Association (ATA), the main professional organization of translators in the United States, has made some important first steps in improving the stature and visibility of the translating profession.

Insensitivity to foreign-language issues also impairs corporate decision-making. A vast number of international marketing managers do not speak a second language. Some have first ventured abroad only after being named to the post of Vice President, International Marketing. Such a person usually has much more pressing and "important" things on his or her mind than translation and product internationalization. The *Wall Street Journal* recently ran an editorial claiming that the model manager of the future would not be an MBA or financial analyst, but rather an erstwhile Russian literature major with extensive experience living abroad. The MIT study advises US employers who want to stay competitive: "Insist that key employees have an adequate understanding of foreign cultures."[4]

A marketing manager will often decide not to translate his product's user interface (documentation, on-line help, etc.) with the rationalization that "they can understand English." (A vice president for international marketing called me recently, asking whether translation was at all necessary, "because isn't 1992 when everyone in Europe is going to speak English?") Even if the user can understand English—as may be the case with application development tools aimed at highly trained engineers—it misses the point. American marketing managers have difficulty grasping that *whether* the end-user can understand English is not the issue. Documentation serves as a marketing and public-relations tool (software reviews in foreign trade publications provide clear proof of this—poorly translated documentation is invariably held up to ridicule). A user interface which speaks to the user in his or her own language says, in effect: our company stands behind this product and will meet you on your own turf. To cite the MIT study: "Companies...will have to develop a new set of international sensitivities. The key fact here is that competition strengthens the hand of the customer, whose celebrated voice often speaks in languages other than English."[5]

great at the University of Cambridge in England. Those who can foresee the exploding demand for foreign-language skills shake their heads, Cassandra-like,

Unfortunately, the American firm's international marketing strategy is likely to be more short-sighted: "I've got a really tight budget for international," the marketing manager might say, "I'll let my distributor worry about it." A graphic designer who sees American CAD software with an English manual, littered with incongruous Dick-and-Jane examples, will often associate this with a lack of commitment on the part of the manufacturer, and will question the service and support that accompany the product. I was actually approached by a software manufacturer who wished to "take the plunge" and translate its manual into French, but with a bare minimum of expense—they insisted I leave all illustrations untranslated (which accounted for almost 50 percent of the document), even though they included such America-specific examples as aerobics centers and ranch-style homes.

### Case Studies

The good news, ironically, is that some of the greatest innovations in doing business internationally—in designing international user-interfaces in particular—are coming from "tongue-tied" America. The following section outlines the latest developments, including discussions with some of the technical and marketing minds leading the internationalization movement.

### Xerox: Creating a Global Standard

Americans, in their headlong rush to develop computer technology, have passed by most of the world. This according to Joseph Becker of Xerox, who is widely regarded as a pioneer in the field of international user-interface design. Becker helped create the multilingual text processing of the Xerox 6085 workstation (the Viewpoint software which runs on this workstation can support over 40 languages).

While developers are making headlines by integrating computers with live television, videodisk technology, and 9-channel sound, most people on Earth cannot even type their own name into a computer. Native speakers of English are so accustomed to typing on a computer keyboard and seeing English text appear on a display screen that they consider this to be a given, says Becker. But we would not take textual interaction for granted if our native language were Chinese or Arabic or Hindi.

Nearly every computer program has some textual interaction with its user, and a vast number of programs still use a purely textual interface. Yet no standards yet exist for typing, sorting, and displaying most of the languages of mankind. As a result, a computer user in Asia or the Middle East or India cannot interact with a computer program in his own language except in limited cases of customized software. And programmers in most of the world cannot put comments, variable names, or literal strings into their source code using their own native language.

Becker believes that the best chance for internationalizing computer textual interfaces lies in the adoption of a single standard text encoding that can handle all of the world's languages. Then all computer text interactions could potentially support input and output in any user's native language, without the need for custom programming in each case.

Xerox adopted such a multilingual text encoding as an internal corporate standard nearly a decade ago. Recently, Becker and a team of engineers from several Silicon Valley companies have come together to design a new encoding, retaining the features that have proved best in practice, while eliminating those that have not withstood the test. This new standard, dubbed "Unicode" (for "unique encoding"), assigns a unique 16-bit number to every character in the world's living written languages. (The old Xerox standard, says Becker, used a run-encoding technique to compress English text back to 7 bits per character, but the time lost in packing and unpacking the code proved to be more precious than the space required to store 16-bit characters.)

"The ASCII standard for English has taught computer engineers the virtues of a simple, fixed-width encoding," says Becker. "We hope that by merely stretching the width of ASCII from 7 to 16 bits, Unicode will retain the power and popularity of ASCII, while generalizing text interaction to accommodate all the world's languages."

On the surface, the task may seem straightforward, but after one takes into account such items as ligatures, Chinese characters, punctuation, and directionality (e.g., right-to-left for Arabic), one has opened a Pandora's box for both linguists and engineers.

Surveying the last decade at Xerox, Becker takes the greatest pride in having overcome some major technical problems—problems which have long since disappeared into the woodwork. For instance, it took five years to develop computer techniques that can automatically present Arabic text with the proper contextual directionality and character shapes. However, as soon as the Arabic subsystem finally worked properly, it became so "transparent" that Arab users ceased to notice it—they quickly came to take for granted the easy typing and display of Arabic text (it had become, in Becker's formulation, an "axiom of computer behavior").

While the developers of a standard international character set may not enjoy the limelight, their work may well be the louder shot heard round the world. The international E-mail market will boom once an international encoding standard is set, Becker claims. Currently, US-resident engineers from Xerox's Japanese affiliate company send their reports in native Japanese script back to the Tokyo home office via E-mail, using the Xerox 6085 workstation. Once they use this tool, they quickly come to regard it as indispensable. Yet few systems today permit international E-mail in languages other than English.

Becker is optimistic in the long-term. The technical barriers to letting people interact with computers in their native languages have been surmounted. Standards are in development—at Xerox, for example—which will finally permit easy world-wide communication on-line.[6]

### Total Solutions: BBN/Slate and ILA

To date, the state-of-the-art multilingual software has been Xerox's Viewpoint. But Bolt Beranek & Newman of Cambridge, Massachusetts, is readying a multilingual version of its popular BBN/Slate software, in an attempt to give Xerox a run for its money [see Illustrations 1 and 2]. BBN/Slate, a WYSIWYG program which has been on the market for two years, in a single application combines document creation (page layout, word processing, spread-sheeting, and graphics creation and handling), electronic mail, and teleconferencing. BBN has licensed new multilingual technology from International Lisp Associates, a spin-off of Symbolics, and will soon be able to support up to 30 different languages in the same document.

One can enjoy all the features of the Slate environment with each language, including "voice annotation"—by clicking on an icon of a loudspeaker one can play back the instructions recorded by a project manager, for example. A US financial officer can electronically send a financial statement to a French subsidiary for review, and have the French accountant speak into a telephone in the language of his choice to record messages.

Herbert Lison, a developer of Slate at BBN, contends that the system is unique because of its focus on communications—as opposed to printed presentation, the domain of programs like Interleaf. When the information presented has a time component, such as stock quotations or a report which needs to be in the London office *today*, Slate has the features to help. Its communications features are "transparent"—meaning that the underlying intricacies are hidden from the user. "Sending a file electronically with Slate is something a secretary can do without any special technical training," Lison claims. Slate runs on the Sun family of workstations, eliminating the need for special hardware (like the Xerox 6085 multilingual workstation). The basic Slate software costs $2,000 for a single user, with an additional $1,500 for the "multilingual engine," and another $750 for each language group (e.g., Middle-Eastern, or Slavic).

Mark Son-Bell of International Lisp Associates, a 2-1/2-year-old spin-off of Symbolics, has helped develop the underlying foreign-language algorithms used in Slate. Son-Bell acknowledges that Xerox was the real ground-breaker in developing multilingual technology, and that Slate's multilingual features are comparable. However, the ILA multilingual technology (originally a Lisp-based implementation, now also available in C) is not tied to the Symbolics hardware on which it was originally created. Xerox requires a specific hardware platform, notes Son-Bell.

A few keystrokes within the Slate environment provide both the keyboard mapping and the user environment, each in the script and language of the user's choice. One can choose an English system (English sorting, menus, etc.) and at the same time enter Hindi from a Hindi keyboard. Further, the system language chosen is intelligent. Switching from the German to the Swedish operating system, for example, changes both the keyboard mapping and sorting (alphabetizing, which differs from language to language). In German, both of the following sorting conventions are in common use:

| 1. | | 2. |
|---|---|---|
| a. oezz | | a. oezz |
| b. ozz | | b. özz |
| c. özz | | c. ozz |

In Swedish, one sorts according to the following scheme:

a. oz
b. zz
c. öz

ILA's algorithms, based on artificial-intelligence technology, give the user great freedom in configuring the system to his particular needs. Take the French convention that capital letters do not take accent marks. If you wanted to type "étude" in all-capital-letters using a conventional word processor, you would simply type a capital "E." In the ILA system you can simply hit the "é" key and let the computer worry about case-sensitivity. Thus, if you select "étude" and select the all-caps function, it will correctly display "ETUDE" without an accent.

The ILA toolkit can also be user-configured to check errors in orthography interactively—ensuring that the initial letter in a sentence is capitalized, for example. One may wish to have ligatures appear automatically. Instead of hitting a special key or command to obtain a ligature (such as æ, œ, fi, and fl), one need only type the normal letter combination (a-e, o-e, f-i, or f-l).

The ILA toolkit—as well as Slate, which incorporates ILA technology—has similar solutions for cases where the appearance of a letter differs based on its location. This is the case in Hebrew, where a "mem" is written differently when it occupies the final position, or in Arabic, where every letter can be represented in four forms. Son-Bell acknowledges the pioneering work Xerox performed in this area as well. In the ILA and Slate systems, if you press the single key for a given "letter," the computer can perform the contextual analysis of which form that letter should take. ILA has used LISP and the Symbolics architecture to apply the same algorithms or "common procedures" to a number of different languages—such as the code which determines if a letter in word-final position can be shared between two languages, as in Arabic and Hebrew. (These same techniques have been incorporated in the C-toolkit in BBN/Slate.)

The same position-sensitive algorithms are applied to Korean, where a letter's position in a syllable block determines the letter's appearance. Korean presents some of the stickiest problems for a language engineer. It contains both the native Korean Hangul, complete with ligatures and positional variants (i.e., letters "look different" based on their position), as well as Chinese characters which are still used in South Korea (as in place names). Hangul syllables are composed according to the following schema:

consonant • vowel • [optional consonant] • [optional consonant]

Thus, a consonant in Korean can appear in only one of three positions (first, third, or fourth), and vowels can appear in final position, or followed by one or two consonants (never first). In addition, each letter (vowel or consonant) takes a different form depending on where in the word it appears (please bear with me, it's worth the effort!) If one types in a consonant, then a vowel, and then a consonant, the computer must interpret whether that consonant entered last was the final consonant in the word (i.e., the first optional consonant above) or the first consonant in a new word (i.e., the previous word had no optional consonants). This is depicted in Illustration 3, where the following letter combination has been entered: M A M A. In step one, the program displays a stand-alone M. In step two, it displays the M-A combination (which, if it were an actual word, could stand alone in this form). In step three, another consonant is entered, which the computer momentarily interprets as the first optional consonant (note how the forms of the first consonant and vowel are altered automatically). Finally, the new vowel entered forces the computer to retract its hypothesis that the previous consonant was the first optional one—it was, in fact, the first letter of a new word, since a vowel could not stand in the fourth position.

Son-Bell and his associates are also working on a universal transliteration and transcription tool—for everything from Romanizing Hangul or Cyrillic, to converting a Romanized version into Arabic or Farsi. Such a tool would help process the mountains of material in Romanized Arabic, Chinese, and other languages produced by scholars that need to be transcribed into their native script. Transcription tools are important way-stations on the path to high-level machine translation. ILA aims to provide a universal transcription/transliteration product that is "table-driven." "Universal" implies a basic architecture which could eventually be tailored to any language. "Table-driven" means that the user can configure the product. This latter factor is critical for transcription, since so many standards and methods of transcription are currently in use—many scholars have their own idiosyncratic methods. With the ILA transcription tool it will not be necessary to buy a separate piece of software for each new language one wishes to transcribe. Transliteration is particularly complicated for some languages. For example, it is impossible to go from a Romanized form into Hangul without morphological information (or some sophisticated semantic analysis). The ILA architecture, with access to a Hebrew dictionary, will ideally be used to transcribe from Hebrew into Roman—currently an impossible task, since vowels are not normally written in printed Hebrew.

Son-Bell had some interesting comments about machine translation. He believes that machine translation has failed thus far because it has set overly ambitious goals, exemplified in the Chomskian search for a "black box" or idealized natural language. "No one has really looked at small-granularity, high-traffic" alternatives, such as translation programs for short fax transmissions. He notes that foreign-language-processing software has a lot of catching up to do after the watershed years of 1988-89 when raw computing power and memory became so cheap and easy to come by. Comprehensive solutions—those linking the input, output, and internal functioning of the computer—are the name of the game, and BBN/Slate is a step in that direction, he says.

### Lotus: Pioneer in Internationalization

Lotus Development Corporation, creator of the popular 1-2-3 spreadsheet, is widely viewed as a pioneer and "old grand-dad" in international user-interface design—even though the company was founded in 1982. Lotus had the foresight to design most of its products as "international" from square-one. This foresight has created products tailored to the needs of individual countries, helping turn international sales into one of Lotus's biggest profit generators. It has also greatly simplified the localization process—by having products that can be easily translated and customized, time-to-market has been radically reduced.

Things were not so straightforward with the first version of 1-2-3 (Version 1a), says David Gurteen, currently responsible for the international design of Lotus's product line. Lotus 1-2-3 Version 1a was a traditionally designed American product—the UK version did not even display the "£" sign, to say nothing of accented characters. To localize it would have taken a Herculean effort, since the code was not created with translation in mind. Nonetheless, many English speakers (and non-English-speakers) bought the product world-wide.

Symphony, introduced in July, 1984, was Lotus's first product designed as "international" from the very beginning. Symphony's first version accommodated international features, such as selection of date, time, currency, and number format. The second major aspect of internationalizing Symphony was in the engineering, where the code was effectively separated from the text which would eventually be translated—critical for efficient localization.

International consumers place incredible demands on a manufacturer to accelerate time-to-market, particularly as a result of rapid communication—the European high-tech trade press profiles the latest American software versions as soon as they are available in the States. When the French user hears that the new version of Symphony has been released in the States, he will not wait patiently until the new translated version arrives. Localization should thus start as soon as possible. The problem, however, is that the earlier one starts localization, the less stable the product becomes (the original product undergoes numerous changes before release, requiring translation revisions). A modification to the new version can spell headaches and additional dips into the corporate piggy bank, resulting in this horrific scenario: resource files are sent to translators (in Dublin or Tokyo, in Lotus's case), they are then returned to the States for modifications, and are finally returned to the translators for modifications. The window of opportunity for translating and making modifications to the translation is very narrow, Gurteen cautions. (Symantec, US-based manufacturer of the Q & A database, came up with a sneaky solution to the problem of translation lead-time. It released Version 3 of Q & A in the States in February, 1989, and shipped the translated version to France in May—calling it "Version 4," so that the French would not think their edition was outdated.[7])

Lotus is one of a handful of US firms with custom-made translation tools to expedite localization (even though Lotus itself does not have an in-house translation staff, but relies on independent contractors). The translator receives the text separated from the code in a standard manner, along with the special translation tool, called a Resource Editor. The Lotus Resource Editor allows the translator to use a split screen to keep track of edits—averting a potential nightmare. The Resource Editor can also ensure that the first word in a command is unique, and that prompts do not exceed the maximum number of characters.

A more specific problem that Lotus encountered was the translation of macros. With the early versions of 1-2-3, a French user could not use a macro written in the States—macros recorded commands under their English names, not according to tokens or resources. Version 3 will ship to France with two resource files: one with the commands in French, and one with the commands in English but with a French interface (allowing the French user to run English macros). In this latter case, the user would have to be familiar with the English commands, as well as having the fingertip memory to execute them (by initial letter)—and there are many such users, says Gurteen. A similar compromise solution was reached with 1-2-3 J, the Japanese version of the popular spreadsheet. Menus are written in Japanese, although the commands are invoked by typing the first character in the English command! Incidentally, 1-2-3 J runs under 5 PC standards in Japan, and markets one version for each platform: IBM PS 55, Hitachi B-16, NEC PC 9800, Fujitsu FMR, and Toshiba J3100.

The long-awaited Version 3 of Lotus 1-2-3 has been engineered as a single product easily adaptable to local markets. Even the US version supports multi-byte characters (necessary for representing Japanese, for example). Lotus has used third-party developers to tackle languages spoken by relatively fewer PC users, such as Arabic, Hebrew, Turkish, and Greek.

Lotus has heavily researched the special features required by individual countries. German accountants use different methods of amortization from Americans, for example, and the financial functions must reflect that. Illustration 4 shows the differing conventions for stock quotation charts in Japan and the US. Americans use a single vertical line to depict the day's trading range, with a left hash mark to denote the opening price of a stock, and a right hash mark for the closing price. The Japanese depict a vertical line intersecting a rectangle. Here, the vertical segment of the rectangle represents the trading range, and the horizontal sides of the rectangle represent opening and closing prices—no shading indicates an "up" day, and solid shading indicates a "down" day.

Unfortunately, Lotus is more the exception than the rule when it comes to internationalization and localization of American products. More symptomatic of the problem is a conversation I had recently with a vice president of international marketing about tailoring his US-made word processor for local markets. "That German hyphenation is sure a tough problem to lick, isn't it?" I queried, outlining for him some of the bizarre rules (when the word "backen" is divided at the end of a line, for example, the "c" is transformed into a "k": "bak-ken"). He cut the conversation short: he was going to call his German distributor immediately and see if he knew anything about this hyphenation business. (Incidentally, linguists Sasha and Margaret Nizhnikov have recently founded a small software firm in New Hampshire, Circle Noetic Services, to write hyphenation algorithms for European languages.)

The multi-byte architecture of 1-2-3 Version 3 permits some fascinating innovations. A worksheet file can now hold a mixture of foreign characters, such as Cyrillic, Japanese, and German. This means that a company with offices in Tokyo and Munich can use the same worksheet, with the headings and captions legible in each user's native language [see Illustration 5]. Those languages not supported by the local version of 1-2-3 simply are not displayed (e.g., the UK user can see the English headings, but not those in Japanese).

Let us conclude our trip to Lotus with some telling confessions from "International Czar" David Gurteen. "Apple is one of the best platforms on which to create well-engineered international products. It provides a lot of international support within the operating system," he admits. The resource files built into the Macintosh make the localization process "much, much easier" and cheaper as well. Gurteen is full of admiration for BBN/Slate, but questions its appeal ("how big is the market for that kind of product?") and warns that the application requires a great deal of memory, resulting in major constraints on the PC level.

### Internationalizing Output: Adobe and Bitstream

US firms are also hard at work on the "output" side, designing computer typefaces for use around the world. We all see and use so many fonts in our daily life that it is easy to overlook the subtleties in creating typefaces for international use, to say nothing of the extensive development time and investment.

How can the "tongue-tied" American produce a typeface that not only represents the language of a foreign nation, but does so in an aesthetically pleasing way? How can a US firm compete with top design talent abroad? The simple truth is that America's leading type houses—including Compugraphic, Adobe Systems, and Bitstream—have strong international connections. Adobe, for example, has worked closely with the German Linotype company in developing typefaces, and has worked closely with Japanese type giant Morisawa in creating its new PostScript kanji font.

Non-Roman writing systems—especially Japanese, with its over 8,000 unique characters in standard use—pose a special challenge to electronic typesetting. Adobe has met this challenge by extending the PostScript language itself. The designers of the kanji fonts (including Masumi Abe, formerly a colleague of Joseph Becker's at Xerox) faced other hurdles, any of which could have been a "deal-breaker": converting the data of existing character outlines, opening the tight connection between font foundries and their typesetting hardware, ensuring versatility of the characters, and supporting the variety of encodings (numerical identification of characters). Two typefaces, a *mincho* (similar to serif) and a *gothic* (similar to sans-serif), are now available. To date, Adobe has licensed these fonts only to OEMs directly; they are not downloadable. Apple, DEC, Linotype, NEC, and Fujitsu are releasing new PostScript printers to support kanji (and other non-Roman writing systems).

The artwork below, created with Adobe Illustrator's Japanese edition, demonstrates the innovation and versatility of Adobe's kanji PostScript fonts [see Illustration 6]. On the applications side, Aldus Corporation is hot on Adobe's heels, with its Japanese versions of FreeHand and PageMaker [see Illustration 7].

I spoke recently with Matthew Carter, head of typeface design at Bitstream and creator of the popular ITC Galliard font. Carter got down to brass tacks about the complexities of designing typefaces for international markets. For Western European languages, Bitstream ships an extended character set [see Illustration 8]. Diacritical marks are provided in both a text and a display form, since larger point sizes (such as 96 point) simply "don't look right" with the "standard" heavier accent mark [note characters 161 and 162 in Illustration 8].

Bitstream provides characters and diacritical marks separately, along with the assembly instructions for positioning them correctly. Illustration 9 shows an outline of the letter "o" fringed with all the available diacritical marks in the appropriate positions.

This is no mean feat. In addition to creating a typeface with a unified look tailored to the American market, designers like Matthew Carter with an eye to the world market must consider the aesthetics of each potential local market. Carter applies to international typography the adage that a chain is as strong as its weakest link: a font is a flop, in his view, "if you've blown it from the point of view of a single language." Illustration 10, from the Swedish typography magazine *Biblis*, demonstrates the obstacles faced by the non-native typeface designer. The author here criticizes a popular typeface from the point of view of Swedish, saying that the designer should have made the dot above the "j" the same size and at the same height as the "umlaut" above the "a" and "o." The reviewer further maintains that the circle above the "a" should be smaller, with its center point at the same height as the center of the newly aligned dots. Otherwise, they may "look funny"—the bane of a designer's existence.

How can a designer assimilate such knowledge? There is no easy solution, Carter says. When asked how he knew his Icelandic characters were on the up-and-up, he notes, "A friend of mine is the leading Icelandic typographer." Carter wishes he, "had a few good Hindi designers here." There is no substitute—save for trial and error—for sitting down with a native expert: "A half-hour with a well-informed Icelander will tell you all you need to know." Carter seizes every opportunity to improve on his designs: "If I run across a Czech or Pole who's well-informed, I sit him right down." Reference works, as well as existing typefaces in a given language, provide additional insights, but are admittedly of limited value when creating a new look with a typeface.

The fraternity of typeface designers is small and closely knit—Carter recently asked Arabic type specialist Walter Tracy, an old friend, to develop some new Arabic faces for Bitstream for use on laser printers. Illustration 11 displays one of Bitstream's Arabic fonts, complete with the four forms each character can take (whether it appears standing alone or at the beginning, middle, or end of a word), as well as the conjuncts which connect characters and allow lines to appear justified. Not only are such faces aesthetically beautiful—even to those who read no Arabic—they also meet the rigorous demands of the Arabic-speaking users.

Bitstream has developed many non-Latin faces, including Cyrillic, Greek (a particular speciality of Carter's), kanji, Devanagari, and Laotian. Carter notes that certain typefaces travel well and others do not, just as, "the French have certain cheeses they like, but that they don't export." Notwithstanding such national differences, Carter contends that the best typefaces sell well everywhere ("bum accents or no bum accents"). Bitstream's technique of providing the diacritical marks separate from the characters is an important step in allowing individual countries to have their own tastes reflected.

### Internationalizing Input: Articulate Systems

One of the biggest eye-openers (ear-openers, more appropriately) in international user-interface design comes from Articulate Systems of Cambridge, Massachusetts. The Voice Navigator is a voice-recognition package (hardware and software) that creates a verbal interface for any existing Macintosh application. It can "learn" a virtually unlimited number of discrete commands. By uttering the words "open checking account balance," "new check," and "amount," the user can update his account balance essentially without resorting to the mouse or keyboard. In a recent demonstration of the Voice Navigator in Boston, composer James J. Romeo nonchalantly beckoned a Macintosh to "play Misty for me"—whereupon a Kurzweil synthesizer faithfully responded with a fully orchestrated version of the old tune.

The Voice Navigator is inexpensive, with a suggested retail price of under $2,000. It is particularly suited for CAD and desktop-publishing applications, as well as for order entry or assembly-line work, bypassing the need for keyboard literacy. And it does not matter which language you use—in a recent demonstration, Articulate Systems Vice President of Sales and Marketing Dr. Stavros Cademenos found that even a visitor from China used the system without any problems (Chinese is a tonal language, not glottal like those for which the system was originally designed). The truism that you should design products from square-one to be adaptable for foreign markets can become a reality much more easily with products like the Voice Navigator—at least for the Macintosh environment. Instead of countless man-hours rewriting code, it may now be possible in many cases to have a voice-interface that is reprogrammed in a fraction of the time, in any language. The special Language Maker program which comes with the Voice Navigator strips out menu items automatically, making it easy to train the computer with the appropriate commands [see Illustration 12]. Articulate Systems is currently developing a single product that integrates voice, fax, and modem technologies—you will soon be able to call up your Macintosh from a trade show in Hannover, give a verbal order, and have your computer fax back important sales documents.

### UNIX Solutions

Many small US companies are hopping on the multilingual software development bandwagon, including a small New Jersey firm which has designed multilingual versions of the UNIX operating system.

While many UNIX applications have been tailored to a multilingual environment, the real solution is on the operating-system level, says IMT Multilingual Systems founder Ray Kasbarian. IMT's Arabix software, for example, provides a full Arabic UNIX operating environment complete with standard UNIX systems functions and facilities. This product is designed to co-reside with UNIX, and does not inhibit any UNIX processes. The Arabic user or developer also has access to an IMT system-level library of features specific to the needs of bilingual users.

IMT currently has UNIX extensions for the Western European languages, Russian, Arabic, and Greek. They provide two main products to support multilingual processing: one for internationalization and one for localization. The IMT core product (Runtime System) comprises the basic multilingual interface technology and is referred to as bilingual/multilingual operating systems extension (OSX). The OSX products provide systems internationalization and contain all of the UNIX system extensions as well as the general multilingual functions and interfaces. They generate the multilingual environments which permit users to operate applications in languages other than English. The IMT Development System Extensions (DVX) aid in localization by providing extraction and indexing tools.

IMT's multilingual UNIX-based technology features: *multilingual extension* (basic operating environment co-resident with UNIX); *bilingual user operations* (ability to toggle between local language and English); *dynamic keyboard assignment* (user can alternate keyboards of different languages at any time during work session); *applications transparency* (simplifies processing binary-level application programs in any language); *multilingual applications management* (indexes prompts and literals to user's language environment); *developers' tools* (to adjust application prompts, literals, and instructions); *multilingual PC links* (MS-DOS terminal emulation programs allow many special functions—like Arabic context analysis—to be located in a networked PC terminal); *international binary implementations* (IMT selects certain general applications and creates special language-neutral international binary versions which can run in any language supported in an IMT environment).

**News from the Translation Front**

A valiant few are struggling to raise the standards of professional translation in the United States. Multilingual software and hardware innovations may get the glory, but translators and documentation professionals are needed to hold down the fort. The Society for Technical Communication has laid the groundwork for creating a standardized form for multilingual publications.[8] A courageous few have targeted a much-overlooked trouble spot—the original "English" documentation to be translated is rarely standard, and often of questionable quality itself. In the words of Goelle Feldman, French technical translator for McCormack and Dodge, "there is one thing that doesn't translate well, and that's ambiguity."

In her article "Preparing Instruction Manuals for Non-English Readers,"[9] technical writer Stacey Sanderlin advocates the use of Controlled English (a simplified version of English) as an alternative to translation: "With Controlled English, non-native readers can actually read a manual in English after special training in the limited language." Such US companies as NCR and Caterpillar have put great stock in the use of Controlled English for technical manuals. Caterpillar created Fundamental English, while McDonnell Douglas produced a limited-word dictionary for aircraft manuals particularly for international use. Kodak has developed an International Service Language, which supposedly takes a non-English-native only two or three months to learn.[10]

Standards for original English documentation—such as the Controlled English Sanderlin advocates—can also play an important role in creating copy which may eventually be translated. Such solutions face practically insurmountable obstacles in the real world, however. Most American companies, with the possible exception of some of the corporate monoliths, lack translation departments, and the documentation department usually has much more pressing concerns than possible translation at some indeterminate date in the future. The other major stumbling block in the implementation of standards is the American educational system. Ms. Sanderlin suggests that writers use simple, declarative sentences and avoid the passive:

> *Write*: "Fill the drilled holes with wood putty."
> *not* "The filling of the drilled holes is accomplished with wood putty."[11]

In spite of Ms. Sanderlin's well-meaning and much-needed call for standards in English documentation, the problem remains that precious few can understand, let alone follow, these directives. Telling a writer to "use the active voice" is a good idea, but it presupposes that the writer: (a) knows what the active voice is (not a good assumption to make, given the current state of our educational system) and (b) knows how to implement that instruction.

Controlled English may appeal to US firms who dream of English as the universal standard, or who actually presume it has already attained that status. But they are quickly learning that the solution is not so simple, both in terms of talent to use Controlled English consistently, as well as acceptance of such a controlled language by end-users.

## Conclusion: Translation in the US

Let us descend for a moment from the heights of multilingual technology to the realities of translation. Having worked as a professional translator and manager of a translation bureau, I have had to respond to the most-asked questions about translation. Below are a few of the answers.

1. *Do you just farm out the work?* This question, usually delivered with uplifted eyebrows, reflects an understandable concern on the part of a translation client. Many translation services justifiably use independent contractors ("free-lance" translators), due to the highly specialized nature

of each job—it is not easy to support a full-time specialist on-staff to translate only Czech medical documents. The owner of a translation service, in the best of all worlds, would love to "farm out" the work without having to worry about quality-control issues. Some give in to this temptation, but they do not last very long. No translator submits work which does not require substantial editing, and running a translation service can (and should) make a hardened cynic out of even the most mild-mannered linguist—you simply learn not to trust anyone. A good translation service is judged by the quality-control mechanisms it develops—particularly important on the jobs requiring a large team effort, where after-the-fact cries of "I thought that *he* was supposed to check that" are all too frequent if a suitable quality-control mechanism is lacking.

2. *Should I have the translation done in this country or over there?* This, too, begs the more important question of "Is the right person translating my document?" Bad translation services abound in Europe and Asia no less than in the United States. There has traditionally been a trade-off between translating "here" and "there." Translating in the US assures greater accuracy due to close contact between translators and product managers or engineers at the client company. A translation created without the translator actually seeing and working with the product—a not unlikely scenario, if documentation for a large piece of hardware is shipped to a translator abroad—usually results in ludicrous misunderstandings. Meanwhile, translating abroad is said to result in more idiomatic translations and adherence to the latest standards. However, this old dichotomy is rapidly losing relevance, with the advent of fax and modem technology. One can now have it both ways, with professional translators working closely with the client on this side of the Atlantic, and translators cooperating on the same project on the other side.

3. *Are your translators native speakers?* This question, one of the most common posed by newcomers to the field, misses the mark. The United States is a country of over 200 million native speakers, only a handful of whom can write well in their native language. Being a native speaker is,

naturally, a prerequisite for translation into a given language—I have met two people in my life whom I would trust to translate into a language other than their native tongues—but it is only the most preliminary of criteria. My desk is piled high with résumés of "native speakers" who are mediocre translators.

The skills required on a typical translation project go far beyond basic linguistic competence. If you were marketing an accounting software package in France, you would need a translator who spoke French as a native, who was intimately familiar with American and French accounting practices, who understood computer processes and the current "lingo," and who could write clean, clear French prose. Or, more likely, you would assemble a team which included all the above talents.

To understand the translation business in the US, one must consider two basic factors. On the one hand, good translation requires incredibly sophisticated skills. Good translators are next to impossible to find. Further, managers of translation services are often themselves not linguists and may not be able to differentiate between a superb and a very good translator (a critical distinction). On the other hand, in spite of the level of sophistication required, translation is usually viewed as a very low-level and routine skill. One typically sends materials to a translation service much as one would send artwork to a print shop: one expects a finished product in return, with no complications and no questions asked.

This scenario has perilous consequences. Translation is a very under-developed business lacking in professionalism in this country. Fewer and fewer people opt for a career in translation due to the low esteem accorded the profession. Little is currently done to improve foreign-language instruction and awareness, impacting both potential translation talent as well as the talent who would potentially require translation.

I have tried to demonstrate in the above pages the need for change as well as the forces currently at work which are bringing about change. There are many grounds for optimism, with much of the impetus coming from US economic success in foreign markets. The most deeply rooted problems require a broad redefining of values and massive educational reform over the long term—and the long-term horizon does not appear to be a part of the natural American landscape.

NOTES

1 See Paul Simon, *The Tongue-Tied American: Confronting the Foreign Language Crisis* (New York: Continuum, 1980), pp. 1-19.
2 *Bank of Boston Survey: Exporting by Young High-Tech Companies*, Prepared by the Staff of the Economics Department, Bank of Boston, 16 August 1988.
3 Michael L. Dertouzos, et. al., *Made in America: Regaining the Productive Edge* (Cambridge, Massachusetts: MIT Press, 1989), p. 50.
4 *Made in America*, p. 150.
5 *Made in America*, p. 141.
6 For further information, see the following articles by Joseph D. Becker: "Multilingual Word Processing," *Scientific American* 251,1 (July, 1984), pp. 96-107; "Typing Chinese, Japanese, and Korean," *Computer* (January, 1985), pp. 27-34; "Arabic Word Processing," in *Communications of the Association for Computing Machinery* 30, 7 (July 1987), pp. 600-610.
7 Ron Wolf, "How Symantec Solved the Problem," *San Jose Mercury News* (31 October 1988), p. 7D.
8 See John Archibald and Alan Darisse, *A Guide to Multilingual Publishing* (Washington, DC: Society for Technical Communication, 1981). See also Fred Klein, ed. *Technical Communication Today*, special issue of *Technical Communication* 29, no. 4 (Fourth Quarter 1982), pp. 4-32. [Both cited in Sanderlin's article, listed below.]
9 Stacey Sanderlin, "Preparing Instruction Manuals for Non-English Readers," *Technical Communication* (Second Quarter 1988), pp. 96-100.
10 Sanderlin, p. 98.
11 Sanderlin, p. 99.

ILLUSTRATIONS, Two Faces of America

**The Enchanted Mouse**

Once there was an ascetic whose wishes always came true. One day as he was sitting on a river bank, a hawk passed by with a little mouse in its talons, and dropped the mouse near the ascetic. Taking pity on it, he wrapped it in his sleeve to take home with him. But then he worried that his wife might object to raising a mouse, so he made a wish for it to change into a little girl. His wish came true, and the mouse changed into a little girl endowed with grace and beauty, and the ascetic hurried home with her and said to his wife:

"Here is my daughter, treat her like your own child."

**الفأرة المسحورة**

زعموا ان ناسكا كان مستجاب الدعوة ؛ فبينما هو ذات يوم قاعد على شاطئ نهر اذ مرت به حدأة في رجلها درصة فوقعت منها عند الناسك. فادركه لها رحمة ، فأخذها ولفها في ردنه ، واراد ان يذهب بها الى منزله. ثم خاف ان يشق على امرأته تربيتها ، فدعا ربه ان يحولها جارية. فتحولت جارية واعطيت حسنا وجمالا. فانطلق بها الناسك الى منزله ، وقال لامرأته:

هذه ابنتي فاصنعي بها صنيعك بولدك.

**鼠精**

從前有一個苦行者，他的願望總是能實現。有一天，當他坐在河堤上時，一隻老鷹從旁邊飛過，將它爪中捉着的小老鼠，掉落在苦行者的附近。

那位苦行者懷著憐憫之心，將這隻小老鼠包藏在他的袖子裏，要帶回家去。但是他又擔心他的妻子可能會反對撫養這隻小老鼠，因此他就下了一個願，祈望將這隻小老鼠變成一個美麗大方的小姑娘。他的願望馬上實現了，小老鼠變成了一個漂亮的小姑娘。苦行者急忙帶着小姑娘回家並對他的妻子說：

「這是我的女兒，請您像親生女兒一樣的對待她。」

Illustration 1. Output from Xerox Viewpoint software, created on the Xerox 6085 workstation

كا ن ممثلنا في مو تمر ا لاطلنطي يكتب عدة مقلات مهة عن او رو با ا لعربية لما صلت
ا ليه مذكرة عاجلة تطلب منه ا لا ينشر هذه ا لمقلات تطلب منه ا يضا عدم ا لبحپ فيها

This passage may be translated as:

*"Our representative at the Atlantic Conference was writing a number of important articles concerning Western Europe when an urgent message reached him requesting that he neither publish nor speak about the articles."*

To: ashaheen
Subject: Spreadsheet for Saudi Arabian Ambassador's Office FY89
Cc:

| | Food | Fuel | Entertainment |
|---|---|---|---|
| Jan-Mar | $567.23 | $289.55 | $174.00 |
| Apr-Jun | 489.76 | 141.03 | 210.45 |
| Jul-Sep | 522.33 | 189.77 | 128.90 |
| Oct-Dec | 538.59 | 236.97 | 165.20 |
| Total | $2,117.91 | $857.32 | $678.55 |

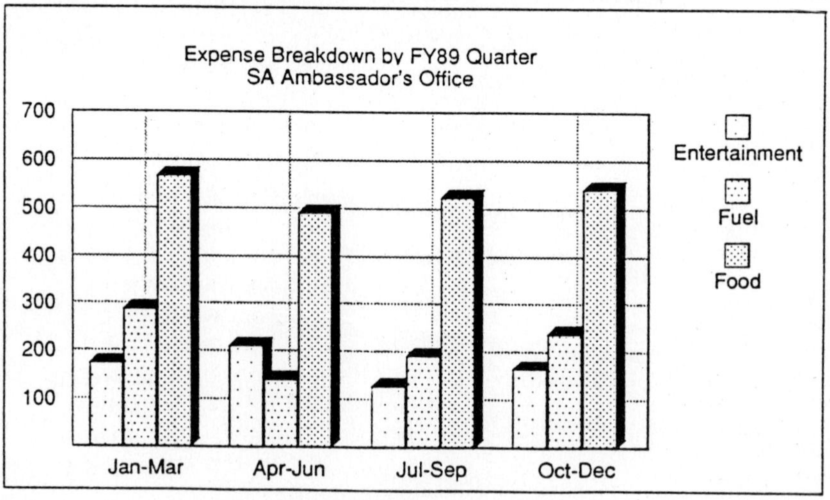


Illustration 2. Output from BBN/Slate software, created on a Sun workstation

ㅁ ;Type ㅁ

마 ;Type ㅏ

맘 ;Type ㅁ

마마 ;Type ㅏ

Illustration 3. Korean text entry (ILA multilingual technology)

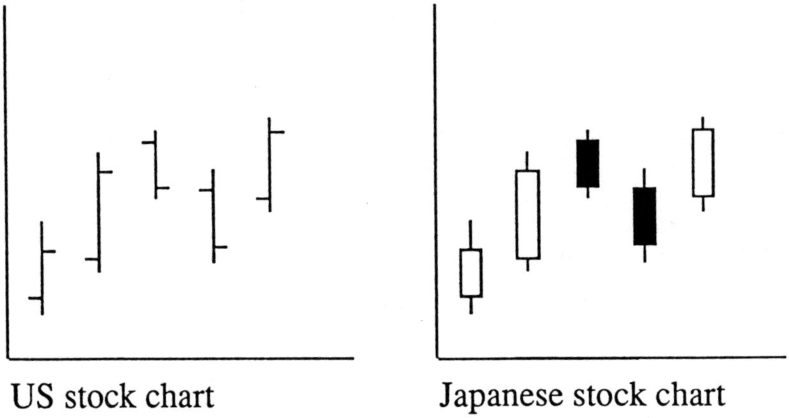


Illustration 4. US and Japanese stock charts

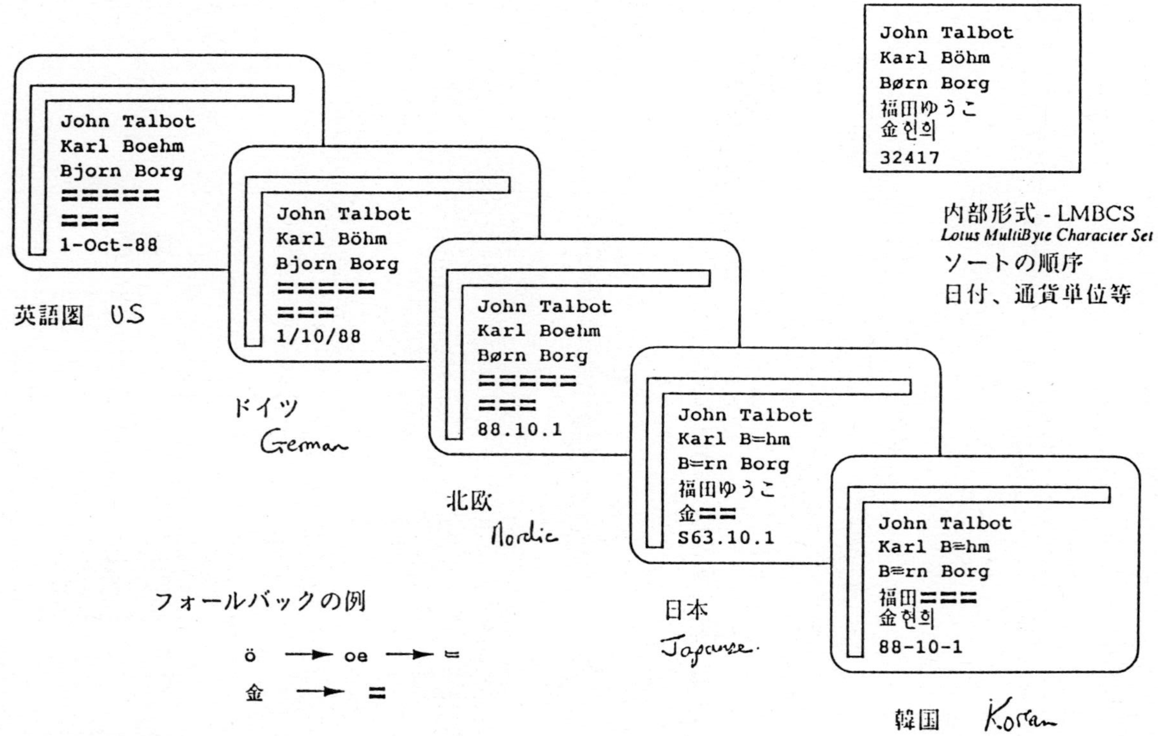


Illustration 5. Lotus MultiByte Character Set in action

Illustration 6. Japanese output using Adobe Illustrator

ビジネス講座:
ハイパーカードの堪どころ
1. メッセージ編

HyperCard

●大重美幸

昨年は、基本的なスタックをいくつか作ることを通して、ハイパーカードを体得してもらいました。今年は切り口を変えて、最低限理解しなければならない部分だけを説明していく予定です。言い方を変えれば、ここさえわかれば大丈夫という勘どころを押さえていきます。
初回は「メッセージ」です。メッセージはハイパートークを理解するための、もっとも大事なキーワードです。メッセージはどこからきてどこへいくのか。メッセージは何を語り、それをどう受け止めればよいのか。これが今回の勘どころです。

Illustration 7. Japanese document created in the Japanese version of Aldus PageMaker

| | | | | | | | | | | | | | | | | | | | | | | | | | |
|---|---|---|---|---|---|---|---|---|---|---|---|---|---|---|---|---|---|---|---|---|---|---|---|---|---|
| 001 | 002 | 003 | 004 | 005 | 006 | 007 | 008 | 009 | 010 | 011 | 012 | 013 | 014 | 015 | 016 | 017 | 018 | 019 | 020 | 021 | 022 | 023 | 024 | 025 | 026 |
| 5520 | 5220 | 5462 | 5990 | 4980 | 4640 | 6000 | 6380 | 2800 | 3840 | 5280 | 4490 | 7480 | 6160 | 6320 | 4820 | 6320 | 5580 | 4800 | 5160 | 6000 | 5340 | 8020 | 5180 | 5060 | 5060 |
| A | B | C | D | E | F | G | H | I | J | K | L | M | N | O | P | Q | R | S | T | U | V | W | X | Y | Z |
| 027 | 028 | 029 | 030 | 031 | 032 | 033 | 034 | 035 | 036 | 037 | 038 | 039 | 040 | 041 | 042 | 043 | 044 | 045 | 046 | 047 | 048 | 049 | 050 | 051 | 052 |
| 6080 | 4380 | 4660 | 3854 | 4880 | 4240 | 2770 | 4520 | 4870 | 2420 | 2300 | 4470 | 2440 | 7280 | 4910 | 4660 | 4760 | 4590 | 3300 | 3460 | 2890 | 4920 | 4270 | 6660 | 4350 | 4280 |
| & | a | b | c | d | e | f | g | h | i | j | k | l | m | n | o | p | q | r | s | t | u | v | w | x | y |
| 053 | 054 | 055 | 056 | 057 | 058 | 059 | 060 | 061 | 062 | 063 | 064 | 065 | 066 | 067 | 068 | 069 | 070 | 071 | 072 | 073 | 074 | 075 | 076 | 077 | 078 |
| 4040 | 4960 | 5000 | 3600 | 4800 | 4800 | 4800 | 4800 | 4800 | 4800 | 4800 | 4800 | 4800 | 4800 | 4800 | 4800 | 4800 | 7360 | 10580 | 1440 | 2400 | 2400 | 2400 | 2760 | 2760 | 1740 |
| z | fi | fl | 1 | 2 | 3 | 4 | 5 | 6 | 7 | 8 | 9 | 0 | £ | $ | ¢ | ƒ | % | ‰ | / | : | . | , | : | ; | ‘ |
| 079 | 080 | 081 | 082 | 083 | 084 | 085 | 086 | 087 | 088 | 089 | 090 | 091 | 092 | 093 | 094 | 095 | 096 | 097 | 098 | 0981 | 099 | 100 | 101 | 102 | 1021 |
| 3480 | 1740 | 3480 | 1740 | 3480 | 4200 | 2920 | 4160 | 3600 | 3600 | 3640 | 3640 | 4320 | 4320 | 4320 | 4320 | 2760 | 4320 | 8640 | 5520 | 5520 | 7480 | 6320 | 8580 | 4380 | 4380 |
| “ | ’ | ” | ‚ | „ | ? | ! | / | ( | ) | [ | ] | * | † | ‡ | § | - | – | — | Å | Å | Æ | Ø | Œ | å | å |
| 103 | 104 | 105 | 106 | 107 | 108 | 109 | 110 | 111 | 112 | 113 | 114 | 1141 | 115 | 1151 | 116 | 1161 | 117 | 1171 | 118 | 1181 | 119 | 1191 | 120 | 1201 | 121 |
| 6260 | 4660 | 7060 | 5260 | 2420 | 2120 | 2120 | 3820 | 3820 | 4200 | 2920 | 4320 | 4320 | 4320 | 4320 | 4320 | 4320 | 4320 | 4320 | 4320 | 4320 | 4320 | 4320 | 4320 | 4320 | 4320 |
| æ | ø | œ | ß | ı | ‹ | › | « | » | ¿ | ¡ | ´ | ´ | ` | ` | ^ | ^ | ¨ | ¨ | ~ | ~ | ˇ | ˇ | ¸ | ¸ | ¯ |
| 1211 | 122 | 1221 | 123 | 1231 | 155 | 156 | 157 | 158 | 159 | 160 | 161 | 162 | 163 | 164 | 165 | 176 | 177 | 178 | 179 | 180 | 1801 | 181 | 1811 | 182 | 183 |
| 4320 | 4320 | 4320 | 4320 | 4320 | 8640 | 3440 | 4220 | 4260 | 4380 | 3960 | 4820 | 4060 | 4660 | 4860 | 4940 | 4200 | 4200 | 5990 | 4490 | 5520 | 5520 | 4980 | 4980 | 4880 | 2440 |
| ¯ | ˘ | ˘ | ° | ° | — | 1 | 2 | 3 | 4 | 5 | 6 | 7 | 8 | 9 | 0 | { | } | Đ | Ł | Ą | Ą | Ę | Ę | đ | ł |
| 184 | 1841 | 185 | 186 | 1861 | 187 | 1871 | 188 | 189 | 190 | 1901 | 191 | 1911 | 192 | 1921 | 193 | 1931 | 194 | 1941 | 195 | 1951 | 196 | 1961 | 197 | 1971 | 198 |
| 4490 | 4490 | 2300 | 4380 | 4380 | 4240 | 4240 | 8980 | 5806 | 4320 | 4320 | 4320 | 4320 | 4320 | 4320 | 4320 | 4320 | 4320 | 4320 | 4320 | 4320 | 4320 | 4320 | 4320 | 4320 | 2348 |
| Ľ | Ľ | ȷ | ą | ą | ę | ę | L·L | l·l | ˙ | ˙ | ˝ | ˝ | ’ | ’ | _ | _ | · | · | , | , | ˛ | ˛ | ˛ | ˛ | - |
| 199 | 200 | 201 | 202 | 203 | 204 | 205 | 206 | 207 | 208 | 209 | 210 | 211 | 212 | 213 | 214 | 215 | 216 | 217 | 218 | 219 | 220 | 221 | 222 | 223 | 224 |
| 2400 | 5240 | 4600 | 4500 | 4640 | 5060 | 4240 | 4120 | 5100 | 5400 | 2520 | 3600 | 4800 | 4120 | 6260 | 5100 | 5240 | 4240 | 5400 | 4660 | 3960 | 4400 | 5180 | 4620 | 6536 | 4660 |
| - | Ø | A | B | C | D | E | F | G | H | I | J | K | L | M | N | O | P | Q | R | S | T | U | V | W | X |

Illustration 8. Extended character set for Bitstream Charter typeface

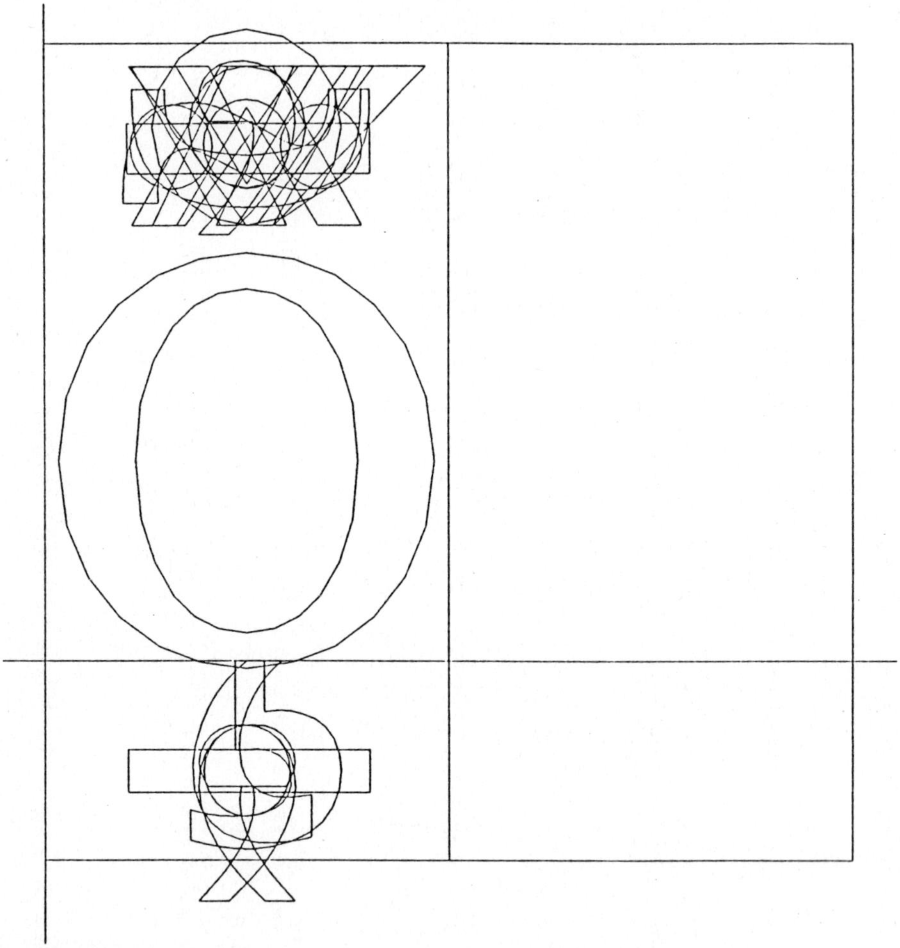

Illustration 9. Positioning of diacritical marks at Bitstream

ijåäö, själ fi

ijåäö, själ fi

Illustration 10. Swedish typeface critique, from *Biblis*

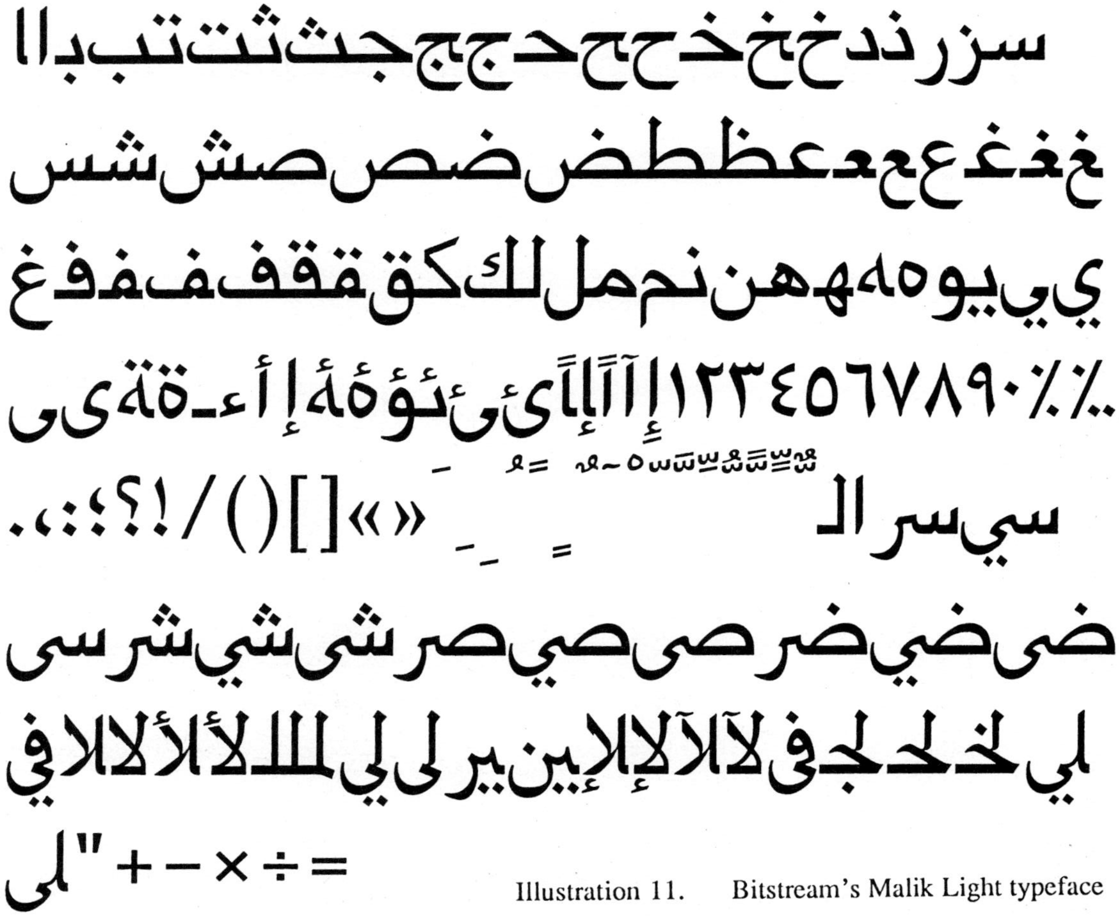

Illustration 11. Bitstream's Malik Light typeface

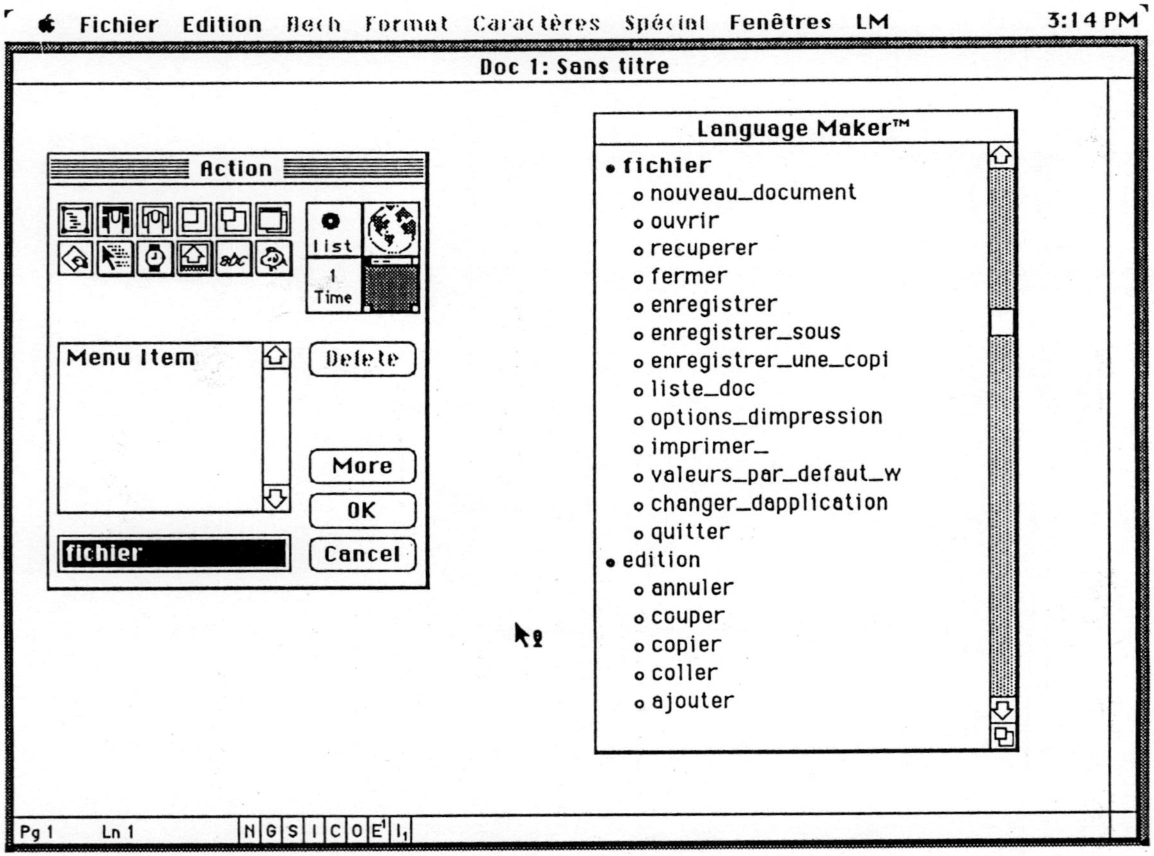


Illustration 12. The Voice Navigator's "Language Maker" program

*Designing User Interfaces for International Use*, edited by J. Nielsen
Elsevier, 1990


# ARRIS: REDESIGNING A USER INTERFACE FOR INTERNATIONAL USE

**M. C. Peterson**
Sigma Design, Inc., Englewood, CO, U.S.A.

## INTRODUCTION

This case study describes the steps taken to adapt the user-interface of a mature, commercially-available software product to meet the requirements of various international markets. It presents the interrelated technical and business issues which were considered during the design phase of this project, details the implementation of the first phase of the adaptation, and discusses issues relevant to future phases.

## THE ARRIS PRODUCT

ARRIS is a computer-aided design (CAD) product made and distributed by Sigma Design, Inc. It is used by building design and management professionals for applications such as architecture, retail space layout and facilities management. ARRIS consists of a base module and eleven add-on modules for functions including model rendering, site design, space planning, asset management and HVAC (heating, ventilation and air conditioning) design.

ARRIS was designed for the UNIX operating system and is sold for personal computers and engineering workstations based on 80x86, 680x0 and RISC (reduced instruction set computer) technologies. The languages utilized are C and Sigmac. (Sigmac is an applications language unique to ARRIS.)

When the software was first sold in 1983 under the name CAD Solutions, it was bundled with proprietary hardware as part of a UNIX-based turnkey system.

The user interface was oriented toward command mnemonics which could be typed or selected from a push-button menu built into the terminal keyboard.

In 1986, the user interface was redesigned to feature color on-screen and pop-up menus selected by a pointing device such as a mouse or a tablet pen. (Examples of ARRIS screens are not included in this paper because of the user interface's required use of color.) At the same time, the software was unbundled from the turnkey hardware, ported to standard, commercial UNIX platforms and renamed ARRIS.

## INTERNATIONAL REQUIREMENTS

When Sigma Design decided to market ARRIS outside of the United States and Canada, we initiated two programs to support this new business activity. One was to locate and authorize a distributor for each country in which we wished to sell ARRIS. The other was to gather requirements from these distributors regarding the internationalization of ARRIS, and to plan the implementation of the necessary features. Key to the success of the implementation was the development of an approach that would clearly balance costs against benefits, best utilize the talents of the staffs of both Sigma Design and the distributors, and most reliably result in the timely delivery of an internationally-oriented ARRIS.

The requirements submitted by our country distributors fell into two categories. One category required modifications to the functional content of ARRIS. While these requirements had some impact on ARRIS's user interface, that impact was not generally relevant to the design of user interfaces for international use and are thus outside the scope of this study. (The requirements included such items as better handling of metric databases, more flexible layout of drawing dimensions to better conform to the various industrial standards and expansions in the scope of symbologies to support diverse building design practices. This category also included capabilities for easily developing and connecting drivers for local brands of graphics peripherals such as video boards, plotters, tablets and hardcopy devices.)

The other category of required modifications included items that directly involved the user interface itself. It is these items that will be discussed in the following sections. Before examining the individual items, it is useful to discuss the overall approach taken to meet the objectives discussed above.

We took an approach that would divide the responsibility for implementation of local versions of ARRIS between Sigma Design and the individual country distributors. Sigma Design was to modify ARRIS to provide the general capacities and utilities for local customization of the user interface; each distributor was responsible for the local customization itself. This approach insured an equitable distribution of work, kept each organization focused on its own area of expertise, and localized the cost/benefit analysis of how much customization is actually required for commercial success in each individual market.

## CHARACTER SETS

ARRIS was originally designed to support the ASCII character set, a seven-bit character set limited to 127 values. While ARRIS allowed up to 26 character fonts to be used for each design project, the ASCII specification limited the number of characters in each font to 127. The ability of ARRIS to support an expanded variety of character sets was not only a frequently-voiced requirement from our distributors, but was also key to meeting a number of other international requirements.

While requirements ranged as high as 10,000 characters, it was determined that support of a 255-character set (eight-bit characters) could satisfy most countries' requirements. Based on this analysis, ARRIS was modified in the following manner.

First, the text subsystem was modified to support full byte (8 bit) characters. This project consisted of inspecting the code and cleaning up any situations which assumed that only 7 bits of each character were relevant.

Second, the text subsystem was modified to extend the range of a font to 65,535 characters. Careful attention was given to the font data storage and handling algorithm so that the amount of data storage allocated for each font was proportional to the number of characters actually specified. This was done to ensure the most efficient performance for each user, and most particularly to ensure that existing domestic users did not incur any performance penalty for a feature they did not need. The actual algorithm employed manages a font as a collection of 256-entry pages.

Third, a special mode was established for the text subsystem when extended fonts (fonts greater than 255 characters) are used. In this mode, a two-byte pair is interpreted as a single character. The first byte is the index of a font page and the second byte is an offset into that page. (In the normal mode, the index is always assumed to reference the first page.) The text subsystem user interface allows a user to specify a text string while in this mode by typing in a series of numbers between 1 and 65,535 delimited by blanks. Local distributors can expand upon this interface by developing custom menus to allow the characters to be picked directly by the user, by developing special input conversion routines, and by other techniques. In all cases, these locally-developed front ends translate the user's input into a series of numbers that are passed to the text subsystem.

In a fourth modification, a character font editor was developed for ARRIS to support the creation local character sets. Local distributors now have the option of bulk-loading the fonts from preexisting descriptions, creating the individual characters by hand using the editor, or using a combination of the two techniques.

One example of the creation of a local character set is the ARRIS implementation of the Japanese Industrial Standard (JIS) character set, which requires support of thousands of characters. The JIS character set orders several individual character sets into a master character set and assigns an integer index to each character. The individual character sets include most of the ASCII characters, two phonetic sets of 55 characters each (the traditional Hiragana and modern Katakana), and several thousand ideographic characters (a subset of Kanji). In CAD applications, the ASCII (Roman) characters are usually used for alphanumeric codes like part numbers, and the Kanji is combined with either Hiragana or Katakana for drawing annotations.

Once the special text mode described above had been implemented, Sigma Design's Japanese distributor wrote a Sigmac program to load the font from a previously-available vector file. After the font was plotted from ARRIS for visual inspection, individual characters were cleaned up as required using the font editor. Since it is apparently not unusual in CAD systems to specify JIS characters by their integer indices, no additional user interface was developed for this first phase. The distributor is currently implementing a front end that will translate input from an ASCII keyboard into Kanakata and Kanji. This front end will then pass the appropriate numeric indices to the ARRIS text subsystem.

## MESSAGES

At the time this project was undertaken, user messages were embedded within the Sigmac applications code. In order to make them available for translation, a new Sigmac output routine was developed.

The nature of this routine differed from the traditional solution in a manner worth noting. In the traditional approach, the message output routine takes an argument which is a numeric index into a message file. The translator then replaces the original message with the translated message. In our implementation, we decided to let the original message itself be the index. Through this method, the source code is more readable by the programmers maintaining it and the relationship between the original and translated messages is self-documenting. The latter feature will become more apparent from the following description of the routine's behavior.

If no compiled message file is present when ARRIS is invoked, a flag is set appropriately and the message routine simply outputs the original. If a compiled message file is present, the setting of the flag tells the message routine to obtain the translated message from the file and output it. The routine accesses the compiled file through an index created by hashing the initial characters of the original message. The text version of the message file is made up simply of entries consisting of the original message followed by the translated one.

Once this routine was designed and implemented, the following additional projects were undertaken.

First, all of the Sigmac source code was converted to replace old message output routines with the new one. This conversion was efficiently accomplished using a variety of automated and manual techniques.

Second, an in-house utility was developed to automatically create the original text message file by scanning the Sigmac source code for instances of the message routine and extracting the original message from each. This approach ensured that we could continually rebuild the message file during the development cycles, and that we can easily rebuild it for each new release or when we add a new module.

Third, a distributor utility was developed that would merge an existing translated message file into a newly-released message file. This was done to ensure that distributors could easily carry their translation work from one release of ARRIS to another.

Fourth, the entire system was designed to operate in the extended font mode. This is simply accomplished by allowing the distributors to specify a translated message as a string of numeric indices.

## MENUS

ARRIS had considerable flexibility in its user interface prior to undertaking specific modifications for international use. It used on-screen menu boxes, the menus made frequent use of icons, and the menus were already defined by external files for easy modification.

After reviewing the distributor requirements, one modification was made to the menu subsystem. The utility which builds the menus from the external definition files was modified to process the original menu box text through the same translation facility that was implemented for messages. Distributors who wish to customize the menus simply by translating the text need only translate the appropriate message file entries and rebuild the menus.

## PROJECT MILESTONES

This first phase of redesigning and converting the ARRIS user interface for international use was accomplished in one year. Sigma Design began to gather requirements through discussions with our international distributors in April 1988. By July of that year, we had agreed upon an external specification and had begun the internal design and implementation of features that would be incorporated into our next general release (ARRIS 5.6). We scheduled deliveries of special pre-releases of ARRIS 5.6 throughout the August-December period so that our distributors could develop their local customizations prior to the general release. (The August pre-release consisted solely of a message file to initiate translations; later releases were increasingly more robust.) After an extensive international quality assurance cycle, ARRIS 5.6 was released in March of 1989.

## FUTURE ISSUES

While ARRIS 5.6 represents an extensive redesign of the ARRIS user interface for international use, it is by no means exhaustive. A number of issues were deferred in the interest of meeting the majority of the requirements in a timely manner.

An ARRIS font character was originally specified by vectors on a 32x32 grid. The new font editor provides a 64x64 option. While the latter resolution is adequate for most characters, very complex characters like those found in Kanji require 128x128 for a quality appearance. The implementation of this resolution and the consistent behavior of characters specified at different resolutions are projects for the next release of ARRIS.

The text of some ARRIS messages are not predetermined, but are constructed during program execution. Providing a translation capability for this class of messages is under investigation.

Currently, keyword input must be given in the original language. A capability for allowing translation of keyword prompts and input is under investigation.

## CONCLUSIONS

ARRIS is now sold in over fifteen countries outside of North America. The ARRIS experience suggests that user interfaces not originally designed for international use can be successfully re-engineered toward that end.

The ARRIS experience also suggests that designers of user interfaces should focus on providing enabling capabilities for local customizations rather than providing the customizations themselves. Attempting to deliver customized versions of a software package is often beyond the expertise of the original authors. It tends to be costly and cumbersome. It usually results in too little or too much customization with respect to local commercial requirements.

The ARRIS case study should be of equal value to those who are designing as well as redesigning a user interface for international use.

*Designing User Interfaces for International Use*, edited by J. Nielsen
Elsevier, 1990


# HYPERTEXT - TOWARDS THE SINGLE INTELLECTUAL MARKET

**Patricia Baird**

University of Strathclyde, Glasgow, United Kingdom

## Introduction

Computerised information systems which enable the storing, retrieving and dissemination of information are pervasive. People accept and use them in many walks of life -- in education, in travel agencies, libraries, banks, department stores etc. A multiplicity of systems exists (some of which are easier to handle than others) to support the presentation of computerised information. For whilst the machine support for each system is standard, users of systems and their cultural and educational backgrounds, vary enormously. Authors/designers therefore have a significant task to ensure that the coming together of users and systems is as trouble-free as possible.The point of contact is known as the user-interface, and whether that be a teletext screen, an online catalogue, a cashline dispenser, an interactive video disc or some other medium, the usability and the ultimate success if the system depends on the conviviality of the interface. The most successful interface is the one which, effectively, 'disappears'; the one which presents the user with a transparent, seamless environment to access the information. It is the information which is important, not the enabling technology. Increasingly, the key to competitive advantage for electronic products in the market place, is the ease with which the information and the technology can be integrated. The design of the front-end, or interface, is vital.

## Hypertext

Hypertexts are novel forms of information management, offering users access to computer-supported systems of non-sequential reading and writing. The hallmark of hypertext lies in the capability of linking disparate nodes of information in a database, creating webs of connected material, enabling end-users to navigate through the database, activating the preset links using a pointing device such as a mouse, roller-ball or touch-screen. The information environment in which the user works is analogous to a full documentation system, where all the references and footnotes and marginal glosses and background information are instantly available along with the original document. The user is thus presented with an enriched information arena where there is no one 'right' way to go through the data; where there are no common commands; where there are no complex instructions to learn; where there need be no intermediary; where the novice user feels at one with the technology, is in complete control and enjoys the experience. The hypertext, in other words, should offer the friendliest of interfaces and be end-user driven.

As well as allowing users access to large complex systems, hypertexts also provide authors with new ways of working, presenting and organising information. The data is organised and tailored, creating a system to satisfy and empower the individual. To revert to Douglas Englebart's call in the 1960s -- our documentation systems should focus on the computer augmenting the person, not the reverse (Englebart, 1963).

**Interactive/user-driven systems**
Hypertexts are interactive. User groups are not always homogeneous. Designers of hypertexts must take these two premises as their starting point. Producing an interactive learning system for a varied user group requires the author to take account of the needs of the user group, and the levels of cognition and comprehension which the group brings to the system. Matching user interface design to user needs is vital to the success of a good hypertext system; matching the user's conceptual model of what the system may contain to what the author has provided is also vital towards the process of intuitive interaction. This is particularly true where the system is designed to meet the information requirements of international users. Continuous tracking and testing of the interface is essential, with subsequent re-vamping of the links if this proves necessary. Authors, however, have an ongoing problem with unequivocally conveying meaning of content and links. The problem centres on the author's ability to distance himself, his own value judgements and his own cognitive activity from the system. As Doland notes (1989):

> What, then, ought we to do to assure that the hypertext becomes an extension of the human mind rather than a channel for it to flow within?...We will have to be aware of the ways in which the structure and content of a hypertext document can create meanings and relationships; we will have to be aware of and comfortable with the notion that there is nothing that is not ideological ... For large research projects it might be well to establish a peer review process of the hypertext document...Users should be able to determine without difficulty the purpose of the linkage.

**Glasgow Online**
To highlight some of the inherent difficulties of creating a user interface which will be of use to the entire community, this chapter will concentrate on *Glasgow Online* , which is a hypertext created by the Department of Information Science at the University of Strathclyde, using Apple's software, HyperCard. Hypertext has been widely discussed and written about in the past two years, since the *HyperTEXT '87* conference at Chapel Hill, North Carolina (1987). The *Glasgow Online* team, comprising 21 people ( rising to 31 later in the project), was established in 1987. The main thrust of the project was not to create new information on the City, but to add value by re-packaging and re-structuring existing information. The end-product is a public domain utility which will be sited with interested agencies and organisations including tourist information centres, public libraries, hotel foyers, air, bus, rail termini, European Information Centres, academic institutions, citizens' advice bureaux. The project's intention is that the database should not be allowed to atrophy, but will

be a regularly updated utility. In its second year, now that the critical mass of data has been achieved, the team has been reduced to two, whose principle tasks will be to enhance and update the database every three months.

Information available on *Glasgow Online* is as shown in figure 1. Mark 1 of the database comprises 16 Mb of information and is expected to grow with each update. The work of the first few months of the project concentrated on identifying, gathering, collating, validating and updating information and data from organisations, businesses, retail outlets, services and other agencies throughout the City.

Figure 1

The design and structure of the database has been an evolving and developing process throughout, and will continue as new data and new methods of presentation become apparent. Creating the navigational paths through the data is relatively straight-forward within HyperCard. Determining what those navigational paths should be is more problematic. The programming language of the software is called HyperTalk and is as near to English, at the first level, to enable non-programmers to link nodes and allow multiple levels of access to the data. No technical expertise or prior knowledge is required. However, as authors ascend the learning curve and become more ambitious regarding presentation, a knowledge of data structures and information management, can certainly help. But to create stacks and present meaningful information within HyperCard, the major restricting influences are imagination and a flair for graphical display of information. The correct mix of text, icons, graphics, animation and sound (all of which is possible with HyperCard) to meet the needs of the intended user group, is the principle task for the hypertext author.

**Transparent/seamless environment**

The interface must be transparent and unobtrusive so that it does not interfere in any way with the user's understanding of the system. Those hypertext systems which will be successful and which will survive will be the ones which will virtually disappear -- which will become transparent enabling technologies allowing access to the information they host. The hypertext should be as unobtrusive as the pencil. No-one marvels at the pencil, yet as an enabling 'technology', it is remarkable -- not *per se*, however, but for enabling the user to produce words on the page, thereby contributing to the communication process.The medium must never obscure the message.

Interface therefore is all important, especially in the construction of a database which is intended as a community information resource. The determining factor in design and structures must not rest with the enabling technology, but on the needs of the intended target population of the finished product. Throughout the first year's development, significant emphasis was placed on testing the database. It has always been the intention of the project team at Strathclyde to be guided by the user group, rather than relying on the technology to drive the development. Since there is, as already noted, no one 'right' way to access a hypertext, then particular attention must be paid to the needs of the intended user group; the prior knowledge they bring to the system; their patterns of cognition; the mental model they have of the structure; their level of comprehension and the ease with which they can recover should they get lost.

**Orientation**

Getting lost in hyperdocuments is a significant problem, which authors of hypertexts must be aware of and address early in system development. The user should know where he is; where he has been; where can he go from here. Hypertext systems, provided careful authoring has been undertaken at the outset, can support tangential thought patterns. Users can choose their own specific navigational paths through the data using preset links to obtain customised information. In a traditional linear learning situation, users do not have or expect all the information available all of the time. Too many choices can lead to disorientation whether the environment is linear or non-linear. So perhaps getting lost in the hyperdocument is not the real problem since, in the normal course of events, some of the people are going to get lost some of the time. The real problem rests with recovery mechanisms and the system's ability to backtrack. The interface must always support the user. The Glasgow system does not yet incorporate full backtrack features, although this is an anticipated enhancement which HyperCard will support. It does, however, allow the user who feels disoriented to exit to the main menu from any card in the system and start again. This, of course, is not ideal but goes some way towards backtracking. The 'Exit' button appears on every card on the system in the same place -- bottom right of the screen. (See figures 1 and 2). This in turn raises the matter of consistency across the system. The hypertext should be structured in such a way that users quickly learn where to expect recurring features, leitmotifs etc. The 'Help' button also appears consistently on every screen in the system beside the 'Exit' button. The use of recurring features aids the learning process for all users and is particularly valuable for non-English speakers who will be looking for familiar landmarks throughout. Familiarity with the system will not be eased if the screen is constantly 'changing its face'.

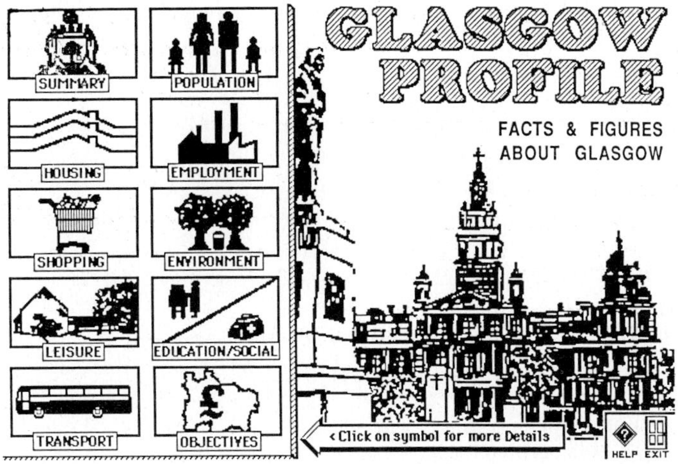


Figure 2

## Guiding clues

Linear text has inbuilt clues which guide the user through the text, e.g. page numbers, paragraphs, footnotes, punctuation, layout etc. Non-linear presentation should not try to ape the prompts of linear text but should adopt clues appropriate to hypertext systems e.g. highlighting, flashing signals, reverse video and others embedded in the text. Authors of hypertexts must be careful not to compromise the software by stepping back from the unique characteristic of hypertext i.e. the capability within non-linear structures, of retrieving customised information along lateral links as well as hierarchical links. The user's attention must be drawn, as it were 'subliminally', to the active areas on screen which open up the navigational routes. Authors should also avoid overall explicitly signalling which way to go next. The user should always have a choice. The 'Help' screen in *Glasgow Online* (figure 3) indicates the variety of cues which guide the user through the system and greatly assists button recognition which allows lateral navigation.

Figure 3

Much of the data is hierarchically structured but to offer hierarchy as the sole means of access, is not true hypertext. This would merely pour existing structures into the hypertext vessel.

**System testing**

If interface is the most important aspect of producing a good hypertext system, then the other side of that coin is testing. Seven test sites were chosen during the first year of the Glasgow project, as well as full HCI testing at the HCI Centre at Heriot-Watt University. Full accounts of the testing have been documented elsewhere (Baird and Percival, 1989 and Hardman, 1989) but it is worthwhile specifying one of the test groups (germain to this present volume) and examining their reactions to the system. During the summer of 1988, the University hosted the Second International Conference of Industrial Mathematicians. Two characteristics predominated -- many of the participants were visiting Glasgow for the first time and, in the main, their first language was not English. The system fulfilled three functions -- demonstrating Apple's HyperCard software; providing an information resource for what was probably the first group of 'tourists' to use *Glasgow Online*, and providing a valuable testing ground for the development team. In the main the conference participants came from various European countries. There were a few from Japan and some African countries also.

Two systems, which were well signposted, were on hand for the three days of the conference outside the main auditorium. No direct invitation was extended from the Departmental testing team to use the database, since voluntary use was considered vital. The impetus to use *Glasgow Online* arose as a direct result of the perceived needs of the participants themselves for information about the City. Having used the system, each user was asked to complete a questionnaire and to make any general comments. Questions centred on ease of use and utility of the system. Some declined to complete the questionnaire, but, based on those who did, an analysis of the results and the observation techniques employed by the research team, over the three day period of the conference, indicated positive reaction and a narrow spread of responses (see figure 4).

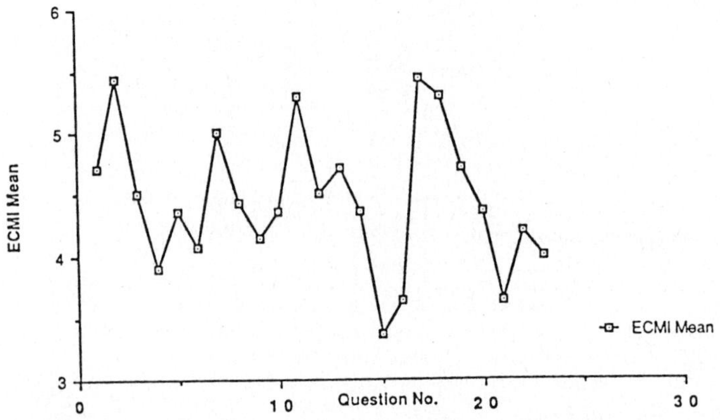


Figure 4

Those who used the system found the information they were looking for, and comments, amongst other things, indicated that they enjoyed the experience of using the system.
The fact that they mostly required the whereabouts and locations of pubs and restaurants was immaterial: the system's use of graphics and icons to complement and elucidate the text enabled *Glasgow Online* to answer real questions for real people. Language was not a barrier.

**Button/icon recognition**
The conceptual design stage of any computerised system for international use poses many problems for authors. Two of the most important are overcoming language difficulties and comprehension of language substitutes. The system's ability to integrate meaningful icons/graphics with text alleviates the problem of providing information for those whose first language is not English and, by extension, the success of the interface depends on users recognising buttons and icons.*Glasgow Online* relies heavily on the use of internationally recognised icons. The intended user group, as has already been suggested, will largely comprise visitors to the City, many of whom are non-English speakers.Therefore the authors have tried to utilise internationally-recognised icons as much as possible instead of relying entirely on text-based information. There are many problems with the choice and recognition of icons and the debate over icons versus text goes on. Yet icons are economical. They depict in a relatively small physical space what would often, spatially, take more text to indicate. Icons also transcend borders and languages. For instance, in the 'Accommodation' stack of *Glasgow Online*, iconic information is used extensively to convey facilities available within hotels in the City (figure 5).

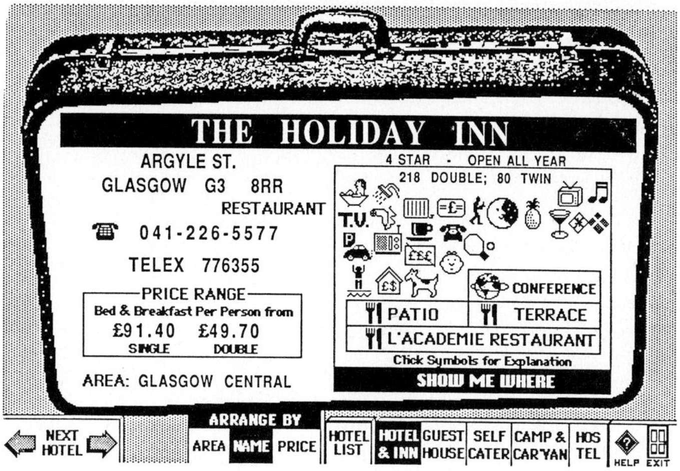


Figure 5

These icons are used and understood globally, but a safety net in the form of an iconic index is provided for those who require it (figure 6). *Glasgow Online*, avoids vast chunks of text, preferring to exploit the extensive graphics capability of the Macintosh environment. This presents a pleasing interface which puts non-English speakers as well as non-computer literate users at ease. For community information, extensive text-based information is inappropriate since literacy/comprehension levels are indeterminate factors.

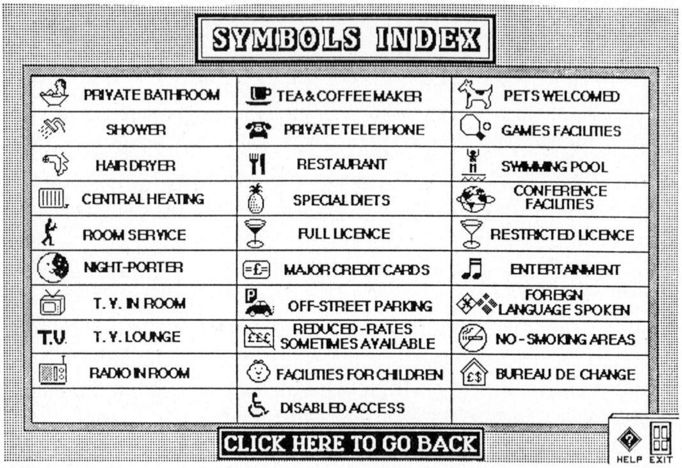


Figure 6

## Translation

Text at certain points, however, is necessary, and the problems and possibilities of automatic translation may have to be assessed. We require a lingua franca to speak to each other globally, and English is universally assuming the position of front-runner in that field. However, it is generally accepted that cultural nuances cannot be divorced from language and that the unique presentation and retrieval of information can best be achieved through individual languages. As we approach 1992, an interesting overview of the future of multilingualism and automatic translation techniques explores the problem of combining language and information within the European context and offers some solutions (Pogson, 1989). In the United States, work being is being undertaken at Dartmouth College to develop an interactive learning program to help students of Chinese. The program is called *Hanzi Assistant* and it has been designed to work with HyperCard. The multiplicity of characters which comprise the Chinese language will be graphically displayed, stroke by stroke, and accompanied by pronunciation recorded by Beijing Chinese radio announcers. The program will also offer a translation and phonetic service within the initial work, which produced a 300 character version. Further funding is being sought to complete a 2,000 character version to be available comercially on CD (Business Week, 1989). So advances in translation techniques together with the advent of software environments which are hospitable to sound features will further ease the interface problems for international users.

## Semantic models

Lateral movement within and between stacks should always be possible and this involves the creation of organisational and referential links. Organisational linkage can be achieved by hierarchies, but also by utilising semantic net theory, which defines meaning within particular fields. Meanings of words become known as they are contrasted with the meaning of related terms. This can lead to structured models of semantic memory which include hierarchies but also include related terms. For instance in *Glasgow Online*, a simple hierarchy may be as shown in figure 7; extension into a semantic model in figure 8.

Art Galleries---Burrell Gallery---Paintings---Impressionists. (Figure 7)

---

Art Galleries---Burrell Gallery---Paintings---Impressionists
I
I
I
William Burrell---Shipping---Heavy Industry
I
I
I
Service Industries (Figure 8)

---

The complexity of the system can be relieved by presenting graphical browsers at various stages in the system showing users the possibilities for connection. A graphical browsing facility would facilitate access to the system particularly for international users, who may not intuitively grasp nuances within language and therefore miss some linking possibilities. Semantic models include terms related by connotations which are not always transparent to non-English speakers.

**Read and write systems**

Hypertexts are systems for reading and writing, and although *Glasgow Online* is a read only system at this stage, the capability is there within the system for users to write to the database, creating their own links, leaving their footprints which subsequent users can benefit from without disturbing the integrity of the original text. This concept, writ large, is Ted Nelson's eventual hope for Xanadu. The most fully developed account of his vision (Nelson, 1987) is contained in the work *Literary Machines* . Such a facility would also act as a self-monitoring device, where users comments on design, interface and links could be used by authors to regulate stacks and extend semantic models when updating.

**Overload**

There is the temptation when creating HyperCard stacks to pack in so much detail to each card that cognitive overload arises. Overload results in loss of clarity, irritation, difficulties with mental processing and should be avoided. In *Glasgow Online*, some cards in particular show a tendency to card clutter, (see figure 9). A decision had to be taken between retaining busy cards, so putting clarity at risk, and the flexibility given to the user to move laterally through the system by means of the multiple icons, shown on figure 9, as button areas. Multiple icon access was adopted as policy, again benefitting international users by relieving them from too much reading. Overcoming the problems of 'busy' cards whilst retaining the icons can be accomplished by filtering techniques and zoom facilities which will be another future enhancement of*Glasgow Online*.

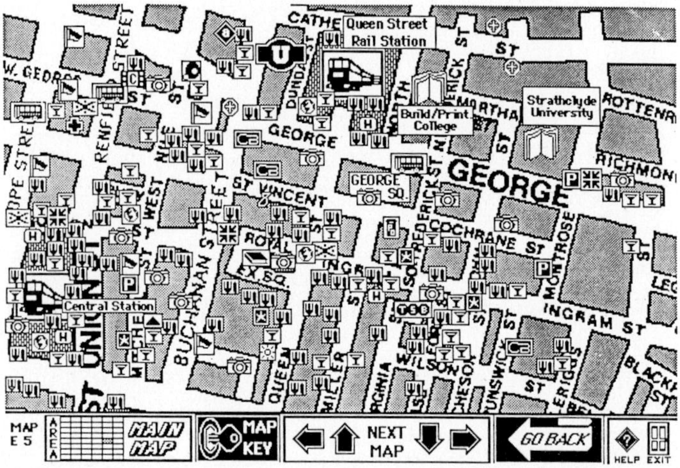


Figure 9

**Future enhancements**
Sound, colour and animation increase the impact and information retrieval functionality of any system. It is expected that a future version of HyperCard will support colour. In the meantime, a third-party development called SuperCard, produced in California from HyperCard, is already on the market. Colour clarifies meaning, and signalling is facilitated by its prudent use. Sound and animation also arrest attention and software such as MacRecorder, a highly commended sound package, and VideoWorks for animation may figure in future versions of *Glasgow Online.*

**Conclusions**
Designing community information systems which traverse borders, have international appeal and support comprehension is a time-consuming, labour-intensive activity. A significant investment in research and testing is necessary before and during development. The questions of consistency of approach, ease of learning, flexibility, familiarity, cognitive overload are often only answered after extensive on-site testing. The important matter of costs, which would be inappropriate to discuss here, is another major factor which requires careful examination. Integration into a hypertext environment does, however, add value to existing information and provides the user with an information arena which other methods of presentation could not support.

**References**

1. BAIRD, P. and PERCIVAL, M. Glasgow Online: database development using Apple's HyperCard. *Hypertext: theory into practice* Oxford, Blackwell Scientific Publications, 1989, pp.75-92.

2. *Business Week* 19 June 1989, p.74.

3. DOLAND, V. Hypermedia as an interpretive act. *Hypermedia* Vol.1, no.1., London, Taylor Graham, Spring 1989, pp.6-19.

4. ENGLEBART, D. G. *A conceptual framework for the augmentation of man's intellect in vistas in information handling* . Washington, D.C., Spartan Books, 1963, pp.1-29.

5. HARDMAN, L. Evaluating the usability of the Glasgow Online hypertext. *Hypermedia* Vol.1., no.1. London, Taylor Graham, Spring 1989, pp.34-63.

6. NELSON,T. *Literary machines* Edition 87.1, San Francisco, CA., Published by the author, 1987.

7. POGSON, G. An in-depth look at Europe's multilingual challenge. *LT Electric Word* no.13, Amsterdam, Louis Rosetto, May/June 1989.

8. *Proceedings of HyperTEXT '87.* Chapel Hill, University of North Carolina, 1987.

*Designing User Interfaces for International Use*, edited by J. Nielsen
Elsevier, 1990


# CREATING INTERNATIONAL APPLICATIONS

## A Hands-On Approach using the Hewlett-Packard NLS Package

**Dave Taylor**

Intuitive Systems, Mountain View, CA, U.S.A.

While there is a fair amount of literature discussing the cultural and sociological differences between countries and the challenge of creating software, hardware, documentation, and packaging for international use, there is very little written about how to actually *do* it. In this section we'll demonstrate the "internationalization" of a simple program through use of a vendor supplied package.

The particular toolkit featured will be the Hewlett-Packard Native Language Support System as found on their entire computer product line. We'll also demonstrate the process of taking a simple program written in the C programming language for the HP-UX Unix operating system, and rewriting it to utilize the NLS package and become more international in scope and capabilities.

### The Problems of International Software

Taking an application and teaching it another language and culture is far more complex than simply going through the source code and changing all the text read in or printed out. Among the various stumbling blocks in the arena of internationalization are:

- The standard 7-bit American ASCII code is insufficient for the portrayal and manipulation of almost any other language, and while extensions into 8-bit ASCII adds support for many of the common European languages, languages using different alphabets like Hebrew, Arabic, or any of the Asian languages require at least 16-bits of identifying information to uniquely differentiate between the hundreds or thousands of different possible characters.

- The sorting and collating of information are also much more complex when languages have ordering rules other than the inherent ordering found in the ASCII character set. This is even demonstrable in English, when programmers have to write special routines to have the sorting algorithms ignore the case of the word (that is, should "Smith" sort before or after "smith"?) Many languages have surprisingly complex collation rules; it is common for character pairs to be treated as a single character. An example of that is the "ch" character in Spanish, which should correctly sort between "c" and "d" in words of that language.

- Transliterating characters from upper to lower case and vice versa is also more complex than it may initially appear; an example of this is shown in the difference between Canadian French and European French. The Canadians consider the correct transliteration of the letter "é" to be "É", but the French prefer for the capitalized character to have the accent removed as in "E". 16-bit languages like Chinese offer even further complications in this regard, with many words not being considered as being in either upper or lower case at all.

- Hyphenation is also an aspect of software applications that, while it isn't often used outside of word processing systems, is something that varies from country to country and language to language. Many languages have hyphenation rules that result in the spelling of the word changing when hyphenated too; an example of that being the German word kuckuk, which is correctly hyphenated not as "kuc-kuk", but as "kuk-kuk".

- Monetary formats are one of the most common differences between different countries, with countries having the monetary symbol as a prefix (the United States and England), a suffix (German or Japanese), or even embedded in the amount itself (Portuguese).

- Numeric formats are a potential problem too, since the format for numeric values can change quite a bit from country to country with even the common "." decimal point being replaced by a "," in many different countries in Europe.

- Time and date formats are also very much a result of the country and language of the user. More than just the names of the months and days of the week, different languages have different expectations for time notation, ordering of information when the date is specified, and so on. Some countries, notably Japan, China and Israel, use their own calendar rather than the western gregorian calendar with which we're familiar.

- Order of presentation isn't constant either; a number of different languages are read from right to left rather than the more common left to right of English and the European languages. This becomes particularly challenging with graphical user interface software.

There are further obstacles to the problems of internationalizing software applications, enough that it's not too much of a surprise that very few programs in the world can interact gracefully and easily in other than the language of the original designers and programmers.

## The Three Most Common Avenues of Solution

Not surprisingly, there are a number of different approaches to creating international software applications and systems. Reflecting the three main phases of software creation, most solutions are applied at either compile-time, link-time or run-time. That is, changes to the software to allow support for other languages can be accomplished via modifications to the actual source code, the addition of external routines that can be linked before creating an actual executable, or the addition of routines that interpolate from the actual run time environment what language is required.

Each of these solutions has strengths and weaknesses – as discussed elsewhere in this book – which can be best summarized by realizing that the difference is primarily that of the end user requirements and the level of programming and technical sophistication of the language and culture translators. For sites that will require multiple language support, for example, compile and link-time solutions would result in the requirement of multiple copies of the program be available, named "program.french", "program.dutch", and so on. In an environment of this nature, run-time language binding is a clear winner.

Many simpler computing environments don't have those exotic needs, however, and in those cases the performance improvements gained by having a version of the application or system tailored specifically to the target language is a significant performance boost, doubly so in smaller and slower personal computing environments.

A more political issue with internationalization is that oftentimes the foreign language versions of the software are marketed and sold by local distributors in the country or territory. These distributors, while they may well have the expertise to create localized versions of the application, oftentimes do not need, or want, to have the entire application source available. In situations of this nature, it makes the most sense for the original application developers to distribute compiled object code versions of their applications with language-specific routines collected in separate files distributed as source to the foreign distributors. They then can modify the specific portions of the package as appropriate, compile the changed modules, and then link the entire set of object files together into a single executable application ready for local distribution and use.

## Other Aspects of Software Internationalization

Worth mentioning is that there are many more aspects to the successful software application than just getting the program itself to work in the target language and culture. More than the obvious requirements that documentation, quick reference cards, and other literature be translated into the language in addition to the software package itself, there are also challenges associated with appropriate advertising and product packaging to be considered.

Most interestingly, however, are the issues surrounding the submission and resolution of customer defects and problems. If vendors rely on their foreign distributors to resolve problems in the local version, they could quickly end up with dozens of different version of the program, making it very complex for the parent company to distribute new versions of the package in the future. If all problems are forwarded to the central application group, they will inevitably prove to have great difficulty understanding what is being reported, since the version of the package used at the main plant will be almost completely different to the one that the customer reporting the problem uses.

The middle ground of having the foreign distributor try to 'translate' the problem and defect reports into the original language of the developers is fraught with perils of its own, most especially the time delays and added burden to the distributor that this imposes; good defect reporting and resolution is measured in days, not months or years. Finally, the foreign distributor could endeavor to fix the problems that are due to localization without bothering the parent company, and could forward those problems that are more fundamental application problems. The spectre of divergent versions of the software again arises in this case, however.

A common way around part of this problem is to utilize numeric error codes to ensure that whatever the localized text may say, the message itself is uniquely identifiable, whether it be in Hebrew, Latin, or Vietnamese. Unfortunately this has a high price in terms of usability and overall customer satisfaction. The most common place that you can see this uniquely numbered message solution is with programming language compilers, where messages like that shown in listing one could be in almost any language and still make sense to the original developer.

The ability for run-time language binding to support multiple languages with a single executable is an excellent middle ground, and it is the most common type of internationalization approach taken on multiuser machines. The Hewlett-Packard NLS system, as we shall shortly see, is of this type, as are the rest of the Unix operating system-based solutions.

```
"test.c", line 7: error 854 - fd undefined
"test.c", line 7: error 104 - incorrect indirection
"test.c", line 8: error 500 - newline in string or char constant
"test.c", line 10: error 30 - syntax error
```

*Listing One: Typical Numeric Error Messages*

## The Hewlett-Packard Native Language Support System, a Closer Look

Before the example application is introduced, let's take a look at the conceptual basis of the HP Native Language Support System. The fundamental idea behind NLS is quite straightforward and is perhaps best introduced by way of analogy; if you were to go to a country where you not only couldn't speak the language, but couldn't even pronounce it, a common way for you to communicate to the locals would be for you to look up the word or phrase you want to use in a two-language dictionary, then point at the entry and let the other person read it.

If we take that idea and change it so that we have an intermediate "link" between the phrases in the two languages, we'd be very close to how the NLS system works. That is, imagine looking up in your phrase book for a particular phrase and finding it is language-independently referred to as "message 4324". Armed with just that number, any number of other people, speaking any language, could then look up "4324" in their own phrase books and find out what you're trying to convey.

While this sounds a bit awkward as a way to communicate with someone in person, it turns out to be ideally suited for computer-based interaction, and is exactly how the NLS system is designed. All textual information is stored in what are called *message catalogs* with messages broken down into *sets* for ease of interaction. Programs then simply request of the NLS system at run time "message 24 from catalog 43" and have returned that particular word or phrase in the current language. Consider illustration one to get a better understanding of how this fits together.

For the more constant cultural and language elements the NLS package has a wide variety of subroutines available to application programmers. These routines have predefined rules about collating order, monetary display formats, dates and times, and many other aspects of specific languages. Within HP's Unix operating system, the following wide range of NLS routines are available for program use:

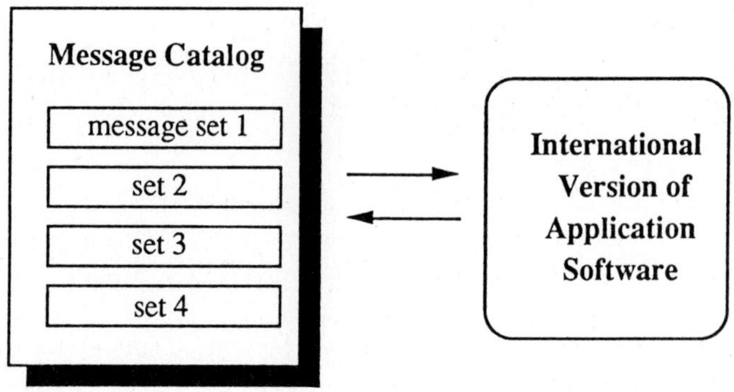


*Illustration One: Conceptual Model of the HP NLS Message Catalog*

Message Catalog Manipulation:

| | |
|---|---|
| *catclose* | close a message catalog |
| *catgetmsg* | get message from NLS message catalog |
| *catgets* | get a program message with program specified default |
| *catopen* | open a message catalog for reading |
| *catread* | get a message, substituting parameters if needed |

Numeric Functions:

| | |
|---|---|
| *cvtnum* | convert local string to internal floating point number |
| *ecvt* | convert floating point number to local string format (note: *ecvt*, *fcvt* an *gcvt* perform essentially the same function, with biases towards different styles of output) |
| *nl_atof* | convert string to double precision number |
| *nl_strtod* | convert string to double precision number |

Date and Time Functions:

| | |
|---|---|
| *nl_ascxtime* | similar to *nl_cxtime* but expects different calling parameters. |
| *nl_cxtime* | output specified date and time as specified by format (this is really the NLS version of the *ctime* subroutine) |

Collation and Comparison Functions:

| | |
|---|---|
| *nl_strcmp* | compare two strings in a language-dependent way |
| *nl_strncmp* | compare the first 'n' characters of two strings in a language dependent way |

| | |
|---|---|
| *nl_tolower* | translate character given into lower case, if needed. |
| *nl_toupper* | translate character given into upper case, if needed. |
| *strcmp8* | compare 8-bit ASCII strings for equality |
| *strcmp16* | compare 16-bit ASCII strings for equality |
| *strncmp8* | compare n-character slices of 8-bit strings for equality |
| *strncmp16* | compare n-character slices of 16-bit strings for equality |

NLS Functions:

| | |
|---|---|
| *currlangid* | return the language ID of the current language in use |
| *idtolang* | map NLS internal language ID to language name |
| *langinfo* | similar function as *nl_langinfo* |
| *langtoid* | does the opposite of *idtolang* |
| *nl_init* | initialize the NLS environment |
| *nl_langinfo* | return information pertaining to current language |
| *strord* | convert string to screen to keyboard order, or vice versa |

Input Functions:

| | |
|---|---|
| *nl_fscanf* | NLS version of the *fscanf* file input parsing routine |
| *nl_scanf* | NLS version of the *scanf* input parsing routine |
| *nl_sscanf* | NLS version of the *sscanf* buffer parsing routine |

Output Functions:

| | |
|---|---|
| *nl_fprintf* | NLS version of the *fprintf* file output routine |
| *nl_printf* | NLS version of the *printf* output routine |
| *nl_sprintf* | NLS version of the *sprintf* output-to-buffer routine |
| *perror* | print system error message in appropriate language |

Character Classification Functions:

| | |
|---|---|
| *nl_isalnum* | true if character is a letter or digit |
| *nl_isalpha* | true if character is a letter |
| *nl_iscntrl* | true if character is a control character |
| *nl_isdigit* | true if character is a decimal digit |
| *nl_islower* | true if character is lower case |
| *nl_isprint* | true if character is printable |
| *nl_ispunct* | true if character is a punctuation character |
| *nl_isspace* | true if character is a "white space" |
| *nl_isupper* | true if character is upper case |
| *nl_isxdigit* | true if character is a hexadecimal digit |

Tools to process 16-bit character input:

| | |
|---|---|
| ADVANCE | increments character pointer one character (not byte) |
| *BYTE_STATUS* | return ONEBYTE, FIRSTOF2 or SECOF2 |
| *CHARADV* | increment character pointer, returning most recently seen character |
| *CHARAT* | evaluates to a character, either one or two byte, as appropriate |
| *FIRSTOF2* | returns true if specified character can be first of two-byte character |
| *SECOF2* | returns true if specified character can be second of two-byte character |
| *WCHAR* | writes a specified character value into a given string |
| *WCHARADV* | write a specified character value into a given string, then increment the string when done |

In addition to this somewhat overwhelming array of programmatic choices, there are also a number of user level commands that need to be included so that the NLS package can be utilised:

| | |
|---|---|
| *dumpmsg* | extracts messages from an existing message catalog |
| *findmsg* | extracts catalog messages from C source programs |
| *findstr* | finds static character strings in C source programs |
| *gencat* | to create a program readable message catalog |
| *insertmsg* | uses findstr output to add calls to *catgets* function |

For the most part, if you're designing an NLS program from the bottom up, you'll only need to use the *gencat* routine to create message catalogs.

## Salary Analysis: A Sample NLS Program

To demonstrate how all the pieces of the HP Native Language Support System fit together, let's look at how a simple exemplary program can be internationalized. The program we'll use is very straightforward; given a list of names and wages, compute the average, highest and lowest salary in the group, then print the list, sorted, and the salary information.

Listing two shows the salary analysis program as it could be written easily in the C programming language for an HP-UX Unix machine. Notice that we've anticipated the addition of internationalization code by isolating the work into separate routines.

```
/**                     non NLS sample.c                          **/
/**              (C) Copyright 1989, Dave Taylor                  **/

/**
This program reads from standard input a list of peoples names and
salaries, then prints the sorted list of names and salaries, ending with a
summary of top, bottom and average wage.                    **/

#include <stdio.h>
#include <ctype.h>

#define String_Length               128
#define List_Size                   100

/* macros for easier code later on */

#define replace_if_higher(a, b)     if (b > a) a = b
#define replace_if_lower(a, b)      if (b < a) a = b

/** Data structure for use within the program  **/

struct user_record {
  char  name[String_Length];         /* who they are, and */
  float salary;                   /* how much they earn */
} employee_list[List_Size];

int   employee_count = 0;            /* number we're read  */

float    total_salaries = 0.0,       /* for min, max      */
         highest_salary = -99999.99, /*  and average      */
         lowest_salary  = 99999.99;  /*   salary values   */

main()
{
        read_in_data();
```

*Listing Two: The non-NLS Sample Program*

```
        process_data();
        output_data();
}

read_in_data()
{
        /** Read in the data from standard input. We'll read each line into
                buffer then scan it to allow our own free input format     **/

        char    buffer[String_Length],              /* input line buffer      */
                name[String_Length];                /* a place for the name */
        float   salary;                             /*      and the salary   */
        int     lines = 0;        /* what line we're on   */

        while (gets(buffer) != NULL) {
                break_down_buffer(buffer, ++lines, name, &salary);
                store_data(name, salary);
        }
}

process_data()
{
        /** Sort the tables, and compute the average, highest and lowest
                salaries in the data set                                  **/

        register int i;                             /* internal counter */
        int     our_string_compare();               /* prototype decl */

        qsort(employee_list, (unsigned) employee_count,
                sizeof (struct user_record), our_string_compare);

        for (i=0; i < employee_count; i++) {
                total_salaries += employee_list[i].salary;
                replace_if_higher(highest_salary, employee_list[i].salary);
```

*Listing Two: Continued*

```
            replace_if_lower (lowest_salary, employee_list[i].salary);
        }
}

output_data()
{
        /** Output the data, timestamped, and the summary information
            at the end too.                                             **/

        register int i;                     /* internal counter */
        long    thetime;                    /* for timestamp   */

        if (employee_count == 0) {
            printf("No employees entered!\n");
            exit(1);
        }

        thetime = time((long *) 0);
        printf("\nEmployee list as of %s\n", ctime(&thetime));
        for (i=0; i < employee_count; i++)
            printf("  %-40.40s   $%.2f\n", employee_list[i].name,
                employee_list[i].salary);

        printf("\nAverage salary = $%g,  low = $%g, high = $%g\n",
            total_salaries/employee_count, lowest_salary, highest_salary);
}

break_down_buffer(buffer, line, name, salary)
char    *buffer;        /* the input line buffer                          */
int     line;           /* what line number we're at in the input file    */
char    *name;          /*  space for the name: value returned            */
float   *salary;        /*  space for the salary: value returned          */
{
        /** Given a buffer in the format "name = salary" break the data
        into two separate fields, and store in the two variables        **/
```

*Listing Two: Continued*

```
        register int i, j, end;

        for (i=0; buffer[i] != '=' && buffer[i] != '\0'; i++)  /* find '=' */ ;

        if (buffer[i] == '\0') {
          printf("Error in input line %d: no '=' delimiter found >\n", line);
          exit(1);
        }
        /** found '=' character, back up to the last letter of name           **/

        for (end=i-1; isspace(buffer[end]) && end > 0; end--)  /* no op       */;

        /** now copy from first to last actual letter of the name             **/

        for (j=0;j <= end; j++)
                name[j] = buffer[j];
        name[j] = '\0';                         /* terminate the new string     */

        sscanf((char *) buffer + i + 1, " %f", salary);       /** read in the wage **/
}

store_data(name, salary)
char    *name;              /* the name of the person we're adding              */
float   salary;             /*                and their salary                  */
{
        /** Add the data to the table, if there's space                         **/

        if (employee_count+1 > List_Size) {
                printf("Too many people to process: limit is %d names\n",
                        List_Size);
                exit(1);
        }

        strcpy(employee_list[employee_count].name, name);
        employee_list[employee_count].salary = salary;
```

*Listing Two: Continued*

```
        employee_count++;
}

int
our_string_compare(first, second)
struct user_record *first, *second;
{
        /** compare the name fields in the two structures given. This
        routine is required because of our utilisation of the
        built in Unix "qsort" quick sort subroutine.            **/

        return( strcmp(first->name, second->name) );
}
```

*Listing Two: Continued*

Some things to notice about the example include that collected at the top of the program are all the buffer size dependencies (the identifiers *String_Length* and *List_Size*), and that the actual data format dependent information is centrally located in one routine: **output_data.** Also, notice that other language dependent algorithms like collation order are located in a single place, the routine **our_string_compare.**

The input format for the data the program uses has been deliberately kept to a bare minimum, both for speed and ease of programming. The sample data file that will be used throughout is shown in listing three.

```
Davis, Jim      =  1000.00
Louie, Nancy    =  2400.00
Carlos, Maria   =   450.00
Vixie, Paul     =  4394.30
Cooper, Ted     =  5000.00
Taylor, Dave    =  8523.17
Charé, Raul     =  7530.25
```

*Listing Three: Sample Input Data*

With only minimal work, this program could be translated into another language, at least for the output strings. However, we're interested in transforming the program into one that can, at run-time, choose which language to use dynamically, and for this we'll turn to the Native Language Support System.

The first step towards NLS-izing the program is to extract all the text messages and other language dependent data, and place them in a message catalog. This is straightforward an the resulting default catalog for the language "n-computer"[1] is shown in listing four.

```
$    This is the message catalog for the sample HP NLS program
$    that we're working with. broken into three different
$    message sets as indicated.
$
$    This version is for language "n-computer"
$

$set 1 normal output messages

1    Employee list as of
2    Average salary =
3     low =
4     high =

$set 2 error messages

1    Error in input line
2    : no '=' delimiter found
3    Too many people to process: limit is
4    names
5    No employees entered

$set 3 character delimiters, etc.

1    =
```

*Listing Four: Continued*

Notice how quite a bit of the output text from the original program has been encapsulated i this small message catalog, including even the delimiter that is used to separate the names from the salaries. Though this message catalog is quite easy to read and understand, it isn

[1] n-computer is "Native Computer" language, or American English.

quite ready to be used by our program. Solving that problem requires using the *gencat* HP-UX user command to create a machine readable file that we'll call "computer.cat":

**% gencat computer.cat computer.source**

The next step is to create a list of mnemonic labels that our program can use to access the different catalogued messages. Since the C programming language has a powerful macro replacement facility, we'll simply create an include file that defines a set of name to number mappings for program use; the file "*symbols.h*" in listing five.

The symbolic reference include file also defines two other values for our program; the default computer language, which we choose to be a slight variant on the standard NLS default of "computer", and a *printf*-style format string that will define the name of each message catalog. In the format string, the '%s' will be replaced by the name of the user-selected language, so if we were using "dutch" the resulting message catalog would be "*dutch.cat*". The **.cat** suffix for message catalogs is a de facto HP internal standard.

```
/**                    NLS symbols.h                    **/
/**           (C) Copyright 1989, Dave Taylor           **/

/**
This set of headers allows for easy and mnemonic references to work
or all the various messages and message sets we now have to be
concerned with. This information is very dependent on the layout
of the individual NLS catalogs.                          **/

/* define the three different sets          */

#define OUTPUT            1
#define ERRORS            2
#define DELIMS            3

/* the messages within the OUTPUT set        */

#define HEADER            1
#define AVG_SALARY        2
```

*Listing Five: The "symbols.h" Header File*

```
#define LOW_SALARY          3
#define HIGH_SALARY         4

/* the messages within the ERRORS set      */

#define PROLOGUE            1
#define NO_DELIM            2
#define TOO_MANY_1          3
#define TOO_MANY_2          4
#define NO_EMPLOYEES        5

/* and the messages within the DELIMS set  */

#define NAME_SALARY         1

/* now some other useful NLS type things   */

#define Default_Language        "n-computer"
#define CATALOG_HOME            "%s.cat"
```

*Listing Five: Continued*

As you can begin to see, with some careful planning, internationalizing your software can be not only a good chance to isolate culture and language specific algorithms and dependencies, but also to further modularize the program itself and create a new version of the software that is quite possibly easier to understand than the original.

## The Missing Pieces of NLS

So far, the Native Language Support System has done an admirable job of allowing us to move things around and restructure our program to support multiple languages. As we continue, we'll see that almost all of what we'll need for the example program is already built in to the NLS package. There is, however, one major deficiency in the system; there is no formatting assistance available for dealing with foreign currencies.

Fortunately we're not left completely high and dry, however, since each language supported by the NLS system has a large body of data specifying information about standard time and date formats, months of the year, and many other items of data. For currency output formats, we're interested specifically in two items: what the radix or "decimal point" is in the local notation, and what the currency delimiter is.

To access the NLS language-specific data the function required is called *nl_langinfo*, and it expects a mnemonic identifier indicating what item of information is requested. In this case we'll obtain RADIX and CRNCYFMT, the latter of which is returned with the first character indicating whether the currency sequence should go before the numeric value, replace the radix symbol, or after the fractional value.

Listing six contains the subroutine *print_nls_currency*, which when given a floating point numeric value, will obtain the format information needed from the NLS database, then output the value in the notation indicated.

```
/**                         NLS money.c                              **/
/**                (C) Copyright 1989, Dave Taylor            **/

/**
This routine allows for simple output of monetary values using the
NLS coded information.  Surprisingly, the HP NLS package doesn't
have a built-in routine to perform this needed function.     **/

#include <stdio.h>
#include <nl_types.h>
#include <langinfo.h>

#include "symbols.h"             /* as shown in listing five, above    */

#define set_equal(a, b)     { char *buffer;  buffer = b;  a = buffer[0];  }

#define Short_String_Length  32

#define Prefix  1                /* possible locations for       */
#define Infix   2                /*  the currency symbol         */
#define Postfix          3             /*     in the string                */

char    *currency_string,  currency_delimiter[Short_String_Length];
```

*Listing Six: The "Money.c" NLS Currency Routine*

```
int     got_currency_string = 0,  placement = Prefix;
char    default_radix = '.';

char *nl_langinfo();
extern double floor();

print_nls_currency(value)
float value;
{
        /** Get the NLS currency format string from the system, then use it as
        the basis for printing the given value. The format for the string
        is the character sequence that delimits currency in the local language,
        prefixed with a '-' if the delimiter should appear before the value,
        '+' if it should appear afterwards, and '.' if it replaces the radix    **/

        float fraction, newvalue;

        if (got_currency_string++ == 0) {          /* haven't yet loaded it    */
                currency_string = nl_langinfo(CRNCYSTR);

                switch (*currency_string) {
                    case '-'    : placement = Prefix;   break;
                    case '+'    : placement = Postfix;  break;
                    case '.'    : placement = Infix;    break;
                    default     :
                printf("Internal NLS error: bad currency format string '%s'\n",
                        currency_string);
                                exit(1);
                }
                strcpy(currency_delimiter, (char *) (currency_string + 1));
                set_equal(default_radix, nl_langinfo(RADIXCHAR))
        }

        newvalue = floor(value);
        fraction = value - newvalue;
```

*Listing Six: Continued*

```
        printf("%s %g%s%c%d %s",
                placement == Prefix ? currency_delimiter : "",
                newvalue,  placement == Infix ? currency_delimiter : "",
                placement == Infix ? "" : default_radix,  (int) (fraction * 100.5),
                placement == Postfix ? currency_delimiter : "");
}
```

*Listing Six continued*

This is the first source listing utilising the NLS package. Notice that we are required to include a few new system header files for the program to work correctly, namely the nl_types.h file which defines various parts of the NLS system, and langinfo.h, which defines the symbolic names used to access the various elements of the NLS language information database.

Notice that when we call the routines to return information from the NLS database that we needn't explicitly specify what language is currently being used. That is because all programs that use NLS routines are required to initialize the builtin package through a call to *nl_init.*

As is becoming obvious, the choice of language is something that one doesn't want to continually specify upon invocation of each of the many programs in the operating system Instead, Unix supports a set of variables within the overall runtime environment, inherited by subprocesses, and easily accessed by any program.

HP's Native Language Support System looks for an environment variable named LANG, which can be set to any of the over twenty languages currently supported. Initializing the NLS system is then a matter of querying for the language, initializing the NLS internals, then attempting to open up a message catalog.

Accessing an individual message from a message catalog is done by using the already opened message catalog – via the *catopen* system call – and requesting a specific message number, from a specified message set. You can see why the mnemonic names we created in the "*symbols.h*" file are useful; a request for "set = ERRORS, message = NO_EMPLOYEES" makes quite a bit more sense than "set=2, message=5".

The actual routine to get the language from the run time environment, initialize the NLS environment, and also open up our message catalog, is shown in listing seven.

```
/**                      NLS initialize.c                              **/
/**              (C) Copyright 1989, Dave Taylor                       **/


/** Initializes the entire NLS system, including opening up our message
        catalog and ensuring that the language specified is not only available,
        but has an available message catalog too.                     **/

#include <stdio.h>
#include <nl_types.h>
#include "symbols.h"

#define String_Length   128

nl_catd         catalog;            /* the message catalog pointer          */
char            *language;          /* what language we're using            */

char *getenv();

initialize_nls()
{
        char filename[String_Length];

        /** get the language from the environment, or use default if none **/

        if ((language = getenv("LANG")) != NULL)
                sprintf(filename, CATALOG_HOME, language);
        else {
                sprintf(filename, CATALOG_HOME, Default_Language);
                language = Default_Language;
        }

        /** now initialize the NLS system with the language specified. **/

        if (nl_init(language) == -1) {
                printf("Language \"%s\" is not currently supported.\n", language);
```

*Listing Seven: The NLS "initialize.c" Source Program*

```
                exit(1);
        }

        /** and open the programmatic message catalog, if possible.  **/

        if ((catalog = catopen(filename, 0)) <= 0) {
                printf("No message catalog available for language \"%s\"\n", language);
                exit(1);
        }
}
```

*Listing Seven: Continued*

Notice how algorithmically the initialization seems to make quite a bit of sense based on what we've already been considering about the NLS system. We'll see this trend continue in the following routines to print messages from the NLS catalog and to return specific values from the message catalog back to the program; listing eight.

```
/**                        NLS  output.c                              **/
/**                 (C) Copyright 1989, Dave Taylor                   **/

/** Allow easy and mnemonic references to messages and data in the program
    message catalog.  initialize_nls MUST be called before either of these routines. **/

#include <stdio.h>
#include <nl_types.h>
#include "symbols.h"

#define String_Length  128
extern nl_catd  catalog;          /* the message catalog pointer        */
extern char     *language;        /* what language we're using          */

print_nls_message(set, message)
int     set, message;
{
        /** print out the specified message,if available.              **/
```

*Listing Eight: The NLS "output.c" Program Source*

```
        char    buffer[String_Length];

        if (catgetmsg(catalog, set, message, buffer, String_Length) == NULL) {
                printf("Problem finding message %d in set %d for language \"%s\"\n",
                        message, set, language);
                perror("catgetmsg");
                exit(1);
        }
        printf("%s", buffer);           /** avoid puts() to avoid carriage-return **/
}

char
get_nls_value(set, message)
int     set, message;
{
        char buffer[String_Length];

        if (catgetmsg(catalog, set, message, buffer, String_Length) == NULL) {
                printf("Problem finding message %d in set %d for language \"%s\"\n",
                        message, set, language);
                perror("catgetmsg");
                exit(1);
        }
        return(buffer[0]);                      /* first character only  */
}
```

*Listing Eight: Continued*

Careful readers of the sample code will notice that all built-in program error messages are being output in English, regardless of what language is chosen by the user via the LANG run time environment setting. This is because we want to be able to have some meaningful error messages in situations where, for example, the message catalog is accidentally removed while the program is running, or similar. This isn't quite as bad as it may initially appear, however, since the NLS system offers native language error messages via the *perror* system call.

Finally, now that we've presented all the new code, let's look at what changes are required to our original program. For ease of finding these changes, all new lines of code are presented in a larger typeface and emboldened. Listing nine contains the new version of the "*sample.c*" file.

```
/**                    NLS sample.c                                  **/
/**          (C) Copyright 1989, Dave Taylor                         **/

/**   This program reads from standard input a list of peoples names and
      salaries, then prints the sorted list of names and salaries, ending with a
      summary of top, bottom and average wage.                       **/

#include <stdio.h>
#include <ctype.h>
#include "symbols.h"

#define String_Length          128
#define List_Size              100

/* some macros for easier code later on        */

#define replace_if_higher(a, b)         if (b > a) a = b
#define replace_if_lower(a, b)          if (b < a) a = b

struct user_record {
        char    name[String_Length];        /* who they are, and  */
        float   salary;                     /* how much they earn */
} employee_list[List_Size];

int     employee_count = 0;                 /* number we've read  */
float   total_salaries = 0.0,               /* for min, max       */
        highest_salary = -99999.99,         /*  and average       */
        lowest_salary  = 99999.99;          /*   salary values    */

main()
{
        initialize_nls();
        read_in_data();
```

*Listing Nine: The NLS "sample.c" Main Program Source*

```
        process_data();
        output_data();
}

read_in_data()
{
        /** Read in the data from standard input. We'll read each line into
            a buffer then scan it to allow our own free input format          **/
        char    buffer[String_Length],             /* input line buffer        */
                name[String_Length];               /* a place for the name     */
        float   salary;                            /*   and the salary         */
        int     lines = 0;                         /* what line we're on       */

        while (gets(buffer) != NULL) {
                break_down_buffer(buffer, ++lines, name, &salary);
                 store_data(name, salary);
        }
}

process_data()
{
        /** Sort the tables, and compute the average, highest and lowest
                salaries in the data set                                       **/
        register int i;                                 /*   internal counter  */
        int     our_string_compare();                   /*  prototype decl     */

        qsort(employee_list, (unsigned) employee_count,
                sizeof (struct user_record), our_string_compare);

        for (i=0; i < employee_count; i++) {
                total_salaries += employee_list[i].salary;
                replace_if_higher(highest_salary, employee_list[i].salary);
                replace_if_lower (lowest_salary,  employee_list[i].salary);
        }
}
```

*Listing Nine: Continued*

```
output_data()
{
        /** Output the data, timestamped, and the summary information          **/

        register int i;                          /* internal counter        */
        long    thetime;                         /* for timestamp           */

        if (employee_count == 0) {
                print_nls_message(ERRORS, NO_EMPLOYEES);
                exit(1);
        }
        thetime = time((long *) 0);
        putchar('\n');
        print_nls_message(OUTPUT, HEADER);
        printf("  %s\n\n", nl_cxtime(&thetime, NULL));

        for (i=0; i < employee_count; i++) {
                printf("  %-40.40s    ", employee_list[i].name);
                print_nls_currency(employee_list[i].salary);
                putchar('\n');
        }

        putchar('\n');
        print_nls_message(OUTPUT, AVG_SALARY);
        print_nls_currency( (float)
                        (total_salaries / employee_count));
        print_nls_message(OUTPUT, LOW_SALARY);
        print_nls_currency(lowest_salary);
        print_nls_message(OUTPUT, HIGH_SALARY);
        print_nls_currency(highest_salary);
        putchar('\n');

        putchar('\n');
        putchar('\n');
}
```

*Listing Nine: Continued*

```
break_down_buffer(buffer, line, name, salary)
char    *buffer;          /* the input line buffer                           */
int     line;             /* line number we're at in the input file         */
char    *name;            /* space for the name: value returned             */
float   *salary;          /* space for the salary: value returned           */
{
        /** Given a buffer in the format "name = salary" break the data
            into two separate fields,,and store in the two variables       **/

        register int i, j, end;
        char delimiter;

        delimiter = get_nls_value(DELIMS, NAME_SALARY);

        for (i=0; buffer[i] != delimiter && buffer[i] != '\0'; i++)  /* skip */ ;

        if (buffer[i] == '\0') {
                print_nls_message(ERRORS, PROLOGUE);
                printf(" %d", line);
                print_nls_message(ERRORS, NO_DELIM);
                exit(1);
        }

        /** now we've found the '=' character, let's back up to
                get to the last character of the persons name          **/
        for (end=i-1; isspace(buffer[end]) && end > 0; end--)      /* no op */ ;

        /** now copy from the first to last letter of the name.              **/
        for (j=0;j <= end; j++)
                name[j] = buffer[j];
        name[j] = '\0';                         /* terminate the new string   */

        sscanf((char *) buffer + i + 1, " %f", salary); /* read in the salary   */
}
```

*Listing Nine: Continued*

```
store_data(name, salary)
char    *name;              /* the name of the person we're adding      */
float   salary;             /*      and their salary                    */
{
        /** Add the data to the table, if there's space              **/

        if (employee_count+1 > List_Size) {
                print_nls_message(ERRORS, TOO_MANY_1);
                printf("%d", List_Size);
                print_nls_message(ERRORS, TOO_MANY_2);
                exit(1);
        }

        strcpy(employee_list[employee_count].name, name);
        employee_list[employee_count].salary = salary;

        employee_count++;
}

int
our_string_compare(first, second)
struct user_record      *first,
                        *second;
{
        /** compare the name fields in the two structures given. This
        routine is required because of our utilisation of the built in Unix
        "qsort" quick sort subroutine.                                    **/

        return( nl_strcmp(first->name, second->name) );
}
```

*Listing Nine: Continued*

As you can see, except for the modifications for output, there are really very few changes to the original program. Part of this is because we designed from the beginning a program that was highly modular, making it easy to isolate the input and output, as well as the specific portions of the code that depend on a particular language.

Among the changes that are worth highlighting, notice that within the routine **output_dat** we had to change the original call to *ctime* to output the current time in a readable format to a routine called *nl_cxtime*. While ctime returns a date format that is easily understood by u – as exemplified by the current date being *Sun Apr 23 15:10:21 1989* – the NLS routine *nl_cxtime* returns the same information, but with the order of information and day and month names translated into the appropriate language. In Spanish, for example, today would be indicated by the *nl_cxtime* routine as *Dom, 23 Abr 1989 15.10.21* Notice especially the change in hour, minute and seconds delimiter in the time value.

The other major internal change is within the routine **our_string_compare**, where we've changed from using the C builtin function *strcmp* to the native language knowledgeable *nl_strcmp*. This is to aid in the correct sorting and collation of languages where the ASCII character encoding isn't sufficient for an implicit ordering. Actually, this particular change would have been beneficial in the original, non-NLS version of the sample program too, because unlike the *strcmp* function, *nl_strcmp* is case insensitive, and would have correctly sorted the word "chicken" between "Cat" and "Coyote".

With all this discussion and the rather overwhelming deluge of program source code in the many listings previous, you're probably starting to wonder exactly what the output of this program might be. Well, before we examine how to create foreign language message catalogs and such, let's have a look at what the output of the test program would be. First off, let's again present the sample input that was presented many pages ago as listing three

Notice that while the input data is free of any currency or monetary indication for the individual wages, it still is not completely international in data format; the radix for the wages i a "." or decimal point. Also, we can now see why having the delimiter set to an "=" and alterable by modification of the message catalog is a step towards portability; proper names can have many different values appear within them, including hyphens, spaces, and many other non-traditional Anglo-Saxon letters, though in common use, it is rare to see a character like '=' used within the context of a proper name. Data, however, isn't constrained to such a limited domain, and even seemingly innocuous delimiters like a colon (':') or hyphen ('–') can be used in unusual ways.

Feeding this data file to the original non-NLS *sample.c* program would result in the output shown in listing ten. Notice in the listing the order of the first three names. Since we were very careful in our process of adding NLS functionality – internationalizing the program – it turns out the listing ten is also the output of the NLS *sample.c* program with the default language of "n-computer".

| | | |
|---|---|---|
| Davis, Jim | = | 1000.00 |
| Louie, Nancy | = | 2400.00 |
| Carlos, Maria | = | 450.00 |
| Vixie, Paul | = | 4394.30 |
| Cooper, Ted | = | 5000.00 |
| Taylor, Dave | = | 8523.17 |
| Charé, Raul | = | 7530.25 |

*Listing Three: Sample Input Data*

Employee list as of Sun Apr 23 15:31:39 1989

| | |
|---|---|
| Carlos, Maria | $ 450.00 |
| Charé, Raul | $ 7530.25 |
| Cooper, Ted | $ 5000.00 |
| Davis, Jim | $ 1000.00 |
| Louie, Nancy | $ 2400.00 |
| Taylor, Dave | $ 8523.17 |
| Vixie, Paul | $ 4394.30 |

Average salary = $ 4185.39    low = $ 450.00    high = $ 8523.17

*Listing Ten: Sample Output for language "n-computer"*

Now let's look at some other languages and see what changes have to be made to our message catalogs, and then what the resulting output of the NLS sample program is, given the input data from listing three.

### British English

The easiest language to start with is one that require no modification of the message catalog, and simply has a different format for the date and time information and currency.

The first attempt to use English, by setting *LANG=english* in our Unix run time environment, will not work however, and instead results in the error message:

**No message catalog available for language "english"**

Which really shouldn't be much of a surprise; you can even go back to listing six and find where this message is printed from within the *initialize_nls* routine that is a part of the program.

What we'll need to do is to create an identical message catalog to the n-computer one we've already got, naming it appropriately so the program can find it:

```
% cp  n-computer.src  english.source
% gencat english.cat  english.source
```

Now we can invoke the program, with the resulting output shown in listing eleven.

```
Employee list as of Sun. 23 Apr, 1989 03:47:21 PM

    Carlos, Maria          £ 450.0
    Charé, Raul            £ 7530.25
    Cooper, Ted            £ 5000.0
    Davis, Jim             £ 1000.0
    Louie, Nancy           £ 2400.0
    Taylor, Dave           £ 8523.17
    Vixie, Paul            £ 4394.30

Average salary = £ 3314.36  low = £ 100.0  high = £ 8523.17
```

*Listing Eleven: Sample Output with Language "english"*

Unfortunately, as you can see, the NLS system doesn't know about exchange rates, so in essence we've managed to give everyone on the employee list a 50% raise! Humour aside, however, programs for the international market must be sensitive to this sort of possible confusion.

## Spanish

The next language that we'll look at is one that is spoken in Mexico, Spain, and many other countries around the world, yet for NLS purposes is specific to Spain. A quick note of caution, however: languages that are similar to a supported NLS language, but not part of the NLS package, are tricky and involves some careful thought. For example, to add support for Australian English might require little more than a change in the monetary output format. Before a product could be shipped closer examination of the differences would still be necessary; Australian collation algorithms might have to deal with Aboriginal names in a unique way that wouldn't be included in any algorithms targeted for the British Isles.

Similarly, we could modify the Spanish language support within the NLS system to allow software to work without difficulty in Mexico and other Spanish speaking countries – notably in South America – but the changes may well be subtle and insidious. The best approach is to check with natives from each of the target countries to ensure that the cultural and social expectations are those of locals.

Let's now look at the message catalog translated into Spanish. Presented in listing twelve, notice that while we're allowed to keep all comments in English, we could also use Spanish or whatever other language we're interested in (perhaps to increase the contextual information surrounding each message to ensure a higher quality translation). The actual NLS message catalog key words like $set, however, are required to be in English for the *gencat* program to be able to recognize them and process the message catalog source correctly.

This remaining language bias is not as inappropriate as it may initially seem, actually, since it is mirrored in the keywords found in almost all of the common programming languages available today. That is, in C one must use "if", "while", and "for", not their equivalents in a local language.

```
$     This is the message catalog for the sample HP NLS program
$     that we're working with. It is broken into three different
$     message sets as indicated.
$
$     This version is for language Español
$

$set 1 normal output messages

1     lista de empleados al
2     Salario promedio =
3      máximo =
```

*Listing Twelve: The Message Catalog for Language "Spanish"*

4 mínimo =

$set 2 error messages

1 Error en la línea
2 : falta el símbolo '='
3 Demasiadas personas: el límite es
4 nombres máxim
5 No indicó ningún empleado.

$set 3 character delimiters, etc.

1 =

*Listing Twelve: Continued*

Running the sample program with the run-time LANG environment variable set to "spanish" results in the output shown in listing thirteen. Notice that the name Chavé has correctly sorted between the name Cooper and the name Davis, since in Spanish "Ch" is considered a single letter, occurring lexographically between "C" and "D".

lista de empleados al Dom, 23 Abr 1989 15.31.51

| | |
|---|---|
| Carlos, Maria | 450,0 Pts. |
| Cooper, Ted | 5000,0 Pts. |
| Charé, Raul | 7530,0 Pts. |
| Davis, Jim | 1000,0 Pts. |
| Louie, Nancy | 2400,0 Pts. |
| Taylor, Dave | 8523,0 Pts. |
| Vixie, Paul | 4394,0 Pts. |

Salario promedio = 4185,28 Pts. máximo = 450,0 Pts.
mínimo = 8523,0 Pts.

*Listing Thirteen: Sample Output with Language "spanish"*

Did you notice that the radix or "decimal point" is a comma, rather than the more familiar period found in English-speaking countries? In addition, this is our first example of a standard currency delimiter that is more than a single character long; Pts. is an abbreviation for Pesetas, the Spanish base unit of currency.

### French

Similarly, we can translate the message catalog into French as shown in listing fourteen, with the resulting output of the program shown in listing fifteen. Notice that in French Charé sorts between Carlos and Cooper.

```
$    Ceci est le catalogue de messages du programme 'HP NLS'
$    avec lequel nous travaillons. Ce catalogue est découpé en
$    trois groupes tel que nous l'avons mentionné.
$
$    Version pour langue française.

$set 1 normal output messages

1    Liste d'employés au
2    Salaire moyen =
3    bas =
4    haut =

$set 2 error messages

1    Erreur dans la ligne d'entrée
2    Delimiteur '=' pas trouvé
3    Trop d'utilisateurs pour ce programme. la limite est
4    noms
5    Pas d'employés entrés

$set 3 character delimiters, etc.

1    =
```

*Listing Fourteen: Message Catalog for Language "French"*

Liste d'employés au dim 23 avr 1989 16h53 40

| | |
|---|---|
| Carlos, Maria | 450,0 FF |
| Charé, Raul | 7530,0 FF |
| Cooper, Ted | 5000,0 FF |
| Davis, Jim | 1000,0 FF |
| Louie, Nancy | 2400,0 FF |
| Taylor, Dave | 8523,0 FF |
| Vixie, Paul | 4394,0 FF |

Salaire moyen = 4185,28 FF  bas = 450,0 FF  haut = 8523,0 FF

*Listing Fifteen: Sample Output for Language "French"*

## Asian and other 16-bit Languages

The NLS program that we've written here performs admirably for any of the many 8-bit languages, additionally including German, Swedish, Dutch, and Italian. If we want to us a language that is completely different in character set, like Arabic or Chinese, however, v need not only to have a message catalog that allows us to support the language in question but we also need to change the way in which we create and store the information itself.

To accomplish this, HP offers an additional layer to the NLS package called the Native Language Input/Output system, or NLIO for short. Running as a layer between the operating system and the user, it can handle such tasks as translating from keyboard representation of an Asian language into the actual ideograms appropriate. Conceptually NLIO appears as in illustration two.

The NLIO system is accessed through a number of user level commands:

| | |
|---|---|
| *nlio* | control Native Language I/O |
| *nlioenv* | set Native Language I/O environment |
| *nlioinit* | initialize Native Language I/O |
| *nliostart* | start Native Language I/O |

The HP support for 16-bit characters is implemented through an internal 15-bit set (which still gives over 32,000 different possibilities for an individual character) and a lot of what the NLIO system does is translate between the internal and so-called external representations.

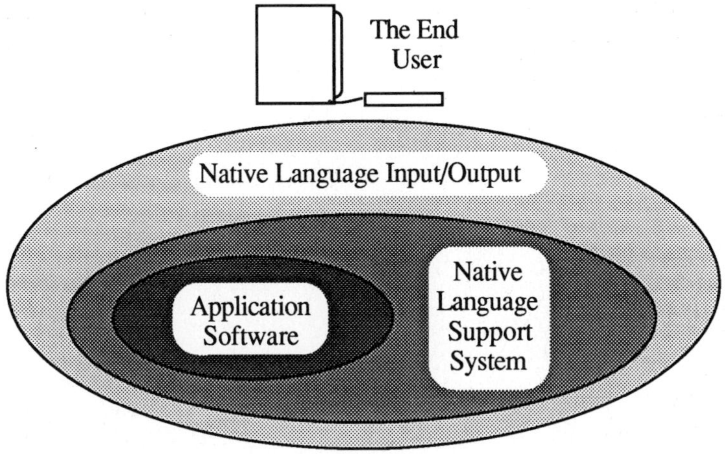


*Illustration Two: The HP Native Language I/O System*

Space doesn't permit more than a cursory explanation of how to enable and use the NLIO system, alas, but suffice to say it is considerably more awkward, and more poorly documented, than the NLS system. Run time modification of the NLIO run-time environment is done through calls to the Unix *ioctl* – I/O Control – subroutine, and between invocations of individual programs, the user can change various elements of the NLIO runtime environment, such as which word or phrase dictionaries are being referenced, through use of the *nlioenv* command.

**To Summarize**

We've now gained a better understanding of the complexities and challenges associated with creating a software package or application that can function anywhere within the world computer marketplace. We've also introduced and demonstrated the HP Native Language Support System and briefly discussed the Native Language I/O subsystem, also from Hewlett-Packard Company.

Those people without Hewlett-Packard HP-UX Unix machines will find that the X/Open Portability Guide suggestions on run time internationalization are very similar to the NLS package, and it should be a fairly straightforward task to bring up the sample application on any of the many vendor platforms that are certified by the X/Open Consortium.

Internationalization is a topic that is just beginning to become important as the world marketplace develops to the point where computers interacting in the local language becomes a necessity. It's only through incorporating the cultural and sociological beliefs and ideals of a place and language that one can achieve a fundamental goal of any international item, be it software, hardware, or any other product; to meet the expectations of the end user, fitting in well to their own cultural and social context.

## References

Apple Corporation, *Developing International Software*, Apple Programmers and Developers Association document #A7G0016, September, 1988.

AT&T Document *Internationalization and AT&T Unix System V*, from AT&T Unix Pacific Co. Ltd, Japan, February 1989.

Burkley, Rodger, *Implementing Kanji Characters on VMS – A Technical Overview*, Digital Equipment Corporation.

Hewlett-Packard Company, *A Tutorial Introduction to the HP NLS System*, in the HP-UX 6.5 documentation suite, November 1988.

Hewlett-Packard Company, *The HP-UX Documentation Suite*, version 6.5 for the series 9000 Unix computer, November 1988.

International Business Machines Corporation, *Software Without Frontiers*, IBM England document # GE-19-5356-0, December, 1984.

Nakajima, Reiji, *GMW Window System and Wnn Japanese Language System*, Kyoto University Research Institute for Mathematical Sciences, July 1988.

X/Open Consortium, *The X/Open Portability Guide*, release 3, April 1989.

*Designing User Interfaces for International Use*, edited by J. Nielsen
Elsevier, 1990


# INTERNATIONAL USER INTERFACE FOR INFOFLEX

**Jakob Peter Nielsen**

Data Reforming A/S, Copenhagen, Denmark

### Abstract

The Danish software house Data Reforming started in august 1988 a project with the purpose to make an international version of the business application INFOFLEX. One of the conditions for exporting a software system is that all text on all screens and reports are translated to the national language. The project involves development of tools to enable translation of the text based COBOL application running primarily under UNIX. This paper contains a description of the implementation which is the result of the work done in the first six months of the project.

## 1 Introduction

One of the key conditions for exporting a software system to be used by non-technical users is that all text on screens and reports are translated to the national language, e.g. German. This is especially true if the application is developed in Denmark with all texts written in Danish.

Data Reforming started in august 1988 a project with the purpose to develop an international version of the business application INFOFLEX. The primary goal of the project was to develop tools to enable translation of the application to other languages than Danish. The primary target languages was German and Norwegian. A second goal was at the same time to develop tools which could ease the development of the user interface part of the application.

Data Reforming's primary business has since 1980 been development and maintenance of the application and "hot-line" support for users. The company today has 15 employees of whom 6 is engaged in development. The distribution of the application takes place through resellers of XENIX/UNIX based micro- and minicomputers.

The INFOFLEX application covers the business areas from wholesale / retail (Point Of Sale) to manufacturing (order / batch production). There is about 850 installations and the estimated number of users is about 3000.

INFOFLEX is developed using RM/COBOL-85 from Ryan-McFarland. The application is developed entirely in COBOL. There is no use of C or assembler subroutines. Together with the RM/COBOL runtime technology this gives a large degree of portability. The application runs with only one source code and one object code on the operating systems UNIX, XENIX, AIX and MS-DOS, on hardware ranging from microcomputers from IBM and Compaq to minicomputers from IBM, Altos and NCR.

New installations primarily takes place on Intel 386 based microcomputers with the SCO Xenix operating system.

The user interface is build using traditional 24 lines times 80 characters terminals connected over serial lines (RS232). The interface is menu driven with a large number of form fill-in screens.

This paper first outlines the various possible solutions to the translation problem. Then a description of the current implementation is given. The paper ends with a discussion of our experiences regarding performance, application and user interface development.

## 2 Solutions

We first discuss four possible solutions to our problem. The various advantages, disadvantages and experiences are outlined.

The four very different ways to solve the translation problem is:

1. Edit text and information regarding layout of screens and reports (e.g. lines and positions) in the COBOL source.
2. Place all text from screens and reports outside the COBOL source. The information regarding layout of screens and reports are still contained in the COBOL source.
3. Place all text and all information regarding layout of screens and reports outside the COBOL application. Access to the text and layout database is then given through special procedures.
4. Place all text and all information regarding layout of screens and reports outside the COBOL application. A special compiler is then used to generate the user interface code, which is then compiled by the COBOL compiler and linked together with the application.

### 2.1 Solution 1

Of bitter experience we know that this solution is the worst solution one can possible chose. A few years ago Data Reforming began, in corporation with a Swedish software house, a project with the goal to make a Swedish version of the INFOFLEX application.

We did not, at that time, possess the tools to enable translation in any other way, than to edit the text in the COBOL source. The reason for not developing the tools at that moment was lack of time and restricted memory (the size of a COBOL run unit was in the old RM/COBOL-74 limited to 64K, runtime included).

The Swedish software house used approximately 2 man years to translate the application except the manufacturing system. The project ended luckily with a running product and a product that the Swedish firm is able to sell.

The biggest problem with this method is, that you create two versions of the source, which you have to maintain. If you find a bug in the Danish version, you have to correct the same bug in the Swedish version or retranslate the portion of code involved. The same thing has to be done when you make an enhancement to an existing function or develop a completely new function. It is our experience, that the two versions very quickly grows completely different.

Another disadvantage is that the translation cannot be done by non-programmers. You have to have some knowledge of the COBOL language to edit the code.

In addition to this there is the problem, that the firm who should do the translation to the foreign language, should have a source licence to the application.

The only advantage with this method, that I can see, is that you do not loose any performance.

## 2.2 Solution 2

Removing all text from the COBOL source is a better solution than the first solution presented. With respect to the application, you only have one version to maintain.

The problem with this solution is that all information regarding layout of screens and reports are still contained in the COBOL source and cannot be changed when you make the translation. This gives no ability of moving, deleting or adding fields. You are stuck with the layout, and even worse, if you have a word in e.g. Danish which translated to German occupies more space on the screen than available, you sometime have to make the most absurd and meaningless abbreviations. A way to get round this problem, is to fill as much space as possible between texts and fields. This is not always possible and in some cases do not look good either.

We have used this method in the application in the programs which creates external forms (invoices, statements etc.). The text on the forms can be translated into several different languages. We have experienced that it is not enough only to change the text, you also have to move, add and delete fields.

## 2.3 Solution 3

This solution does not have many of the deficiencies of the two previous solutions, but this solution adds many interesting aspects (or problems!).

The aspects are:

- Is it possible to make a general tool that could be used to support the current user interface without loosing flexibility ?

- How to specify the layout of the screens and reports. Should it be done the traditional way by using lines and positions or should be done in a more what-you-see-is-what-you-get way ?
- How should the application gain access to and use the information specified outside the application ? How should the "special procedures" be designed ?
- How big will the changes be in the existing programs ?
- Will there be any loss of performance ?

Early in the project, we decided to use this solution. The rest of this paper is therefore devoted to answering the above questions. Shortly, one can summarize our experiences:

- There must be made a lot of trade-offs concerning the development of a general versus a flexible tool.
- It is not easy to develop a way of specifying the layout information outside the application. Using i.e. lines and positions is not a good solution. Things are in favor of a WYSIWYG method.
- The interface to the "special procedures" must be developed as simple as possible. The access to the text/layout information should be hidden from the application.
- In the current application there is a tight coupling between the user interface specific code and the function specific code. There is a large job ahead in separating the two parts and using the developed user interface tool.
- Yes, there will be a loss of performance. Making things more general costs. Time is used to access the text/layout information, but also to process the information.

## 2.4 Solution 4

This solution came up as an idea in the end of the project. Though, we have no experiences with the method we see the following difficulties:

- There is still the problem of making a way of specifying the layout information.
- There is the question of which code to generate. If we are going to generate a lot of code automatic, it surely have to be good!
- A code generator should be developed to perform the translation from the layout information to the user interface specific COBOL code. This is not an especially easy task.
- Linking the generated code to the application can only be done by dynamic linking, i.e. by a call at run time.

- The translator should have access to a COBOL compiler and should have some knowledge of the COBOL programming language.

### 2.5 Selection of Solution

Early in the project we decided to use solution 3. This was due to our experiences with the two other solutions (1 and 2), but also because this solution seemed to contain the biggest technical challenge.

If we have had the choice between solution 3 and 4, I think solution 3 would still be the winner. At Data Reforming, code generators have the reputation of generating lots of inefficient code, totally impossible to maintain. When we presented our solution, the first question we were asked was: "This doesn't involve code generation, does it?".

## 3 Implementation

This section describes the prototype system that we have implemented during the first six months of the project.

Figure 1 gives an overview of the prototype system.

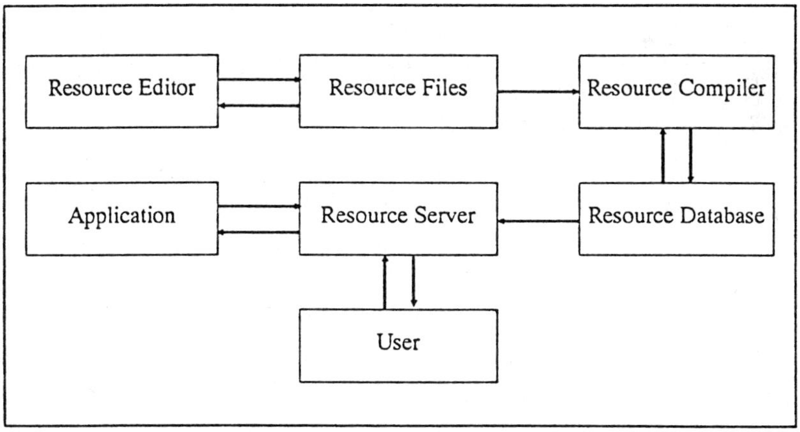


Fig. 1: System overview

### 3.1 Resource Files

The implementation is based on the idea that all information regarding text and layout is placed outside the application. This section describes the way we have chosen to represent this information.

The text and layout information from the application is placed in ordinary text files ("ASCII files"). It is the intension, that for every program in the application there shall exist a text file for every translation of the text in this program. A file containing text and layout information is called a *resource file.*

In addition to the resource files for the programs in the application, there should exist some resource files called *standard resource files*. These resource files contains general information such as system parameters, general error messages etc.

The information is structured according to a certain syntax. The basic idea is, that the resource file is divided into a number of paragraphs. A paragraph starts with a line containing a '#' followed by a *keyword* and additional information, which identifies the information in the paragraph. A paragraph ends with a line containing a '#' followed by the keyword 'END'. Some special paragraphs only contains the identification information. These paragraphs are only one line long and does therefore not end with '#END'.

The current implementation supports the following keywords / paragraphs:

| Keyword | Contents of paragraph |
|---|---|
| PROGRAM | Identification of which program the resource file belongs to. |
| LANGUAGE | Identification of which language the texts in the resource file is a translation to. |
| PANEL | Translation of a screen. |
| BOX | Definition of boxes in a screen. |
| HEADER | Translation of a header on a report. |
| FOOTER | Translation of a footer on a report. |
| LINE | Translation of a so called line in a screen or on a report. |
| FIELDS | Definition of names and attributes to fields in a screen or on a report. A field is for example an entry field, where the user is supposed to enter a value. |
| SEQUENCE | Definition of a sequence of fields in a dialog. |
| TEXT | Translation of free texts. |
| ERROR | Translation of messages (error messages, warnings etc.). |
| SYSPARM | Definition of global system parameters (date/time formats etc.). |

There are some constraints on the order in which the above paragraph may appear in the resource file. For example, a PANEL paragraph including fields should always be followed by a FIELDS paragraph.

### 3.1.1 Program & Language Identification

Every resource file should contain a program and a language identification, i.e. an identification of which program the file belongs to and an identification of which language the texts in the file are a translation to.

This is done by using the keywords PROGRAM and LANGUAGE. The program / language is identified with a name of up to 3 characters. Figure 2 is an example of a resource file for the program "P18". The text in this resource file is translated to English "ENG".

```
#PROGRAM, P18
#LANGUAGE, ENG
```

Fig. 2: Program and language identification

### 3.1.2 Screen Layout

Layout of screens is specified using the keyword PANEL in the resource file. A screen is identified with a name of up to 20 characters.

The screen is written in the PANEL paragraph exactly as it is to be shown, when used in the program. The first line in the paragraph corresponds to line number 1 on the screen.

It is possible to specify attributes to the characters in the screen. The attribute controls how the character will be shown on the screen. It is possible to specify that the character should be shown blinking, in reverse, with high intensity, with low intensity or a combination of the above effects.

Attributes are specified by typing two masterspaces (@) at the end of the line which should be attributed. The following line is then interpreted as an attribute line. The attribute line is not displayed on the screen.

A field is placed in a screen by typing underscores (_) in the position, where the field should be located. The length of the field is determined by the number of underscores. Therefore, the underscore character cannot be used as a normal character in the text.

Figure 3 shows an example of a screen specified by the PANEL keyword. The C, E and D in the text "(Create, Edit, Delete)" are shown in reverse when the screen is shown on the users terminal.

```
#PANEL, MAINT1


        Maintenance of items

        Function       _            (Create, Edit, Delete) @@
                                     R        R      R

        Item number    _______

        Item text      ________________________

#END
```

Fig. 3: Screen layout

It is possible to include boxes in a screen. This is done using the keyword BOX. A box is displayed using the graphic characters from the extended character set.

A box is displayed between two fields. One field for the upper left corner and one field for the lower right corner. If the two corner fields are in the same line, only a line is displayed.

A box can be given several attributes. It is possible to specify, that the box is displayed using single lines, double lines or spaces (no box shown). A box can be showed in reverse, with high or low intensity.

Figure 4 shows an example of a screen with four fields named B1S, B1E, B2S and B2E. Two boxes should be displayed - box number 1 with single lines between fields B1S and B1E - box number 2 with double lines between fields B2S and B2E.

Figure 5 shows the result when the screen is displayed.

```
#PANEL, EX3

    _
          This is box number 1
                                                  _

    _   This
        is
        box
        number
        2
               _

#END

...

#BOX
BOX1, B1S, B1E, SINGLE.
BOX2, B2S, B2E, DOUBLE.
#END
```

Fig. 4: Specification of boxes

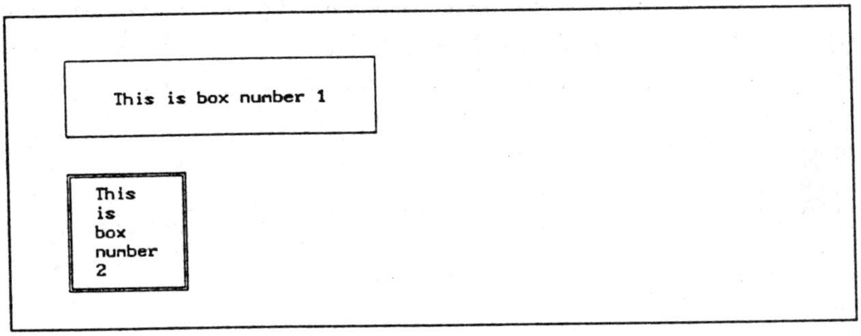


Fig. 5: Screen with boxes

A special screen should be defined in the standard resource file. This screen is called the *standard screen* and can be displayed before a normal screen is displayed. The standard screen contains texts and fields, which is included in every screen in the application. An example of a text displayed in every INFOFLEX program is the INFOFLEX name.

### 3.1.3 Line Layout

Several screens in an application contains a partial layout, which is used in several places in the screen. Figure 6 shows an example of a screen containing output from a query. The lines used to display item numbers, texts and prices are based on the same partial layout.

```
Query on items              Page  1 of 10  More    - +

Item no.   Text                                  Price
-------------------------------------------------------
ABD-24B    Alphabike 24" Blue                   250.00
ABD-24Y    Alphabike 24" Yellow                 350.00
COR-23B    Campeotto 23" Black                  175.50
COR-23Y    Campeotto 23" Yellow                 340.00
COR-23W    Campeotto 23" White                  450.00
XYZ-23W    XYZ Bike 23" White                   890.00
-------------------------------------------------------
```

Fig. 6: Screen with lines

A partial layout of this kind is called a *line*. A line can consist of up to 10 real lines. Lines are specified using the LINE keyword. Nearly the same syntax as in the PANEL paragraph is used. The difference is, that attributes in lines are currently not supported. Figure 7 is an example of a line to be used in the screen from figure 6.

```
#LINE, ITEM-LINE
_________  ____________________________  ________
#END
```

Fig. 7: Specification of line layout

The actual location of a line on a screen is controlled by the application program.

### 3.1.4 Report Layout

Layout of reports are specified using the keywords HEADER, FOOTER and LINE. The HEADER keyword is used to specify the layout of the head on the report page. The FOOTER keyword is used to specify the foot on report page. The LINE keyword is used to specify the layout of the different lines on the report.

A *standard header* and a *standard footer* should be defined in the standard resource file.

Figure 8 shows an example of a report to be specified. Figure 9 shows the corresponding resource file.

```
KVIK BICYCLES INC.

TRANSACTIONS    DEPT. 1           DATE 89.07.26 PAGE  1

  DATE     NUMBER   ACOUNT  TEXT                     AMOUNT

89.01.10  000001   12100   CASH PAYMENT             345.00
89.04.15  000002   10100   INVOICE                   10.00
89.05.16  000003   10100   CREDIT NOTE              -45.00
89.06.27  000004   13300   CASH PAYMENT              12.00
                                                -----------
TOTAL                                            322.00

USER: PL  PRINTED: 11.00 AM
```

Fig. 8: Report

```
#HEADER, TRANS-HEAD

______________________________

TRANSACTIONS    DEPT. _           DATE ________  PAGE __

  DATE     NUMBER   ACOUNT   TEXT                     AMOUNT

#END

#FOOTER, TRANS-FOOT

USER: __   PRINTED: ________

#END

#LINE, TRANS-LINE
________  ______  _____   __________________  ________
#END

#LINE, TRANS-TOTAL
                                                -----------
TOTAL
                                                ___________
#END
```

Fig. 9: Report layout

## 3.1.5 Field Definition

Two basic field characteristics are determined by the contents in the PANEL, LINE, HEADER and FOOTER paragraphs: Field location (line / position) and field length. The field name, type and attributes should also be specified in the resource file. This is done using the FIELDS keyword. A PANEL, LINE, HEADER or FOOTER paragraph containing fields should always be followed by a FIELDS paragraph.

The sequence of the fields in the paragraph is determined by their location on the screen. The sequence is found by reading the screen from the upper left corner and then line by line to the lower right corner.

A field is named with a string of up to 20 characters.

The *field type* is either an accept, a display, a default or a dummy field.

*Accept fields* are fields which can be used to input (accept) and display values.

*Display fields* are fields which can be used to display values.

*Default fields* are fields, which are not on the screen / report. The field is included in the FIELDS paragraph because the application program references to it. If the program want input from the field a default value is returned - hence the name default field.

*Dummy fields* are used as a reference to locations in the screen / on the report. Fx. if the application program should determine where to start displaying the lines in figure 6, a dummy field is used as a reference to the first line.

The field attributes falls in four groups: display, accept, input and editing attributes.

*Display attributes* controls how values in the field are shown on the screen. A value can be show with a beep, blinking, in reverse or with high/low intensity. The display attributes make sense for fields in screens only.

*Accept attributes* control the cobol's accept statement. It is possible to specify that input to the field should always be terminated by the enter key, that it is possible to edit the value and that the value, if it is a text, should be converted to all upper case letters.

*Input attributes* are used to control translation of one character input (used in menus and function choices) and to determine which function and special keys the user is allowed to press in the field.

The *editing attributes* controls how a field value is edited. Most of the editing attributes are used in the editing of numeric values.

For numeric values it is possible to specify that the number is shown with separators between thousands, shown with sign, with leading zeroes or not shown at all if the number is zero. In addition to this, it is possible to control the number of decimals and whether the number should be rounded before it is displayed.

The rest of the editing attributes is used in editing date and time values. Date values can be shown with and without separators between day, month and year. Time values can be shown with and without seconds.

Every field attribute is assigned a default value, therefore it is not necessary to explicit specify all but a few attribute values to a field definition.

The use of the FIELDS paragraph is illustrated in the following example.

Figure 10 shows a screen specified with PANEL. The fields in this screen should be given names and attributes.

Figure 11 shows the corresponding FIELDS paragraph.

```
#PANEL, SCREEN1
                                        Date ________  Time _____

   Function  _      (Create, Edit, Delete)

   Number    ________

   Text      ____________________     Group     __
             ____________________     Discount  _____

   Price     __________               Location  _______
   Cost      __________               Supplier  _______

#END
```

Fig. 10: Screen with fields to be defined

```
#FIELDS
DATE      , DISPLAY, DATE1.
TIME      , DISPLAY, TIME1.
FUNCTION  , ACCEPT , TRANSLATE "CED" "123".
NUMBER    , ACCEPT , UPPER, TAB, REVERSE.
TEXT-1    , ACCEPT.
GROUP     , ACCEPT , ZERO.
TEXT-2    , ACCEPT.
DISCOUNT  , ACCEPT , DEC=2, ROUNDED.
PRICE     , ACCEPT , DEC=2, THOUSAND.
LOCATION  , ACCEPT.
COST      , ACCEPT , DEC=2, THOUSAND.
SUPPLIER  , ACCEPT.
WEIGHT    , DEFAULT.
#END
```

Fig. 11: Field definition

The field named DATE is assigned the type DISPLAY which means that the program can display a value in the field. The editing attribute DATE1 indicates that a date to be displayed in this field should be edited with separators between day, month and year.

The editing attribute TIME1 in the field TIME indicates that a time to be displayed in this field should be edited without seconds.

The one character field FUNCTION is to be used for input of a function choice (Create, Edit or Delete). The field type is therefore accept. The phrase TRANSLATE "CED" "123" tells the application, that when the user enters a C, E or D the application program should receive either 1, 2 or 3.

Characters entered in the field NUMBER are converted to all upper case (Accept attribute UPPER) and input to the field should always be terminated by hitting the enter key (Accept attribute TAB). The field values are shown in reverse video (Display attribute REVERSE).

Numbers shown in the field GROUP are edited with leading zeroes (Editing attribute ZERO).

Numbers shown in the fields DISCOUNT, PRICE and COST are edited with two decimals (Editing attribute DEC=2). Numbers shown in the field DISCOUNT are rounded before they are displayed (Editing attribute ROUNDED). Numbers in the fields PRICE and COST are edited with separators between thousands (Editing attribute THOUSAND).

The field WEIGHT is not included in the screen but can be used by the application program.

### 3.1.6 Sequences

The sequence in which the application program should accept input from the fields in a screen is not necessarily the same as the one given by the sequence of the fields in the FIELDS paragraph. Fx. the application program using the screen in figure 10 should not accept input from the fields in sequence NUMBER, TEXT-1, GROUP, TEXT-2, ... but should accept input from the fields in the sequence NUMBER, TEXT-1, TEXT-2, ....

The keyword SEQUENCE can be used after the FIELDS paragraph to specify the correct sequence of the fields: Figure 12 shows the SEQUENCE paragraph corresponding to the FIELDS paragraph in figure 11. It is possible to define more than one sequence for a screen.

```
#SEQUENCE, SCREEN1-SEQ
FUNCTION
NUMBER
TEXT-1
TEXT-2
PRICE
COST
GROUP
DISCOUNT
LOCATION
SUPPLIER
#END
```

Fig. 12: Definition of a sequence

Sequences are used by the application program not only when the application program accepts input from the user, but also when the application program shows field values to the user, either on the screen or on reports. The SEQUENCE paragraph is therefore used after both PANEL, LINE, HEADER and FOOTER paragraphs.

### 3.1.7 Free Texts

In addition to the texts in screens and on reports, it is possible to define so called *free texts*. These text strings are named and can be up to 80 characters long. It is possible to specify attributes to the characters in a text. This is done the same way as in the PANEL paragraph. The keyword used to specify free texts is TEXT.

Up to nine variable fields can be included in a text. These fields are filled with values by the application program before the text is used. A variable field is placed in the text by using "#1" for field number 1, "#2" for field number 2 and so on.

Figure 13 contains a specification of two free texts. The text INV-TXT contains variable field number 1 (#1). When the application program displays this text, the word "INVOICE" is shown with high intensity and the variable field is substituted with a value delivered by the application program.

```
#TEXT
INV-TXT,  "Invoice number #1" @@
           HHHHHHH
CDN-TXT,  "Credit Note"
#END
```

Fig. 13: Definition of free texts

### 3.1.8 Messages

Error messages, warnings and other messages are defined using the ERROR keyword in the standard resource file.

A message consists of a text of up to 80 characters. It is possible to include variable fields in a message. This is done the same way as with free texts.

Figure 14 shows an ERROR paragraph in a standard resource file.

```
#ERROR
ERR-CUST,  "Customer #1 not in customer file"
ERR-DISK,  "Error reading drive #1"
#END
```

Fig. 14: Definition of error messages

### 3.1.9 System Parameters

When we discussed editing of date, time and number values in the section describing definition of fields, there was no discussion about date, time or number formats, fx. the order of the day, month and year in dates.

These language specific editing rules are determined by the *system parameters* defined in the SYSPARM paragraph in the standard resource file. In addition to date, time and number formats the SYSPARM paragraph contains information on how to interpret answers to Yes/No questions and specification of which character the application should use as prompt character in entry fields.

Three different date formats can be used: Day/Month/Year, Month/Day/Year and Year/Month/Day. The separator character to be used between the day, month and year can also be specified.

For time values is is possible to specify, that the time should be shown in 24 hours format or in 12 hours format with AM and PM.

For numbers the thousand separator and decimal point can be specified. There are 4 possible combinations for the thousand separator / decimal point: Period / Comma, Comma / Period, Space / Comma and Space / Period.

For Yes/No questions it is possible to specify up to 5 characters which should be interpreted as Yes and up to 5 characters which should be interpreted as No.

There is no system parameters which contains information regarding collating sequences, special characters etc. These aspects are assumed to be handled by the COBOL runtime.

Figure 15 shows an example of SYSPARM paragraph.

```
#SYSPARM
SYS-PROMPT       , .
SYS-YES          , OS
SYS-NO           , N
SYS-DATE-FMT     , C
SYS-DATE-SYM     , /
SYS-TIME-FMT     , A
SYS-DEC-KONV     , B
#END
```

Fig. 15: System parameters

The line SYS-PROMPT in the SYSPARM paragraph sets the prompt character to the period (.).

SYS-YES and SYS-NO specifies that the characters "O" and "S" (for "Oui" and "Si") means Yes and the character "N" means No.

The date format is set to Year/Month/Day by the line SYS-DATE-FMT and the separator character between day, month and year is set to the slash (/) character by the SYS-DATE-SYM line.

The time format is set to 24 hours by the line SYS-TIME-FMT.

Comma is used as the thousand separator and period is used as the decimal point. This is set by the line SYS-DEC-KONV (The Danish abbreviation for Decimal Convention).

## 3.2 Resource Editor

The resource files can be edited with a normal text editor (such as the UNIX 'vi' editor) or a word processor. To do this, the translator has to know the resource file syntax. In addition to this, using a normal editor does not give complete WYSIWYG appearance of the screens and the reports.

To ease editing of the resource files, we have developed a special *resource editor*. The resource editor requires only a minimal knowledge of the resource file syntax and gives WYSIWYG appearance of the screens and reports.

The resource editor is currently developed in RM/COBOL-85.

Figure 16 shows the resource editor when the user is editing the screen from figure 10. Figure 17 shows how the resource editor can be used to define field characteristics and attributes.

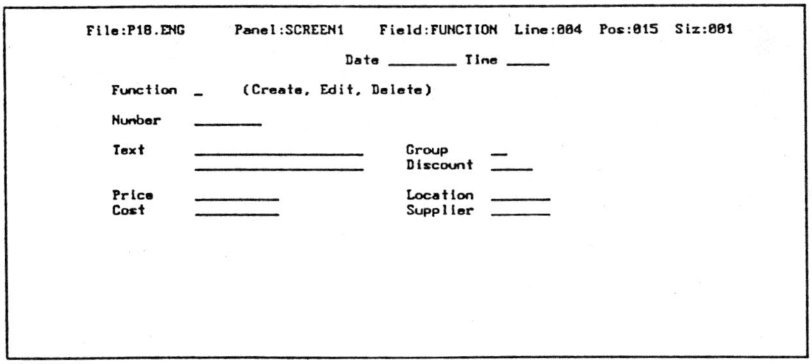


Fig. 16: Resource editor

```
File:P18.ENG       Panel:SCREEN1     Field:FUNCTION  Line:004  Pos:015  Siz:001

    Function  _      (Create, Edit, Delete)

    Number    ________

    Text      _____________________    Group    __

+---------------------------------- Field information --------------------------+
|Field     : FUNCTION                x SIGN        BEEP          x BACK          |
|Type      : ACCEPT                  x THOUSAND    BLINK         x DUP           |
|Line      : 004                     x ROUNDED     REVERSE       x SHOW-DUP      |
|Position  : 015                       ZERO        HIGH          x SDUP          |
|Size      : 001                       BLANK       LOW             SDUP-STOP     |
|Integer   :                         1 TIME        OFF           x CANCEL        |
|Decimals  : 0                       1 DATE        TAB             CANCEL-STOP   |
|                                                x UPDATE          NEXT          |
|                                                  UPPER           HELP          |
|Translate                                                         PROMPT        |
| - from   : CED                                                   BACKWARD      |
| - to     : 123                                                   FORWARD       |
+-------------------------------------------------------------------------------+
```

Fig. 17: Field definition with resource editor

## 3.3 Resource Compiler & Database

The resource files gives a good basis for editing the layout of the screens and reports. Being normal flat sequential text files, they can be edited with a simple text editor.

When it comes to using the text and layout information in the application programs, the unstructured resource files are not good enough. Together with the lack of random access to the resource files , a lot of work on these files has to be done before the information can be used. This processing can easily be done once and for all and does have to be done at run time. One of the tasks is for example to find the location of the fields in the screens and on the reports.

To convert the resource files to a file with indexed and fast access and to do the processing of the information contained in the resource files a special *resource compiler* has been developed.

The resource compiler reads the resource files and generates an RM/COBOL-85 ISAM file called the *resource database.* The resource database is common for all programs in the application.

Using the RM/COBOL-85 ISAM file gives both the advantage of indexed access to the text and layout information, but it also gives the advantage of the RM/COBOL-85 file compression.

The resource compiler has been developed in RM/COBOL-85.

## 3.4 Resource Server

All access to the text and layout information in the resource database and all access to the user, either via the terminal or printed reports, is given through the so called *resource server.*

The resource server is a collection of procedures, which work on the information contained in the resource database. The resource server is currently developed using RM/COBOL-85.

The interface between the application program and the resource server is via the COBOL CALL mechanism, which means that dynamic linking is used (linking at run time).

The application program calls the resource server with a function name and a collection of parameters. The function name tells the resource server which procedure to execute. The control returns to the application program after the resource server has performed the requested function.

Often used information from the resource database is loaded into the resource server, when called the first time by an application program. Field characteristics and attributes are among the data loaded into the resource servers memory. Screens and report headers / footers are loaded from the resource database every time they are used.

## 3.5 Application Programs

This section describe the programming interface between the application programs and the resource server.

The procedures in the resource server falls in the following groups:

- Initialization and closing
- Screen handling
- Field handling
- Editing field values
- Display field values
- Data entry
- Sequence handling
- Line handling
- Browse functions
- Report handling

The following sections shortly describes the procedures used in the application programs. The COBOL examples shown does not directly use a CALL to invoke the resource server. Instead a dummy procedure with the same name as the resource server procedure is performed. The only job these dummy procedures has to do is to move the function name to the function name parameter and then call the resource server.

### 3.5.1 Initialization and Closing

The first thing an application program should do is to call the resource servers initialization procedure. After use of the resource server the application should call the closing procedure.

The resource server contains procedures for initialization and closing for the whole application and procedures for initialization and closing for a single application program.

The initialization procedure for the whole application is called with the name of the language to be used. The procedure opens the resource database and loads information common to all of the application programs (System parameters, standard fields etc.).

The closing procedure for the whole application closes the resource database. Figure 18 shows the COBOL code, which should be used to call the initialization and closing procedure for the whole application.

```
* Initialize Resource Server
  MOVE "ENG" TO RES-LANGUAGE.
  PERFORM RES-INIT-SYSTEM.

  ...

* Close Resource Server
  PERFORM RES-CLOSE-SYSTEM.
```

Fig. 18: Initialization and closing for whole application

When an application program is started it calls the initialization procedure for a single application program. The name of the application program calling the procedure is given as a parameter.

Often used information which belongs to the application program is loaded from the resource database. Fx. characteristics and attributes to all fields are loaded.

Figure 19 shows the COBOL code, which should be used to do the initialization and closing for a single application program.

```
* Initialize Resource Server for program "P18"
  MOVE "P18" TO RES-PROG.
  PERFORM RES-INIT.

  ...

* Close Resource Server for program "P18"
  PERFORM RES-CLOSE.
```

Fig. 19: Initialization and closing for single program

### 3.5.2 Screen Handling

This group of procedures is used to display information from the resource database on the screen. The following functions are implemented:

- Display the standard screen
- Display screen
- Display prompt in entry fields
- Delete screen
- Delete contents of box
- Display free text
- Display message

The standard screen can be shown alone or before a normal screen is displayed. Before the standard screen is displayed the screen is cleared. The fields in the standard screen are filled with values provided by the resource server.

When the application want to display a screen it passes the name of the screen together with a flag indicating whether the standard screen should be displayed to the resource server. The resource server gets the screens texts from the resource database and displays them on the users terminal. Figure 20 shows the COBOL code involved to display a screen from the resource database.

```
* Display screen MAINT1 together with standard screen
  MOVE "MAINT1" TO RES-PANEL.
  SET RES-STD-PANEL TO TRUE.
  PERFORM RES-SHOW-PANEL.
```

Fig. 20: Display screen

When a screen is displayed only the texts are displayed. A procedure is provided to display prompts in entry fields and to blank display fields.

### 3.5.3 Field Handling

The application program can request all known field characteristics and attributes from the resource server. This is done calling a special procedure.

A field is identified by the name of the screen, head, foot or line which the field belongs to together with the field name.

### 3.5.4 Editing Field Values

A field value can be either a text, number, date, time, Yes/No answer or function choice.

Editing of field values is done by the resource server with regard to field attributes and system parameters.

The procedures to edit the different field values are used in the following way: First the application program gets the field attributes, then the editing function is called and out comes the edited value. The value is represented as a text string.

Numbers, dates and times are edited as described in the previous sections.

Yes/No answers are translated from the Danish "J" for Yes and "N" for No to the characters specified in the system parameters for Yes/No questions.

Function choices are translated with the help of the two strings specified by TRANSLATE.

### 3.5.5 Display Field Values

A field is either in a screen, head or foot on a report or in a line. Seen from the applications point of view, the operations are the same whether a field value should be shown on the screen, in the head or foot on a report or in a line. Where a field value should be shown is therefore given as a parameter to the procedures showing field values. This parameter is called the *route*.

The procedures looks up the field characteristics and attributes and edits the fields using the procedures described in the previous section. After the editing the edited value is displayed on the screen or moved into the head, foot or line.

If the field is a dummy or default field no value is edited or shown.

Figure 21 shows how to display the number 10 in the field "GROUP" in screen "SCREEN1" (From figure 10).

```
* Route all field values to the screen
  SET RES-DISPLAY TO TRUE.

* Display field value in screen "SCREEN1" field "GROUP"
  MOVE "SCREEN1" TO RES-PANEL.
  MOVE "GROUP"   TO RES-FIELD.

* Field value is the number 10
  MOVE 10 TO RES-NUM.

* Show number
  PERFORM RES-SHOW-NUM.
```

Fig. 21: Display field value

### 3.5.6 Data Entry

Data entry from the users terminal is handled by six procedures, one of each type of field value (text, number, date, time, Yes/No answer, function choice). These six procedures are called *input procedures.*

The name of the screen, the name of the field and the value of the field before the entry is given as parameters to the input procedure. The input procedure returns the new field value and a parameter indicating which function or special key the user pressed, if any.

The user should type the field value according to the formats defined by the system parameters and the field attributes. The application program always receives the new field value in the same format regardless of how the user entered the value. For Yes/No answers and functions choices the users input is translated.

The input procedure validates and edits the new field value. For Yes/No answers and function choices upper and lower case letters have the same meaning.

Figure 22 shows the code to call the input procedure for entry of a text.

```
* Entry from screen "SCREEN1" field "TEXT-1"
  MOVE "SCREEN1" TO RES-PANEL.
  MOVE "TEXT-1"  TO RES-FIELD.

* The old field value is the text "Alphabike 23 White"
  MOVE "Alphabike 23 White" TO RES-TXT.

* Call input procedure
  PERFORM RES-INPUT-TXT.

* The input procedure returns RES-TXT and RES-INP-KEY
```

Fig. 22: Field entry

### 3.5.7 Sequence Handling

Sequences are for example used to determine in which sequence the application program should accept input from the entry fields.

Procedures are provided to start a sequence and to find the next field in a sequence.

Figure 23 shows the code necessary to accept input from the fields in the screen from figure 10.

```
* Start the sequence "SCREEN1-SEQ"
  MOVE "SCREEN1-SEQ" TO RES-SEQ.
  PERFORM RES-START-SEQ.

* Get the first field in the sequence
  PERFORM RES-NEXT-SEQ.

* Accept input from the fields until the sequence is finished

  PERFORM UNTIL RES-SEQ-END

      EVALUATE RES-FIELD

*         Accept input from the FUNCTION field
          WHEN "FUNCTION"
              MOVE FUNCTION TO RES-FUNC
              PERFORM RES-INPUT-FUNC
              MOVE RES-FUNC TO FUNCTION

*         Accept input from the (alphanumeric) NUMBER field
          WHEN "NUMBER"
              MOVE NUMBER TO RES-TXT
              PERFORM RES-INPUT-TXT
              MOVE RES-TXT TO NUMBER

*         Accept input from the TEXT-1 field
          WHEN "TEXT-1"
              MOVE TEXT-1 TO RES-TXT
              PERFORM RES-INPUT-TXT
              MOVE RES-TXT TO TEXT-1

          ...

*         Accept input from the WEIGHT field
          WHEN "WEIGHT"
              MOVE WEIGHT TO RES-NUM
              PERFORM RES-INPUT-NUM
              MOVE RES-NUM TO WEIGHT

      END-EVALUATE

*     Get the next field in the sequence
      PERFORM RES-NEXT-SEQ

  END-PERFORM.
```

Fig. 23: Field entry with a sequence

When the above code is used to drive the input from fields, it is not necessary to recompile the COBOL source if the order of the field is changed. It is only necessary to edit and recompile the resource file.

The user is normally given the possibility of typing a special key called the field back key. Typing this key means, that the user want to go back to the previous field in the screen. The management of this facility is taken care of "behind the scenes" when a sequence is used.

### 3.5.8 Line Handling

Lines are used either for field entry or for output to the screen or to reports (the printer). A group of procedures is provided for handling lines.

When lines are used for field entry the input procedures are used as described above. The only difference is that the number of the screen line where the first physical line of the line should be located is move to a parameter.

When lines are used for output the whole line is filled with values before it is sent to the terminal / printer.

Fields are filled with values using the procedures to show field values. The route parameter is set so that all output is directed to the current line.

### 3.5.9 Browse Functions

Figure 6 showed the output from a query program. These programs normally has the same basic structure:

- Initialization. Open files etc.
- Get records from the database and show them on the screen. Handle page breaks etc.
- Closing.

The code used to handle page breaks is (or should be) the same in all query programs. To free the application programmer from the tedious task of writing this code, and to give the user of the query program some additional facilities, a special group of procedures called *browse functions* has been developed.

The extra facilities are for example the ability to scroll forward and backward in the output from the query and to use the so called *zoom function*. The zoom function gives the user the possibility to point at a record and then for example receive additional information. In addition to the scroll and zoom functions, a text search function is also provided.

Management of the above facilities is done by the resource server alone. When the user has selected a record using the zoom function the application program receives an identification of the selected record (the key). Compared to using traditional programming techniques, nearly no additional code is needed in the application program, if the browse functions are used.

The application program uses the browse functions in the following way:

- An initialization procedure is called. The name of the screen which should be used as background is given as a parameter. The screen can contain fields to be used to show page number, number of pages of output, scroll information etc. In addition to these fields the screens should contain a box indicating where to display the output from the application program. A parameter tells the browse functions if zoom shall be available to the user.
- The application program gets a record from the database.
- The output is generated using a line.
- The application program sends the generated line to the browse functions together with an identification of the record. The line is displayed by the browse functions and the scroll, zoom and text search facilities managed.
- The control returns to the application program when the browse functions want the next record, the user want to stop the query or has selected a record using zoom.
- When all records are read, a closing procedure is called. The control returns to the application program when the user want to stop the query or has selected a record using zoom.

### 3.5.10 Report Handling

Output to the printer is handled the same way as output from query programs. Procedures are provided to handle page breaks and to print headers and footers on every report page.

The procedures are used in the following way:

- The initialization procedure is called. The name of the report is given as a parameter. The initialization procedure gets the standard header and footer from the resource database together with the header and footer defined for the report. The fields in the standard header and footer are filled with values. After calling the initialization procedure, the application program should fill the fields in the reports header and footer.
- The lines on the report are generated and one by one sent to the report handling procedures. If the application want a page break in the report a special procedure is called.
- When all output is sent to the the report handling procedures a closing procedure is called.

# 4 Conclusions

## 4.1 Implementation Status

The result of the initial project is a prototype implementation based on five parts:

| | |
|---|---|
| Resource Files | External representation of text and layout information based on ASCII files. |
| Resource Editor | Editor dedicated to edit resource files. |
| Resource Compiler | Compilation of resource files. |
| Resource Database | RM/COBOL-85 Index file containing compiled text and layout information. |
| Resource Server | Procedures to access resource database and handle interaction with the user. |

The developed prototype system has been used to develop a small example application. The example, which demonstrates the various features of the implementation, has been translated from Danish to English without any recompilation of the COBOL source. The only changes necessary was the translation of the texts in the applications resource files.

Although a number of existing INFOFLEX programs has been converted using the developed techniques, the implementation has not been used "in real life". This is primarily due to problems regarding performance.

## 4.2 Performance

We were aware that separating text and layout information from the COBOL source would give some performance overhead. Fx. getting a text from a file and displaying it on the screen intuitively takes longer than just displaying the same text when it is included in the COBOL source.

The goal of the initial project was to develop a working prototype. The primary focus was functionality - not performance. Sadly, we ended up with a prototype showing an unacceptable performance.

In the end of the project we started "tuning" up the implementation, but nearly no matter what we did to the code, the performance still remained the same. We have experienced, that the main reason for this is the COBOL CALL mechanism used between the application programs and the resource server. Tests have indicated that a call between two COBOL programs is much slower than a call between a COBOL program and a subroutine written in C. This problem is currently being investigated by the COBOL manufacturer.

## 4.3 Application Development

One of the main ideas behind the implementation was that the programming interface used by the application programmer should be as simple as possible. The concepts should be simple and use of the techniques should not make the application programs unnecessary complex.

The developed tools eases many of the application programmers tasks, for example:

- Display of text on screens and reports should not be hardcoded into the COBOL source. Screens and reports are painted using a text editor.
- The programmer is relieved from using cursor positions when displaying information or accepting input.
- It is much easier to change a fields location on a screen or report. When moving a field using traditional tools, the programmer normally has to change cursor positions in several places in the COBOL source. Using the developed tools the field location only has to be changed in the screen / report layout in the resource file.
- Handling of output from query programs and generation of reports is taken care of by the resource server.

## 4.4 User Interface Development

The developed techniques alone cannot assure good and consistent user interface. A number of elements in the implementation can help to achieve a consistent user interface. These elements are for example consistent handling data entry (Yes/No questions, function choices, dates etc.) and error messages. At the same time, features such as the browse functions, zoom and text search can help to enhance the user interface.

The use of resource files together with the resource editor provides a better basis for designing good screen and report layout compared to using a lot of COBOL statements.

Developing a good user interface for an application such as INFOFLEX is in it self a big project. We plan to run such a project parallel with the implementation of the developed tools.

## 4.5 Future User Interfaces

Implementing the developed techniques in the INFOFLEX application is perhaps the most costly and time consuming part of the whole project. The tools, we have developed, are able to support the current character based user interface. One can ask the question, whether it is reasonable to invest a large amount of time and money in the development and implementation of a tool to support a user interface, which looks a bit old fashion compared to the new graphical user interfaces.

At the moment, a big discussion is going on in the UNIX community regarding standardization of the user interface. The discussion primary focuses on the question of whether it is going to be the OSF's Motif or AT&T/Sun's Open Look which should be the standard user interface of the future. One thing is for sure, the two interfaces are both graphical and both based on the X Window System.

As far as I can see, the debate has not really touched the question of which applications should use the new types of graphical interfaces and how applications using traditional character based techniques should migrate to the new technology.

I personally think, that the use of graphical interfaces will not be limited to application such as computer aided design. The time will come, when the users asks for a standard user interface. The graphical user interfaces seems to be the answer.

Our project has not addressed the question of how to migrate the INFOFLEX application to the new user interfaces or whether it should be done at all. Our problem is, that we cannot just change from the old technology to the new technology from one day to another. First the necessary tools should be available on the majority of our current INFOFLEX environments, second the application should be converted, a task which is not especially easy and requires a lot education of development personnel, and third, and perhaps most important, we still has to support the current INFOFLEX installations. We have an obligation to update the INFOFLEX users who have bought the traditional technology.

Running parallel development on two versions of the application is not the best solution. A better solution might be to develop a tool, which could support both the old and the new technology. The current implementation could be a good starting point.

## 5 Acknowledgments

Altos is a registered trademark of Altos Corporation.

AT&T is a trademark of American Telephone & Telegraph Information Systems.

UNIX is a registered trademark of AT&T.

COMPAQ is a registered trademark of Compaq Computer Corporation.

INFOFLEX is a registered trademark of Data Reforming A/S.

Intel is a registered trademark of Intel Corporation.

AIX and IBM are registered trademarks of International Business Machines Corporation.

X Window System is a registered trademark of Massachusetts Institute of Technology.

MS-DOS and XENIX are registered trademarks of Microsoft Corporation.

NCR is a registered trademark of NCR Corporation.

OSF and OSF/Motif are registered trademarks of the Open Software Foundation, Inc.

RM/COBOL and RM/COBOL-85 are registered trademarks of Ryan-McFarland Corporation.

SCO is a registered trademark of the Santa Cruz Operation, Inc.

Sun and Open Look are registered trademarks of Sun Microsystems, Inc.

*Designing User Interfaces for International Use*, edited by J. Nielsen
Elsevier, 1990


# USER INTERFACE FOR ASIA

**Piyawadee Sukaviriya and Lucy Moran**

The George Washington University, Washington, DC, U.S.A.

## 1. SOCIAL-CULTURE : AN ESSENTIAL USER INTERFACE FACTOR

The state-of-the-art user interface technology, mostly developed in the United States and European countries, has begun to take into consideration variations in individual computer end-users. How to make computers sensitive to different classes of users has been a topic of research for several years. Differences among users such as levels of expertise, relative familiarity with an application, familiarity with related concepts, individual cognitive skills, and individual learning speeds, for example, have been analyzed and incorporated in run-time user models. As part of a good user interface architecture, it is now possible to incorporate a user modeling component to support the different dialogues which suit particular users best. As a result, human-computer interface technology has progressed one step closer to the ideal user-friendliness.

However, research on user-computer interfaces as mediators between people and machine has not yet begun to explore broader cultural differences among users which may be critical factors in determining how software tools can best accommodate different user groups and needs. Analogous to the device-dependence/device-independence metaphor of graphics packages or domain-dependence/domain-independence metaphor of knowledge representation, it may prove wise to develop user interface software tools to distinguish between facets which are culture-dependent and those which are culture-independent. An ideal interface would have a generic user interface in which, as part of the log-in procedure, the user indicates the language to be used for the session, the type of culture or cultures she is comfortable with, and perhaps others. The interface then establishes some initial settings and interacts with the user in the language chosen in the behavior that this particular user would expect from a computer. We are still far from such an ideal situation. Those who must deal with cross-cultural implication of software products, such as Asian countries developing for both at-home and Western markets, or Western vendors marketing internationally, will likely be among the first to take interest in and be aware of cross-cultural aspects of user interface technology.

The development and improvement upon any general methods for defining users and tasks will contribute to addressing this aspect as well. This paper takes a brief look at this issue by focusing on some contrasts between Asian and English-speaking cultures and some analysis of how these differences could have an impact on the adaptability of user interfaces. Section 2 presents some general discussion of variations in forms of verbal and visual communication among and within Asian countries and how these have already affected certain hardware and software design decisions. Thailand, the home country of one of the authors, Piyawadee Sukaviriya, is presented as a particular example. Section 3 goes into more depth about the pertinence of these cultural differences to different aspects of user interfaces. An experiment done to explore differences in command language preference among three language groups, two Asian and one English-speaking, is presented in Section 4. The experiment represents an effort to observe cross-cultural factors which may affect the usefulness of user interfaces to different groups of users.

## 2. VERBAL AND VISUAL COMMUNICATION IN ASIAN COUNTRIES

Numerous facets of a particular society together form its culture. Geographical location, interactions with neighboring countries, internal political warfare, mineral resources, agriculture, and diverse other factors all play a role in shaping each unique culture and the people who conform to it. While these factors influence strongly the language and style of communication between persons of a culture, they may or may not affect the way a computer user of a particular culture interacts with a machine. Little is known in this socio-computer territory, and many observational studies and experiments are needed to form guidelines in creating culturally appropriate user interface technology.

In this paper, we will discuss some of the communication forms of cultures and suggest links between these forms and the forms which user interface design might take at several levels. Thai culture will be used as an example several times in this chapter to reflect how unique characteristics in a culture can influence user interface design choices. Thai people are by no mean the representative of Asia and the authors do not attempt to convey such a message. We are simply drawing on the knowledge of one of the authors, Piyawadee Sukaviriya, who has the advantage of being a representative of the Thai culture and has experienced the country's efforts to adapt to the new computer technology. The intended global message to get across from using Thai examples is to give an idea of how Asian cultures, which are strongly rooted in many different contexts for thousands of years, can be unexpectedly very different. Each culture has its idiosyncrasies — some of which are factors necessary to consider in building an appropriate user interface for that culture. Looking at individual cultures as well as Asian cultures as a group may shed light on potential problems which may otherwise be overlooked by user interface developers from different cultures.

## 2.1 Verbal Communication

> "Language interacts with every other aspect of human life in society, and it can be understood only if it is considered in relation to society." [Encyclopædia Britanica, 1986]

One of the biggest problems among Asian countries is the fairly large variety of languages spoken in different parts of the continent. Out of 39 countries listed in Rand McNally World Atlas, only 7 countries use and have one official language [World Almanac, 1989] — 3 use Arabic, the other 4 use Burmese, Thai, Korean and Japanese, exclusively. In China, though a number of Chinese dialects are spoken, 70% of the population speak Mandarin Chinese. 24 out of 39 countries in Asia use 3 or more languages.

Major languages used in Asia include: Farsi, Hindi and Urdu, which are Indo-Iranian languages of the Indo-European branch; the Altaic languages of Turkish, Japanese and Korean; the Semitic languages of Arabic and Hebrew; the Sino-Tibetan language of Chinese; the Austro-Asiatic languages of Vietnamese and Khmer; and the Tai languages of Thai and Lao [Encyclopædia Britanica, 1986]. In addition to these languages, there are also a large number of dialects spoken in different parts of Asia. Because Asian languages come from a variety of families, they differ tremendously from one country to another.

In the context of generating common components for language interfaces for Asian countries, there is not much at the surface level, ie. the lexical level, of which a software tool can take advantage. Character sets exist with not much in common. However, at the syntactic level where native language constructs can be used in computer-user interactions, a few global observations about these languages give us some clues to commonalities.

One observation is on the declarative sentence syntax pattern — which components of a sentence precede which others. Of the major Asian languages explored, the subject-predicate pattern (similar to English) where a subject precedes its predicate is observed†. However, there are differences in the predicate arrangement such that either action precedes object or object precedes action. Differences in expressing noun classification is also observed. Both the modifier-modified and modified-modifier pattern are observed.

The following are some of the other interesting characteristics found to be common among several Asian languages: the absence of gender in nouns; the absence of articles; the absence of number in nouns such as the use of the same form in "one bird" and "two bird"; and the absence of tense in the verb form such as in "I go yesterday." There are three orientations in writing style: top-to-bottom character sequence and right-to-left line sequence, right-to-left character sequence and top-to-bottom line sequence, and left-to-right character sequence and top-to-bottom line sequence (similar to Western style). Languages which use the top-to-bottom character sequence, which are Korean, Japanese and Chinese, have become accepted written in the left-to-right Western style.

Obviously, these kinds of commonalities can be exploited in designing user interfaces for applications such as macro building facilities, database query languages, and any command language or limited natural language interpreters for Asian countries. Experience with the Thai community's adaptation of Western technology and their human-computer language communication needs sheds light in what other software design decisions may be guided by cultural factors.

### 2.1.1 Example Case of Thai Language

The Thai language consists of 44 consonants, 32 vowels and 4 tonal markers. Similar to many Asian languages, Thai uses no tense, no plurals, no articles and no gender in nouns. The alphabet set has a unique script and a word, as in English, is a combination of consonants, vowels and tonal markers. The composition of consonants and vowels are mostly from left-to-right and the next line is below the previous line (top-to-bottom). Some vowels are placed on top of the preceding consonant; some are placed below the preceding consonant. The remaining vowels are placed in the left-to-right character sequence. A tonal marker is always placed on top of the previous consonant.

† The observation holds true as a result of comparing major Asian languages such as Chinese, Japanese, Arabic, Farsi, Korean, Thai, Hindi and Urdu. The assumption may not hold true if all known Asian languages are compared — work which has not yet been attempted by the authors.

If a vowel has already been placed on top of the previous consonant, the tonal marker will be placed on top of that vowel. Figure 1a and 1b show examples of a tonal marker, placed in one instance on top of the previous consonant and in the other instance on top of a vowel respectively. Such a case is the only time tonal marker placement is context-sensitive. In early 80's, to display Thai on a conventional character-based computer screen, four English text lines had to be reserved — one for the main composition, two above and one below to accommodate all possible occurrences of vowels and tonal markers.

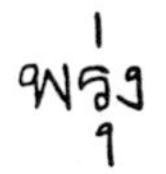

**Figure 1a**: An example of the tonal marker, ่ , placed on top of a consonant in Thai.

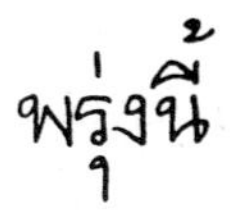

**Figure 1b**: An example of the tonal marker, ้, placed on top of the vowel, ี, which is already placed on top of a consonant in Thai.

Currently, a combination of hardware and software solutions have been employed in Thailand to provide Thai character generation. The same technology of superimposing Thai characters on the English keyboard used in the typewriter industry has been used on the computer keyboard. In order to utilize the maximum space on a computer screen, the character generator mechanism has been modified to generate Thai characters when accepting corresponding ASCII or EBCDIC code from an English keyboard. All possible combinations of consonants, vowels and tonal markers have been coded—each code represents either a consonant, a combination of a consonant and a vowel, a combination of a consonant and a tonal marker, or a combination of a consonant, a vowel and a tonal marker. Each code represents a unique dot-matrix definition to be displayed on the screen. To accommodate all combinations regardless of their validity, two bytes were previously used but lately dropped after use of the eighth bit of the ASCII code was adopted and it was decided to encode only valid combinations. A graphics screen technology which depends totally on character generation from software will not require such a hardware solution.

There are two solutions on the software side to feed proper character codes to the screen. One is in the case where a fixed content of text is to be displayed and the content can be predetermined prior to run time. An example in this case is when static menus of an application are to be generated in Thai. The text content to be placed in the application menus is input in one straight line regardless of the character types. The input text is then preprocessed by a special software patch to generate corresponding ASCII/ EBCDIC codes which are then embedded in the target application code. This solution is very similar to compilation in programming languages. The application, absolutely unaware of what is being generated on the other end at run-time, sends the code to the output device which is already equipped with a Thai character generator. The user then sees Thai menus at the interface level and interacts with the application as if it knew about the Thai interface.

The other software solution is a response to the situation where text content cannot be determined prior to run time. Word processing and data entry are the two obvious examples. In this case, Thai designers added intelligence into the target software so it would know the rules for placing consonants, vowels and tonal markers and the error conditions when these rules do not apply. Applications such as word processors, databases and spreadsheets have been modified to incorporate such intelligence. The ongoing trend is embedding this intelligence in the hardware, therefore allowing each software application in English to handle the Thai alphabet set without any required modifications in the application code.

However, these hardware and software solutions are rather ad hoc and have a short life. When hardware technology evolves, these solutions will not be usable on a new machine. Developers will have to start over again if the same solution is to be used — both from the hardware and the software sides, which is obviously an impedance to a new technology transfer. Moreover, while a user interface can be viewed as having 4 levels according to Foley and Van Dam's language model [Foley et al., 1982] or even 7 levels according to Nielsen [Nielsen, 1986], these solutions only touch on one level — the lexical level which is considered to be the most straightforward level in the user interface technology. A great deal of knowledge about cross-cultural differences relevant to each level of these interaction models needs to be acquired and understood, and systematic solutions need to be developed which utilize such knowledge and are appropriate or transferrable to future user interface technology.

### 2.1.2 Computer Display of Asian Language Scripts : Static Display

To illustrate how written scripts of Asian languages greatly differ from one to another, a simple made-up Macintosh style dialogue box as shown in Figure 2a is used.

This least complicated example is translated into Chinese, Korean, Arabic, Urdu and Thai as shown in Figure 2b through 2f respectively.

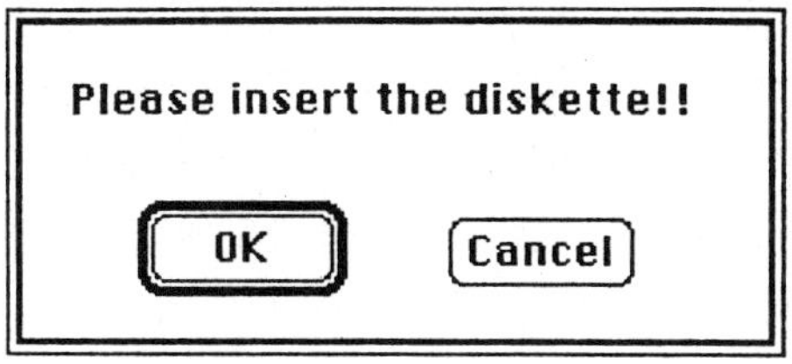


**Figure 2a**: A dialogue box in English.

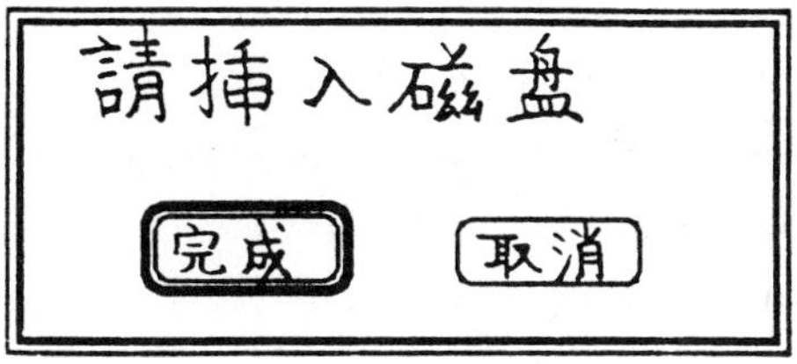


**Figure 2b**: The dialogue box in Figure 2a translated into Chinese.

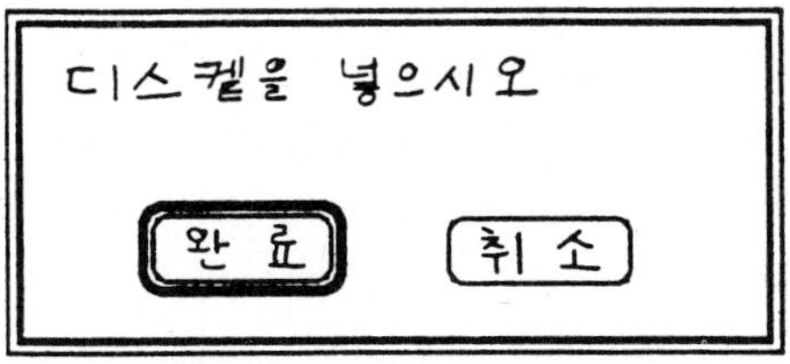


**Figure 2c**: The dialogue box in Figure 2a translated into Korean.

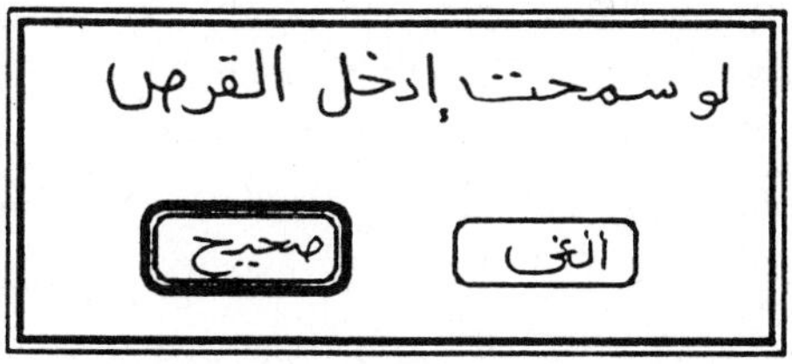


**Figure 2d**: The dialogue box in Figure 2a translated into Arabic.

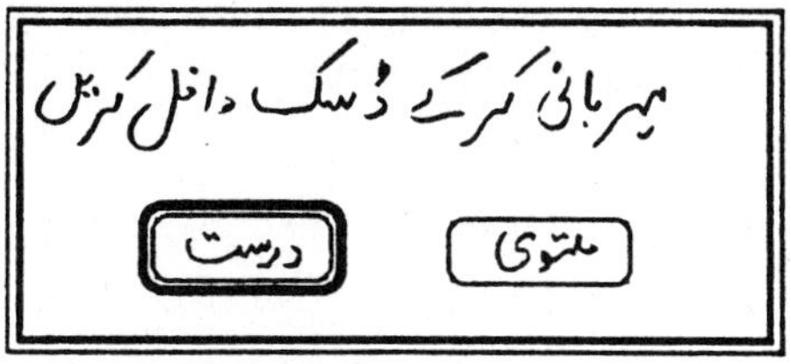


**Figure 2e**: The dialogue box in Figure 2a translated into Urdu.

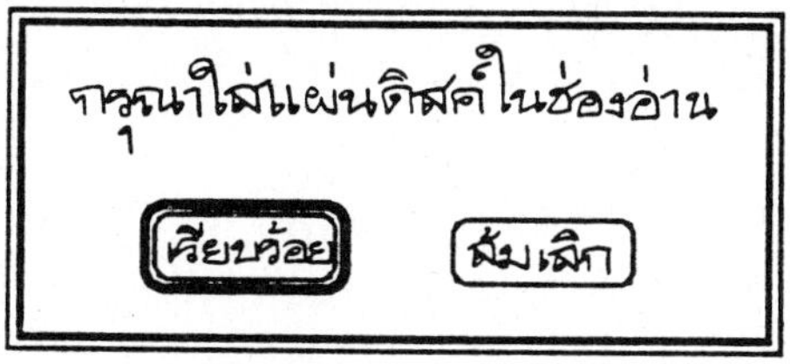


**Figure 2f**: The dialogue box in Figure 2a translated into Thai.

As shown in the examples, some languages are or look more graphical than others. The obvious lexical constraint on the output side is such that some languages require a higher resolution graphics screen than do others. The characteristics of one language's script imposes a minimum requirement of screen resolution to maintain its readability. Beyond that, a tradeoff between screen resolution and the amount of information displayed on the screen can be negotiated.

Another lexical issue lies in the creation of several user interface components such as dialogue boxes, menus, error message windows, places for titles such as window names, file names and menu names which depends on the size of the text displayed. A user interface presentation component such as one proposed in [Kim, 1989] which has sizes of interaction objects as modifiable attributes is desirable to allow flexibility in multiple-language interface presentation. Kim also proposed multiple writing orientations in his design, orientations such as right-to-left character sequence which then influence the user interface presentation style to use right-justified menus automatically. Such a flexibility will increase the appropriateness of user interfaces for Asians even further.

### 2.1.3 Computer Display of Asian Language Scripts : Dynamic Feedback

In some Asian languages such as Korean, the placement of consonants and vowels is very context-sensitive. In Korean, for example, the placement of a consonant depends on both what comes before and after it. In other words, the placement of a consonant sometimes can only be determined after its following consonant or vowel is known. This complicates the interface further regarding what will be the appropriate lexical feedback before the following character is entered. The Korean language example shows that the character display problem is not limited only to the lexical level of a user interface dialogue, it sometimes presents itself at the semantic level as well. Becker in [Becker, 1985] proposed how Korean dynamic feedback should appear on the computer screen suggesting embedded semantic knowledge within the Korean software.

Japanese, similar to Chinese, has the problem of a large character set. The Japanese and Chinese character sets are so large that, if an English-like keyboard is to be used, a large table of equivalent keys representing unique Japanese characters or some coding schemes have to be used with it [Becker, 1985] putting the burden on the user to remember how to indirectly type in a character. A technique currently used in Japan allows users to type in Japanese phonemes from an English-like keyboard. The phonemes are then interpreted by a software patch and Japanese characters are displayed as feedback on the screen [Suwa, 1989]. Certain problems still exist such as the interpreter's inability to distinguish between two different words with the same pronunciation. A consideration of context would certainly help the automatic screen feedback but would add remarkable sophistication to the interpreter since the problem in this case concerns itself with the conceptual understanding of the language interface as well. The advantage of the Japanese technique is the continuing use of a standard keyboard to enter Japanese words. A similar technique is also used for Chinese character input [Huang,

1985, Becker, 1985] using numeric codes to represent Chinese phonetic symbols. The Chinese technique makes it a bit harder for the user to remember the coding scheme.

Another example from the Thai language raises a rather different but related issue to screen display. Thai has a peculiar way of writing all words in one sentence with no space between them. No period at the end of a sentence is used and a space is used instead of a period at the end of the sentence. In other words, space is valid only between two sentences but not within a sentence. Line breaks can, however, be inserted in a sentence in between word boundaries or using hyphenation rules. The use of no space in sentences makes it invalid for a word processor to justify text by adding spaces in between words. Until now, either justifying is done completely manually or the final text has no justification. In this case, the characteristic of the language suggests a slightly different appearance in an interface. To make an interface appropriate, the justify option in a word processor when used in Thai mode should be inaccessible. Similar examples supporting this view can be drawn from right-to-left Asian languages where a user interface with right-justified and pull-left menus would be more appropriate, and the absence of uppercase or lowercase in several Asian languages where displaying a menu option to switch case is inappropriate.

The above examples suggest that, in order for a user interface to be prepared for different unique features present in particular languages, the user interface software tools need to have a structured control mechanism allowing end-product display and feedback preferences as well as allowing the logical control of the product's user interface to be adaptable to the target language of the interface.

## 2.2 Difference in Perception

Languages communicated verbally and in written text are only one form of exchanging information. They thus far reveal a vast difference across different cultures. What about pictures and images? A number of experiments in the field of visual communication have been conducted to find supporting evidence for significant differences. Fussell and Haaland found that, in Nepal, three-tone drawing (a line drawing with shading and internal detail) produced more correct identifications of images among subjects than black-and-white photographs of the same images or the same drawings without shading and internal detail [Fussell et al., 1978]. Ahmad found that perception of size, color and shape varied according to native language and his subjects' familiarity with the pictures used [Ahmad, 1978]. Cook discovered among his Papua New Guinean subjects a tendency to scan a series of picture frames in circular fashion, clockwise or counter-clockwise, rather than the familiar Western left-to-right, top-to-bottom style [Cook, 1980]. Other related experiments can be found in [Goldsmith, 1984].

Though their experiments only indirectly suggest clues for implementing culturally appropriate computer-user interfaces as a medium of visual communication, the underlying motivation is the same — discovering differences among cultures which affect choices for effective visual communication. Knowledge of cross-cultural differences can be used to aid the process of various kinds of technology transfer, be it the process of instructing students in different cultures how to use new medicine, teaching villagers to understand healthy nutrition or promoting the use of computers in various problem-solving activities. Hopefully, these findings will provide guidelines for more effective cross-cultural visual communication, be it communication between human and human or between human and computers.

What these experiments do for user interface researchers is suggest the current view of "the user" needs to be enhanced. A traditional view of an adaptable user interface considers a user as an individual whose experience grows with time spent using computers. As a result, the user interface aspects which should vary among cultural groups have been ignored. For most language oriented environments, users are assumed to speak or at least understand English. Language translation for some non-English languages has been employed to create the look of interfaces which appears to bridge the language difference gap at a superficial level. With the emergence of graphical interfaces, user interface developers tend to take things for granted even further. For example, for some user interface developers, a typical user has (or at least has seen) a mailbox whose shape is as shown in Figure 3a which, whenever its flag is up as shown in Figure 3b, indicates mail arrival. For some other developers, the typical user has a trash can at home whose shape is a straight cylinder with a lid always closed on top as

**Figure 3a**: Mailbox icon with no mail.†

**Figure 3b**: Mailbox icon with mail.†

† Courtesy of Sun Microsystems Inc.

shown in Figure 3c, and trash can be dumped in the can while the lid is still closed as shown in Figure 3d. In actual fact, a trash container in Thailand and perhaps in many Asian countries is normally a basket which looks similar to the icon in Figure 3e always with some flies on top of it to be more realistic.

**Figure 3c**: Trashcan icon [††]

**Figure 3d**: Trashcan icon while a file is being trashed. [††]

**Figure 3e**: A different trashcan icon. [†††]

†† Courtesy of Apple Computer Inc.
††† Drawn by Piyawadee Sukaviriya.

Cross-cultural aspects of conventional language oriented user interfaces are not yet understood, and the new dimension of graphical interfaces adds additional complexity in looking at cross-cultural factors in the user interface context. Though graphical interfaces and direct manipulation have been accepted as better user interfaces, especially for novices, we are not yet in the position to state whether their cross-cultural factors are the same as or different from the conventional language oriented user interface. Research on user-computer interface has exploited knowledge from other disciplines such as psychology to help understand computer users. That view, though useful, normally assumes a hypothetical user population of a homogeneous culture. An enhanced view where users are considered as cultural groups such as the one taken by visual communication researchers will provide insights into how visual interface software tools should be structured. Some knowledge of contrasts between Asian and Western language users already exists as a rich resource for researchers. Experiments combining cross-cultural visual communication with the use of computers would be beneficial to user interface designs for different cultural user groups.

## 3. USER INTERFACE CONTEXT

### 3.1 Command Language Interface

In a command language oriented system where an interface is only concerned with a limited textual form of communication, the problem is to consider whether translation of commands is required for more effective use of computer software. The solution to this language problem is not always as simple as mere translation of commands and parameters, since some computer terminologies involving a particular application or system do not have a direct translation in the adopting society. Words such as "diskette", "disk drive", "zooming" or "panning" have no direct translation in Thai, for example. Attempts to translate these words in Thai often result in phrases explaining what the words mean and users often drop their use after they are familiar with the English-based terminologies. One reason is Thai's lack of a rich vocabulary from which new words can be expanded. However, using English terminology as a fall-back assumes a limited group of users who can recognize the English letters and read some English words. Such an assumption will not hold true for Asian persons in general.

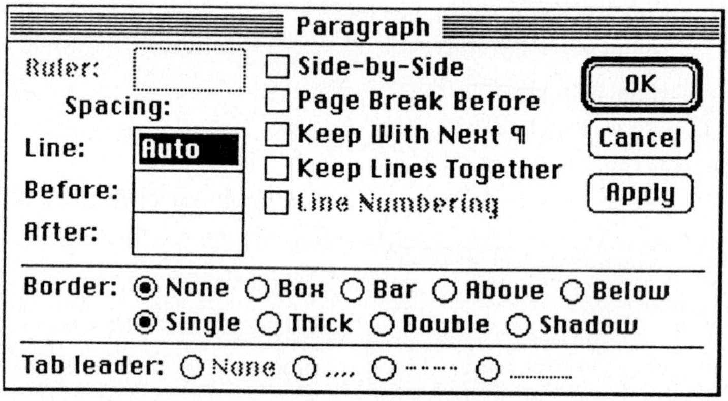


**Figure 4**: The dialogue box used as a subject for command language translation. Screen shot © 1984-1987 Microsoft Corporation. Reprinted with permission from Microsoft Corp.

The dialogue box in Figure 4 is from Microsoft® Word for the Apple® Macintosh® version 3.01 when the option **Paragraph...** is selected from the **Format** pull-down menu. Four persons including one of the authors who translated the dialogue box in Figure 2a into different languages were also asked to translate Figure 4 dialogue box as well. A common problem contributors have is no direct translation of some of the English words in Asian languages, for example, **Tab leader** in all languages tried (Arabic, Korean, Thai and Urdu) and **Page Break** in Thai. In this case, contributors used phrases to explain the function of the words, some of them were rather lengthy. Another common problem is when a direct translation is not understandable, for example, **box** in Korean and Thai, **Bar** in Arabic and Thai, **Ruler** in Thai. The direct translations of these words refer to the physical objects they represent, and are not applicable to the word processing context. Again, the solution is either to elaborate the functions they represent or to find a more appropriate word. All of our contributors finished the translation with no confidence that they would be totally understandable.

Similar attempts to translate Western terms in the field of mathematics failed in Thailand in the late 60's when translation of geometric terms used in secondary schools called for an introduction of new words which are not among contemporary words. The example demonstrates that careful selection of words is needed if English command language is to be translated into a local language. A mere translation or just coming up with new words may work sometimes and may not sometimes.

Another important point concerning a command language interface is the similarity/difference between the syntax of the command language and the syntax of the native language of users. English uses subject-action-object pattern which dominates the design pattern of most command languages, despite the fact that the syntax pattern varies from one natural language to another. The experiment in Section 4 reveals an empirical study of the relationship between command language syntax preference and the native language of a user.

### 3.2 Natural Language Interface

The state-of-the-art natural language interface designs are still centered around the idea that text can be parsed linearly, character by character, and be understood by using both morphological knowledge, the knowledge of the surface syntactic structure, and semantic knowledge and contextual information [Allen, 1988]. In some Asian languages which employ two-dimensional composition in written language constructs such as Chinese, Korean and Thai, this approach cannot be applied immediately. Consider Chinese as an example. Words and/or characters in Chinese consist of lexical and morphological elements formed in two dimensions. In other words, a visual unit of a written text is not necessarily a character normally understood in English— it can be a character, a word or a part of a word. In the particular case of the Chinese language, either lexical knowledge is required to decompose a two-dimensional structure, or a large dictionary of words has to be used to analyze Chinese inputs. Chu in [Chu, 1986] proposed a knowledge base for Chinese characters which exploits the knowledge of

Chinese lexical and morphological compositional rules to aid the process of understanding written Chinese, the natural language for the Chinese population and a number of minorities in several countries in Asia.

Different syntactic knowledge is also required. As mentioned earlier, syntax patterns vary in different languages used in Asia. Subject-action-object and subject-object-action are the two dominant patterns while both modified-modifier and modifier-modified are used among Asian languages. Other details varied from one language to another are such as the use of honorifics in verbs in Korean, the use of particles added to the ends of objects in Japanese as propositions (making one object appearing in two different contexts look superficially like different words), and the use of particles at the end of a sentence to indicate a question in Thai. These details have to be incorporated in the syntactic knowledge of the natural language parser of that particular language.

## 3.3 Graphical Interface

The use of graphical symbols does not solve the interface design transfer problem among language groups. Rather, it takes a detour away from the language problem into a second problem of varying picture perception in different cultures. A well-analyzed example is the use of icons which do not convey precisely the same meanings in all cultures. However, the scope of a graphical interface should not concentrate only on details of individual icons — the whole context of a graphical user interface, such as: left-to-right, top-to-bottom or circular sequencing; relative positions of two pieces of pictorial information; the highlighting mechanism; preferences of certain shapes; and prohibited use of certain shapes should be taken into consideration.

Interestingly, effectiveness of communication via pictures is said to depend on how rich a culture is in images [Goldsmith, 1984, p. 414]. If this is true, Chinese, whose written language characters are largely developed from transformations of real-world objects into two-dimensional graphics [Chu, 1986], will communicate more effectively in iconic interfaces than in command language interfaces. The assumption is certainly empirical and is subject to experiment.

Goldsmith addressed other issues such as image acceptability, use of color, use of context and emphasis, and sequencing of pictures as factors of research findings relevant to defining cultural differences which may impact graphical interface design. An unsolved question is how to design an interface so it can accommodate user's preferences of iconic symbols used in a particular software, as well as accommodating preferences for the factors Goldsmith discussed.

Graphical interfaces usually exploit graphical input devices such as a mouse or a joystick, which take away the language-oriented influence of an input device such as a keyboard, and encourage a direct manipulation [Shneiderman, 1983] style of human-computer communication. This invites users to more involvement with objects they are operating on. With this different style of user interface (or with this different nature of input devices), language conciousness may possibly be greatly diminished and thus change the way users, regardless of their cultures or native languages, perceive computer problem-solving tasks. This issue is touched on by the experiment presented in Section 4.

### 3.4 Other Interfaces

Based on known knowledge of Asian verbal and visual communication, the use of other forms of interfaces by Asians may or may not be affected by cultural factors depending on the way such interfaces tie to the use of both communication media. In addition to command language and natural language interfaces, interfaces directly related to verbal and visual communication include voice interfaces and use of animation on screen to convey meaning. Obviously, some of what applies to verbal communication applies to voice interfaces, and some of what applies to visual communication applies to animated interfaces.

Other interfaces such as non-speech audio, gestural, use of various input devices such as joystick, trackball, touch panel, data glove, etc., have less to do with verbal and visual communication except for the fact that most interfaces involve screen feedback of either one form or the other. Analyzing these other interfaces within the general context of user interfaces for Asia cannot be fruitfully done due to their characteristics unrelated to the traditional studied forms of human communication. Such interfaces call for direct control experiments of the interfaces within the target cultural groups.

### 3.5 Conceptual Framework

Our analysis would not be complete without some mention of the top layer of the Foley and Van Dam's user interface language model [Foley et al., 1982] — the conceptual level, the level which is least understood by computer scientists who are concerned with user interface technology. Obviously, little can be said at this stage about the impact of cultural differences on the appropriateness of a conceptual definition of an application. The discussion with our subjects in the following experiment led us to believe that an already defined conceptual framework of an application software can be perceived differently among both individuals and cultural groups. Again, commonalities and differences in the conceptual perception of various applications, if possibly drawn and differentiated, will be invaluable knowledge. The question is whether it can then be used and how it can be used in user interface research and designs.

## 4. EXPERIMENT ON CROSS-CULTURAL INFLUENCES ON COMMAND LANGUAGE SYNTAX PREFERENCE

The experiment to be presented was a pilot project focused on one aspect of user-computer interface: appropriateness of alternate designs for a user-computer command language at the syntactic and lexical level. Appropriateness is a context-sensitive judgement, dependent on who the user is, what the task is, and where and with what equipment the task is being carried out.

The objective of this experiment was to test one small element of the computer technologies developed in English-speaking cultures: user-interface dialog for a selection task. We tested three specific hypotheses: 1) a person's natural language influences their preferences for computer command syntax, 2) the specific input device used influences preferences for computer command syntax, and 3) a person's cultural background influences preferences for numeric over English alphabetic code.

The experiment served another purpose beyond the hypotheses tested. It created a context for systematic observation of users and for gathering information from users concerning user-interface dialog through questionnaires and discussion.

### 4.1 Hypotheses, Dependent and Independent Variables

The three hypotheses previously mentioned were translated into the more specific terms in the experiment that follows:

1. Given a computer task which involves specifying an action to be performed on an object as well as specifying the object, and given that a subject has the choice to specify either **the action first and the object second**, or **the object first and the action second**, the subject's choice will be dependent on her linguistic background;
2. Given the task and choice specified in hypothesis 1, a subject's choice will depend on whether her input is entered via a spatially-oriented device (locator and data tablet) or a linguistically-oriented device (keyboard); and
3. Given the choice at the keyboard to enter the action command using a numeric code versus using an alphabetic code, and given that all objects are specified using a numeric code, non-English speakers will prefer a numeric code.

Dependent variables were **command syntax order** (object-action or action-object) and **choice of alphabetic or numeric** command. Independent variables were cultural background, input devices, two available command codes, and the task type.

## 4.2 Subjects

Since cross-cultural issues were to be explored, the cultural linguistic background of our subjects was our primary selection criteria. Subjects were chosen from three cultural/linguistic groups: American (English speaking), Thai (Thai speaking), and those from Indian subcontinent (Urdu, Hindi, Persian or Telugu speaking). The Indian subcontinent languages represented have a common grammatical structure distinct from both Thai and English in their ordering of a request or command. In expressing a phrase which contains a verb (action) and an object, such as "Move the chair" or "Delete the file" in English, the Indian subcontinent languages employ the **object-action** pattern while both English and Thai employ the reverse **action-object** pattern. This distinction present in an available population of diverse cultural backgrounds encouraged us to develop a hypothesis that such a difference in linguistic background may influence people's preferences for computer language syntax.

Two subjects participated in a pilot run of our experiment, and then 30 were used in our formal conducting of the experiment. Of the 30, 21 were males and 9 were females. Two of the subjects were under 18 years of age, seven were between the ages of 18 and 21, another seven were between 22 and 25, 13 were between the ages of 25-35, and one subject was over 35 years of age. Two of the subjects considered themselves left-handed, one was ambidextrous, and the rest were right-handed. Five of the subjects were non-students, working full time, and the other 25 were part-time or full-time students mostly in graduate school. The average years of education of our subjects is 17 years — hence this sample represents a college-educated population. Half of our subjects were engineering or computer science students with some background in either computer hardware or software, while the other half had little or no computer-related course work. Half of the subjects indicated they had experience in programming writing at least one 150-lined or more program. One half of the subjects had access to personal computers, which on the average were used equally to play computer games, to program, to write with a text editor, or to use some software packages other than a game or a text editor.

Half of our subjects had only minimal typing skills while the rest had varying levels of skill, averaging between 30-50 words per minute. Only one subject could be considered an expert typist. One third of the subjects had some experience with a pointing device — either a mouse or a joystick. Most of that experience came from playing games with joysticks. None of the subjects could be considered mouse experts, nor could any be considered expert computer users in general.

In summary, half of our subjects represented the right-handed, college-educated, male population of students who are moderate computer users and moderate typists in their 20's, while the other half reflected a range of characteristics distinct from our "average" subjects.

## 4.3 Experimental Design and Procedure

Each subject performed two simple design tasks — one using a locator and data tablet as input device and the other using a keyboard. The two tasks were similar: selecting 32 out of predetermined 64 shapes contained in a grid of 64 boxes on a color monitor with the goal of creating a design of the subject's choosing. Both tasks were divided into 32 or more unit tasks of making a shape **visible** or **invisible**. At all times, two commands, **make-visible** and **make-invisible**, were available to subjects to perform the unit tasks. In the first task performed by each subject, all 64 shapes were visible, and the primary activity was to make 32 undesired shapes invisible to create a design. In the second task, all shapes were invisible and the major activity was to make 32 desired shapes visible. Both **make-visible** and **make-invisible** commands were available all the time so the subjects would not be afraid of making errors in the design and, as a result, would pay less attention to the command syntax they preferred. Figure 5 and 6 illustrate the grid and shapes the subjects worked with.

The underlying program of the experiment was written to accept the **make-visible** and **make-invisible** commands in both **action-object** and **object-action** patterns. The object in both cases was the shape to be made visible or invisible.

Half of the subjects in each cultural group performed the tasks using the locator first, then the keyboard; the other half of the subjects used the keyboard first, then locator. This was done to help protect the data from being biased by a possible transfer effect.

Subjects were given written guidelines explaining what they were to do. Each subject had 14 practice trials before their 32 recorded ones for each performance. Included in the practice trials were specific "structured" practice trials leading the subject through every possible correct combination of inputs, one each time.

## Task with the Locator

Figure 5 shows the screen prompt when the locator† was used. To cause visibility or invisibility of a shape, the subject had to select the box marked **RETURN** by clicking the locator button. The subject then could either select a shape in the grid then one of the action boxes or an action box then a shape. To help the reader understand the experimental unit tasks using the locator, visualize either one of the following selection sequences as a valid command input:

<RETURN> <a shape> <an action box> < RETURN>

<RETURN> <an action box> <a shape> < RETURN>

The action boxes were labeled **TURN ON** or **TURN OFF** for **make-visible** and **make-invisible** respectively. The subject then selected **RETURN** to complete the unit task.

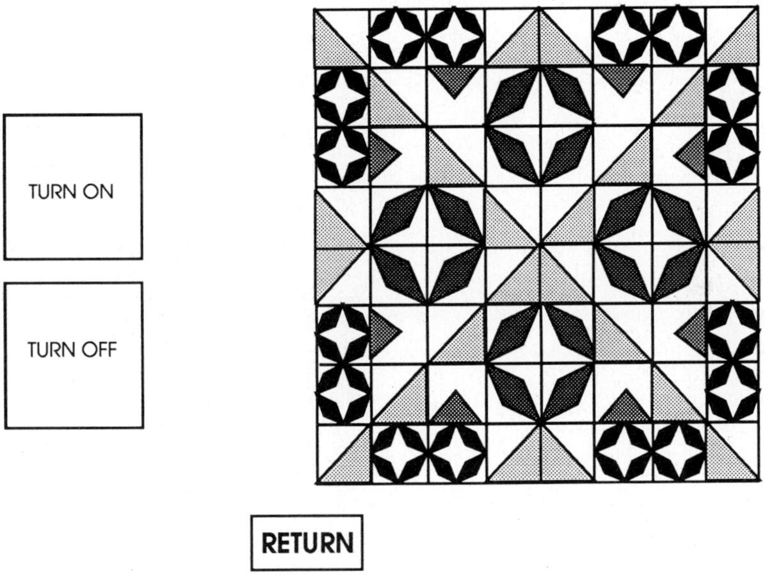


**Figure 5**: Screen display for the task with locator

The RETURN box was positioned on the screen half way between the center of the grid and the center of the "action" boxes. This was designed to ensure no preference of shorter distance to either the commands or the shapes. The RETURN box was also

† Locator is the name we use to refer to a hand cursor device used with a flat surface data tablet to indicate the cursor position on the screen. The hand cursor used in the experiment had four buttons. A selection was made by placing the cursor on top of an object, then pressing the button designated for selection. The subjects were informed which button to use in the written guidelines.

centered below both the shapes and the actions to enforce a similar "upward" motion to both actions and shapes.

## Task with the Keyboard

Figure 6 shows the screen prompt when the keyboard was used. Notice that this time shapes are numbered from 01 to 64 so each could be recalled by keyboard input. To cause visibility or invisibility of a shape, the subject entered two alphanumerics which represented a command, then a space, then another two alphanumerics to specify a shape, followed by the Carriage Return key. The following shows two valid keyboard command input sequences:

YY <space> 34 <CR>
29 <space> 99 <CR>

The subject could also enter a shape number first, then a space, and then the command code, and the Carriage Return key. The **make-visible** action could be specified with either **yy** or **88**, while the **make-invisible** action could be specified with **nn** or **99**.

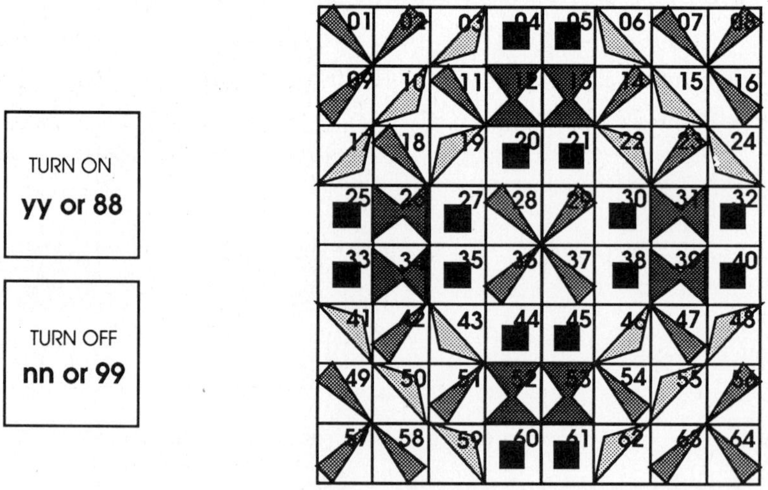


**Figure 6**: Screen display for the task with keyboard

The experiment was designed so that the number of keystrokes to specify an action or an object was the same to eliminate the possible preference of typing a short word before a longer word. Each command was also made a repetition of the same key, either a numeric or an alphabetic key, to ensure the same ease in entering the command.

Certain words or codes would be more familiar to prior computer users — such as **dd** for make-invisible (delete) or **add** or **create** for making a shape visible. For this reason, **yy** (yes) and **nn** (no), and **turn on** and **turn off** were chosen so that prior experience with computer codes would not be a significant influence in our subjects' choice of command preference.

Order of syntax and type of command code chosen when using the keyboard were recorded. Originally, time to complete each unit task and the total task time were to be recorded. However, the unreliability of computer response time rendered such data meaningless. Time recording was eliminated after our fifth subject.

### Questionnaire Completion

When the subjects were finished with their two tasks, they filled out a post-experiment questionnaire. In addition, non-Americans subjects filled out an additional questionnaire concerning the introduction or presence of computer technology in non-English speaking countries.

## 4.4 Data and Data Analysis

Since data collected in the experiment were frequency counts, hypothesis tests using Chi-square distribution were chosen to compare our observed frequencies with expected frequencies. Table 1 shows how data are tabulated. The data collected are displayed in contingency tables 2 through 8.

| | DEPENDENT VARIABLES | | |
|---|---|---|---|
| INDEPENDENT VARIABLES | Var A | Var B | |
| Var 1 | data (exp. frequency) | data (exp. frequency) | Row Total |
| Var 2 | data (exp. frequency) | data (exp. frequency) | Row Total |
| Var 3 | data (exp. frequency) | data (exp. frequency) | Row Total |
| | Column Total | Column Total | Grand Total |

**Table 1**: The Contingency table model used indicating the meaning of numbers in respective rows and columns.

**1st Hypothesis: Choice of command syntax is influenced by culture.**

| | COMMAND SYNTAX CHOICE | | |
|---|---|---|---|
| LINGUISTIC GROUP | Action-> Object | Object->Action | |
| American | 75 (92.7) | 85 (67.3) | 160 |
| Thai | 75 (92.7) | 85 (67.3) | 160 |
| Indo (Misc.) | 128 (92.7) | 32 (67.3) | 160 |
| | 278 | 202 | 480 |

**Table 2**: Data observations from the keyboard task. The data are drawn from 5 subjects in each linguistic group who used keyboard to TURN ON objects as their first task.

| | COMMAND SYNTAX CHOICE | | |
|---|---|---|---|
| LINGUISTIC GROUP | Action-> Object | Object->Action | |
| American | 128 (91.3) | 32 (68.7) | 160 |
| Thai | 106 (91.3) | 54 (68.7) | 160 |
| Indo (Misc.) | 40 (91.3) | 120 (68.7) | 160 |
| | 274 | 206 | 480 |

**Table 3**: Data observations from the keyboard task. The data are drawn from 5 subjects in each linguistic group who used keyboard to TURN OFF objects as their second task.

| | COMMAND SYNTAX CHOICE | | |
|---|---|---|---|
| LINGUISTIC GROUP | Action-> Object | Object->Action | |
| American | 58 (70) | 120 (90) | 160 |
| Thai | 55 (70) | 105 (90) | 160 |
| Indo (Misc.) | 97 (70) | 63 (90) | 160 |
| | 210 | 270 | 480 |

**Table 4**: Data observations from the locator task. The data are drawn from 5 subjects in each linguistic group who used locator to TURN ON objects as their first task.

| | COMMAND SYNTAX CHOICE | | |
|---|---|---|---|
| LINGUISTIC GROUP | Action-> Object | Object->Action | |
| American | 68 (57.7) | 92 (102.3) | 160 |
| Thai | 70 (57.7) | 90 (102.3) | 160 |
| Indo (Misc.) | 35 (57.7) | 125 (102.3) | 160 |
| | 173 | 307 | 480 |

**Table 5**: Data observations from the locator task. The data are drawn from 5 subjects in each linguistic group who used locator to TURN OFF objects as their second task.

Our first hypothesis is that choice of command syntax is influenced by natural language background. More specifically, we hypothesized that our subjects from the Indian subcontinent would have choice patterns for command syntax which would vary from the choice patterns of the other two cultural groups. This turned out to be true; at the $p < 0.05$ level of significance our hypothesis failed to be rejected.

Interestingly enough, an observation revealed that the Indian subcontinent subjects heavily favored the object-action pattern when the shapes were visible and the primary action was making the shapes invisible. On the opposite, these subjects favored the reverse action-object pattern when the shapes were invisible and the action was primarily making the shapes visible. One of the subjects commented that when the shapes were invisible, "they weren't objects." This brings up an interesting questions of how a computer task and its simple components are defined by different cultural groups, and whether there are significant differences in such definitions for certain tasks. As it turned out in our experiment, some of our Indian subcontinent subjects did not feel they were performing the task we thought we had designed (selecting an object, and selecting an action to be performed on the object) when the objects were attached to the "invisibility" attribute.

Our second hypothesis states that our subjects' preferences for command syntax would be influenced by input device used. In other words, the nature of an input device whether it is spatially-oriented or linguistically-oriented would have influence on the choice of command syntax. With the $p < 0.05$ level of significance, this hypothesis failed to be rejected. When using the locator which is spatially-oriented device, subjects tended to "point" to the object first, then specify the action to be performed later. When using the keyboard, subjects tended to have a linguistically-oriented response which is specifying action first in American and Thai subjects and specifying object first in Indian subcontinent subjects.

Though the hypothesis failed to be rejected, observation and discussion with subjects provided interesting insights into how the subjects approached the design tasks differently than what was expected. The selection task via keyboard was expected to be influenced totally by the subjects' linguistic background. However, some of the subjects approached the keyboard task as a cognitive dissonance problem of doing a spatial task looking at graphical feedback while entering commands as a "linguistic" string. They solved the problem for themselves partly by clustering their selections. That is, they would stare at the screen, decided a few shapes they wanted to turn on/off, "memorize" the shape numbers, then looking at the keyboard where they would do a series of

**2nd Hypothesis : Choice of command syntax is influenced by input device.**

| | COMMAND SYNTAX CHOICE | | |
|---|---|---|---|
| INPUT DEVICE | Action -> Object | Object -> Action | |
| Keyboard | 552 (467.5) | 408 (494.5) | 960 |
| Tablet with Locator | 383 (467.5) | 577 (494.5) | 960 |
| | 935 | 985 | 1920 |

**Table 6**: Observations grouped by the independent variable of input device.

commands quickly. The subjects would naturally enter the shape numbers first so to reduce the memory load, thus tagging the action code was an easier mental task to be done after. This accounted for 3 subjects preferring an object-action sequence when entering their choices from the keyboard.

Our last hypothesis was that our non-American subjects would prefer a numeric code to an English alphabetic code for a command. The non-Americans did show patterns of choice significantly different from the Americans, but the dominant choice of all subjects was for the alphabetic code. Additional data gathered from the post-experiment questionnaires revealed that a number of subjects, both American and non-American, thought **yy** meant "yes" and **nn** meant "no" which were easier to remember than the number codes. However, 88% of the non-Americans in their questionnaires thought a numeric code would be easier to learn than an English alphabetic one for a menu selection or a command in a non-English speaking country. This suggested that an experiment to look at meaningless English alphanumeric code choices, perhaps with a longer list of commands to be learned and used, should be explored.

In addition, the post-questionnaires revealed that it was easier for some subjects to remember the shapes distinct from the actions if they remembered one coded in letters and the other in numbers. For some others, they preferred the numeric codes because the numbers were closer on the keyboard to the shape numbers than were the letters. The latter may have to do with the subjects' low typing skills where the keyboard task was approached spatially. In these two cases, cultural background did not seem to make a difference in determining if a subject fell into one of these groups.

**3rd Hypothesis : Choice of command code is influenced by culture.**

| LINGUISTIC GROUP | TYPE OF COMMAND CODE<br>Numeric | <br>English Alphabetic | |
|---|---|---|---|
| American | 107 (119) | 213 (201) | 320 |
| Thai | 138 (119) | 182 (201) | 320 |
| Indo (Misc.) | 111 (119) | 209 (201) | 320 |
| | 356 | 604 | 960 |

**Table 7:** Observations of choices of code, grouped by linguistic group.

| LINGUISTIC GROUP | Action Type: | TYPE OF COMMAND CODE<br>Numeric | <br>English Alphabetic |
|---|---|---|---|
| American | TURN ON: | 43 (62.7) | 117 ( 97.3) |
| | TURN OFF: | 64 (56) | 96 (104) |
| Thai | TURN ON: | 79 (62.7) | 81 ( 97.3) |
| | TURN OFF: | 59 (56) | 101 (104) |
| Indo (Misc.) | TURN ON: | 66 (62.7) | 94 ( 97.3) |
| | TURN OFF: | 45 (56) | 115 (104) |

**Table 8**: Observations in each linguistic group, grouped according to the order of input devices used to consider "trends" between Americans and non-Americans in choice of code. Interestingly, more non-Americans choices were for alpha code when "TURNing OFF" visible shapes, while more Americans choices were for alphabetic codes when "TURNing ON" invisible shapes.

## 4.5 Summary of Experiment

The experiment results bore out the first and the second hypotheses. The subjects' choice of command language syntax were influenced by the linguistic background. However, when an input device with spatially-oriented nature was used, the command language syntax was influenced by the nature of the input device. The data did not show the preference of non-English command codes by the non-American subjects.

The experimental results as well as the observation and discussion with subjects all suggested interesting further directions for cross-cultural experiments. But equally important is that the experimental setting proved productive for generating dialogues and interests in the questions of appropriate computer technology across cultural boundaries.

This was a pilot experiment. Many factors were discovered about the experimental process which suggested how the experiment might be more tightly controlled. One such improvement is to have a more carefully designed task which allows for less individual differences in defining the experimental task — by having all shapes sharing the same attributes either visible or invisible, and by introducing time constraints for each unit task to inhibit clustering of selections, for example.

Our results suggest that people do establish preferences for command language syntax which are both culture-, task- and input device-sensitive. This discovery encourages us, and hopefully the user interface research community as well, to explore further into this unknown territory of cross-cultural differences in using computers.

## 5. Conclusions

One important conclusion drawn is that this and similar experiments can be useful bases for more carefully defining the issues regarding portability of computer technology across cultural boundaries. We have gained a better understanding of the etics vs. emics debate which exists in the field of anthropology: some understandings can be reached by cross-cultural comparisons, while other phenomenon can only be understood within a particular cultural context. Relating this to human factors issues, we can see examples of each. Looking at English keyboard use may not help the Chinese overmuch in designing Chinese character input devices. But looking at differences across cultures in choices of command syntax, or perhaps looking at how quickly items are selected in a row order vs. column order list, might yield very useful insights into appropriateness of certain interaction technologies in different cultural environments.

Asian countries are very diverse in their languages, their societies and their behaviors. This almost guarantees very differing thinking processes — the processes which user interface researchers and cognitive psychologists try to accommodate in the design of human-computer dialogues. Approaching user interface problems with a model of a user as culturally homogeneous, though distinguished by individual class characteristics, will perhaps ease the pain of transferring computer technology from experts to novices. But it will not fully help transferring computer technology from one culture to another. We are sure the attempt to understand the latter will provide useful feedback into the process of understanding the former as well.

The question we would like to leave to user interface researchers and developers to think about is whether it is too much to ask for a single user interface framework to accommodate idiosyncrasies in different cultures so that the interface front-end can be as pleasant as one would like it to be, regardless of a user's culture. Or the question is whether we have not begun to explore this territory and it is now the time to do so.

## Acknowledgement

We would like to thank all of our international friends who contributed to the language difference aspects of this research especially Viraf Bankwalla and Zamir Iqbal for Urdu script, Yan Cheng for Chinese script, Gyu Moon for Korean script, and Sayed Hussen and Abdelhamid Gaafar for Arabic script. An international environment such as one at the George Washington University allows the research in the area of cross-cultural factors in user interfaces to be possible. Without it, the research in this area may never be envisioned.

We would like to thank the Indian Student Association at GWU who helped us draw subjects from the Indian population. We also would like to thank all of our subjects for their time participating in our experiment without being paid. Their injectures and comments are also useful for future studies in this area.

Lastly, Piyawadee Sukaviriya would like to thank Prof. James D. Foley, her advisor, for allowing her to spend her time writing this article rather than doing her dissertation. This research is partially sponsored by the National Science Foundation.

## REFERENCES

Ahmad, M. 1978. "The Effect of Language on the Identification of Pictorial Stimuli." *Programmed Learning and Educational Technology*. Vol 15/ I. pp. 35-41.

Allen, James. 1988. *Natural Language Understanding*. California : The Benjamin/ Cummings Publishing Company, Inc.

Becker, Joseph. 1985. "Typing Chinese, Japanese, and Korean." IEEE Computer. Vol. 18, No. 1, January. pp. 27-34.

Card, Stuart.; Moran, Thomas P; and Newell, Allen. 1983. *The Psychology of Human Computer Interaction*. Hillsdale, New Jersey : Lawrence Erlbaum Associates.

Chu, Kai. 1986. "The Cognitive Aspect of Chinese Character Processing." in *Visual Languages*, edited by Chang, S.; Ichikawa, T; and Ligomenides, P.A. New York : Plenum Press. pp. 349-392.

*Communication, Language and Meaning: Psychological Perspectives*, edited by Miller, George A. 1973. New York : Basic Books.

Cook, B.L. 1980. "Picture Communication in Papua New Guinea." *Educational Broadcasting International*. Vol. 13/2. pp. 78-83.

Foley, James D. and Van Dam, A. 1982. *Fundamentals of Interactive Computer Graphics*. California : Addison-Wesley Publishing Company.

Fussell, D. and Haaland, A. 1978. "Communicating with Pictures in Nepal: Results of Practical Study used in Visual Education." *Education Broadcasting International* vol. II/I. pp. 25-31.

Goldsmith, Evelyn. 1984. *Research into Illustration : An Approach and A Review*. Cambridge, London : Cambridge University Press.

Huang, Jack K. 1985. "The Input and Output of Chinese and Japanese Characters." IEEE Computer. Vol. 18, No. 1, January. pp.18-24.

Johnson, Robert. 1976. *Elementary Statistics*, 2$^{nd}$ Edition. North Scituate, Massachusetts : Duxbury Press.

Kennedy, J.M. and Ross, A.S. 1975. "Outline Picture Perception by the Songe of Papua." *Perception*. vol. 4. pp. 391-406.

Kim, Won C. 1989. *Automatic Design: the User Interface Presentation Component*. A dissertation proposal. Dept. of EE&CS, The George Washington University.

Mendenhall, William. 1979. *Introduction to Probability and Statistics*, 5th edition. North Scituate, Massachusetts : Duxbury Press.

Suwa, Motoi. 1989. Personal communication. An interview with Mr. Motoi Suwa from Electrotechnical Laboratory, Japan, at CHI'89 Conference, Austin, Texas. May 3.

Nielsen, Jakob. 1986. "A Virtual Protocol Model for Computer-Human Interaction." *International Journal of Man-Machine Studies*. Vol. 24. pp. 301-312.

*The New Encyclopædia Britanica*. 1986. vol. 22 Macropædia : Knowledge in Depth, 15th edition. Chicago : Encyclopædia Britanica, Inc.

*Parsing Natural Language*, edited by King, Margaret. 1986. London : Academic Press.

Pelto, Pertti. 1970. *Anthropological Research: The Structure of Inquiry*. New York : Harper and Row.

*Rand McNally Cosmopolitan World Atlas*. 1972. Chicago : Rand McNally and Company.

Shneiderman, Ben. 1983. "Direct Manipulation : A Step Beyond Programming Languages." *IEEE Computer* Vol. 16, No. 8. pp. 57-69.

*The World Almanac and Book of Facts*, edited by Hoffman, Mark. S. 1989. New York : World Almanac.

# INTERNATIONAL USER INTERFACES

**Rosalie A. Zobel-Pocock**

Commission of the European Communities. Directorate-General XIII, Brussels, Belgium

ABSTRACT

This section introduces the requirements of operating systems and applications able to interact with the user in his or her native language. These requirements are examined in the context of UNIX System V (*), the only operating system to have been successfully modified to support multiple languages on one system.

The example of Japanese Language Input is used to highlight the differences between user interaction in a European language and in a language written in a very different script.

Finally a vision of future is explored, in which a person can converse (and write) in one language to another person on the other side of the world, who hears (and reads) in his or her own language.

(*) Unix System V is a trade mark of AT&T Bell Laboratories in the USA and other countries.

## 1. INTRODUCTION

Until about four years ago it was assumed that to use a computer system one had to speak English. Commands and responses, issued in a terse form of technical English, were extremely difficult for even native English speakers to understand. No thought was given to the needs of non-English speaking users throughout the world. This situation represented the ultimate in the neglect of basic human factors issues for computer users in those regions.

The historical reasons are obvious. The first large computer manufacturers were from the United States, and set the trend for others. The initial use of computers was in scientific and technical applications, and it could be safely assumed that English was understood in this environment. As the use of computers spread to the millions of non-technical workers in offices and business, it became essential to offer user interfaces which communicate in the users' native languages.

This section of the tutorial concentrates on the requirements for international user interfaces, which implies not only the support of international features in the operating system, but also in their use applications programmes and utilities.

## 2. REQUIREMENTS OF MULTI-LINGUAL OPERATING SYSTEMS

The essential requirements of a multi-lingual operating system are :

- Supplementary code-sets to allow the use by an application of multiple character symbols in addition to the conventional use of the ASCII code-set for English.

  These code-sets must not be confined to traditional 7-bit and 8-bit code-sets. At least 16-bit code-sets are needed for the languages of Far Eastern countries (Japan, China, Korea). In order to represent all existing Chinese characters a 24-bit code-set is required. The reason is that at least 4000 Chinese characters are used in written Japanese and Chinese documents.
- Device drivers which map the internal code-sets of the operating system to the external code-set, and therefore conventions, of a particular device (e.g. Japanese printer). This may be classed as a virtual terminal function.
- Operating system commands, responses and error messages in many languages. This implies keeping tables of messages in different languages separate from the operating system code which uses them.
- Language selection at the user-level to allow users of different languages to use the same system at the same time in their own language. A single user should be able to switch from language to language during a single task. This implies the support of the requirements of multi-lingual applications, as supplied in the next section.

## 3. REQUIREMENTS OF MULTI-LINGUAL APPLICATIONS

Multi-lingual applications must not only be able to interact with the user in a specific language, but must in addition pay attention to local conventions. Applications should be designed to be portable and convention-independant. This requires operating systems utilities and interfaces to support both implicit and explicit invocation of such conventions.

Local conventions which must be supported are :

- Collating Sequence. More than one collating sequence for a specific code-set must be provided. Utilities which sort must be modified to allow different collating sequences, and tools must be provided to support the definition of these sequences.
- Character Classification. Character classes must be defined by language. Utilities are required which return an indication of which code-set a particular character comes from.
- Date and Time Format. The capability to enter and display the date and time in the local place is required, in the local language and format. All utilities and services which operate with date/time must support this.
- Numeric Representation. The capability to define rules for numeric editing (such as decimal delimiter) must be provided.
- Currency Representation. The capability to specify rules and formats for editing local currency must be provided.
- Toolkits. These must be available to support different languages and cultures. Icons (e.g.

waste-bin, buttons, menus) may need different representations in different cultures. Most existing toolkits have been designed for the Western culture, and are not appropriate in the East. Eastern toolkits require different cognitive analysis from those used in Western cultures.

- Device Handling. Applications (e.g. word-processors) must take into account writing conventions in different cultures. For example, in Arabic and Hebrew writing is from right to left, in traditional Chinese and Japanese from top to bottom and right to left.

The simple display handling of such features is an independant virtual terminal (device driver) function. However, there are implications in, for example, a word-processing application.

- Ergonomic Aspects. In Far Eastern languages large high-resolution screens are required in order to be able to read the complex character sets. Special input methods are required to allow the easy entry of these complex character sets at the terminal.

It should be noted that convention independance is possible in some applications, and between some languages, and has been used in some applications. For example, a simple copy utility may be built which can be used in English, German, French, even Chinese. More complex applications may be impossible to design in this way. For example it has not so far been possible to design a single, integrated word-processing package which can be used in English and Japanese. The two languages, their display, and conventions are so different that it has been necessary to design the two word processors independently.

Similarly operating systems applications should be designed so that dialogues with the user are based on tables which can be easily interchanged.

## 4. EXISTING INTERNATIONAL SYSTEMS

Most computer manufacturers have implemented international features in their operating systems and applications in an ad hoc manner, dictated by the immediate needs of specific markets or users. Operating systems have been modified to support specific languages, without any account being taken of the overall requirements of internationalisation. In the Far East, Western manufacturers were forced to supply Japanese and Chinese-language systems due to the local competitive environment, which already provided such features. In Europe, since the marketing issues were less critical, little was done by manufacturers, except for character-set support. Local applications developers provided applications where possible in local languages and conventions.

In recent years, due to pressure for a standard operating system for all sizes of computer worldwide, the needs of multinational companies, and the need to minimize software development effort, the UNIX System V operating system has been modified to support in one system many of the internationalisation requirements described above. This activity was heavily influenced by the X/OPEN Group in Europe, the Japan UNIX Advisory Board, and user groups in China and the Middle East. An attempt has been made to provide a single operating system kernel, which is useful anywhere in the world, with the addition of appropriate national supplements (e.g. message tables, code-sets). This has not been performed for any other operating system.

## 5. INTERNATIONALISATION OF UNIX SYSTEM V

Internationalisation has been provided in UNIX System V in the following way :

- Messages and text from the kernel, utilities and applications programs are separated modularly to support various national languages (at present English, French, German, Italian, Japanese, Chinese, Korean, Thai).
- Local conventions for date and time, collating sequences, numeric and currency representations are supported transparently depending on the language selected by the user.
- Sixteen-bit and eight-bit code-sets are supported.
- Language selection is provided at the user level. Different users may use the system at the same time in their respective languages.
- The device driver is solely responsible for mapping an external code-set to an internal code-set and vice versa. External code-sets are those code-sets generated by input/output devices (e.g. terminals, printers). An internal code-set is a transformation of the external code-set into a code-set recognised by the operating system.

### 5.1 The UNIX System V Code-Sets

A code-set template is used to transform external code-sets into a code-set understood by UNIX, its utilities and applications. The internal coding method is based on the ISO 2022 and ISO 6937/3 standards for code extension techniques, which suggest the following two alternative techniques for shifting between code-sets :

. single-shift
. locking-shift

The single-shift is a single byte used to announce a temporary shift to another code-set. The byte, or for 16-bit code sets 2-bytes, immediately following the single-shift code are interpreted as part of a new code-set. Subsequent characters are interpreted as belonging to the primary code-set.

The ISO standard defines two single-shift characters :

. SS2 hexadecimal 8e
. SS3 hexadecimal 8f

The locking-shift technique may be used to temporarilly shift-in and shift-out of code-sets. It consists of a pair of character sequences that allow a new code-set to be used for more than one character. Whilst in the context of a locking-shift sequence, all characters, with the exception of single-shifted characters, are assumed to belong to the new code-set.

Because of context sensitivity the locking-shift has not been used in UNIX System V. The single-shift method has been choosen.

In addition to using the single-shift, the eighth-bit is used to distinguish between the primary code-set and characters in one of three supplementary code-sets. By using the combination of eighth-bit and single-shift characters, the internal coding method specifies a template which allows four code-sets to exist simultaneously :

Set 0 (primary) OXXXXXXX (always ASCII)
Set 1 (supplementary N° 1) 1XXXXXXX or
1XXXXXXX 1XXXXXXX
1XXXXXXX 1XXXXXXX 1XXXXXXX
Set 2 (supplementary N° 2) SS2 1XXXXXXX or
SS2 1XXXXXXX 1XXXXXXX
SS2 1XXXXXXX 1XXXXXXX 1XXXXXXX
Set 3 (supplementary N° 3) SS3 1XXXXXXX or
SS3 1XXXXXX 1XXXXXXX
SS3 1XXXXXXX 1XXXXXXX 1XXXXXXX

Designating the exact value is by code-set designation. This variable is dynamic and accessible/modifiable at the operating system, utility and application levels to satisfy the need to support multiple code-sets. It is also available at the file level, so that files encoded in different code-sets can exist in the same system.

Code-set designation meets the following requirements :

- Code-set designations are supported at file level. Each file contains its own set of code-set designation values.
- At file creation time, all files are designated with a system-wide default value.
- Code-set designations are changeable dynamically.
- The code-set designation should contain information on :
  . the width of a character in the code-set
  . the specific code-set designated
- Code-set designation information is transferrable with the file content across networks.

In addition to code-set designation, a language-designation is needed to specify the overall profile of the user's environment. This variable, stored in the user profile, denotes the language and local conventions for that user. It is initially assigned at login time, but can be changed at any time by the user.

Supplementary code-sets are assigned at the user's discretion when processing these Extended UNIX Codes (EUC), the system first checks the most significant bit of the first byte to determine if it is in the primary or a supplementary code-set.

## 6. THE EXAMPLE OF JAPANESE LANGUAGE INPUT METHOD

The example of Japanese language input at a terminal is interesting, since it is probably the most different from English. Nevertheless, it fits the model of levels of abstraction described in Chapter 2 of the tutorial i.e. dialog management, abstract imaging, device sharing, physical independance.

### 6.1 Dialogue Management

In Japan four character sets are normally used in a single written document :

- **Romaji** : Roman character, as in English. These are rarely used in Japanese, but may be used to quote from foreign texts etc.

- **Katakana** : a phonetic characters set of less than 64 characters used to represent foreign words in Japanese.
- **Hiragana** : a phonetic character set of less than 64 characters used to represent Japanese modifiers (post-positions). This is necessary since the Japanese language does not easily fit the Chinese character set. It is more heavily modified than Chinese.
- **Kanji** : the Chinese characters used as the root of all Japanese nouns, verbs etc. For each Kanji there are several sounds, and for each sound in Japanese there are several Kanji. Over 4000 Kanji are in everyday use in Japan. Many other archaic forms exist.

Attachment 1 shows an example of a page of Japanese incorporating all four character sets. These character sets are represented in UNIX System V by using the primary code-set for ASCII (Romaji), supplementary set I for the kana scripts, and supplementary set 2 for Kanji. Supplementary set 3 may be used for archaic or foreign Chinese characters (Gaiji).

It is obviously extremely difficult to input Kanji from a keyboard, due to the enormous number of characters. Therefore Japanese is input in Katakana and/or Hiragana, and a special dialog management programme (or input method) is used to convert from Katakana to Kanji. Due to the one to many mapping, several Kanji exist for each input phonetic sound, entered as one or more Katakana. The user must choose the correct one from a number of Kanji characters displayed on the screen. In some cases there are more than 20 to choose from.

Advances in artificial intelligence have made it possible to automate much of this dialog handling. Kanji can now be chosen by the dialog handler from the context, and user intervention is only required where ambiguity exists. This has speeded up Japanese typing so that the language can be typed almost as fast as Western languages.

### 6.2 Abstract Imaging/Device Sharing

Windowing systems are used similarly in Japan. Any commands for manipulating windows or images is also in Japanese.

### 6.3 Physical Independence

The four external code-sets used on a Japanese terminal are converted by the device driver into 16-bit and 8-bit internal code-sets for processing by UNIX. The method used in UNIX System V is known as STREAMS. The UNIX OS itself is totally independent of the character set displayed at the device. The device driver, or virtual terminal for the screen, handles the device-dependencies.

### 6.4 System Defined Words in Japanese UNIX

UNIX System V defines a number of special words used to identify, for example, system resources, user and group names, peripherals etc. These are known as system defined words.

In the Japanese version of UNIX (JAE 2.0) some system defined words are used only with the primary ASCII code-set, mainly for the needs of network management worldwide. These inlcude :

- User names
- Group names
- Passwords
- Names of devices, terminals, printers, tapes etc
- System names
- Process ID numbers

Some system defined words may be specified using either ASCII character set or combinations of characters from the primary and supplementary character sets. These include :

- File names
- Directory names
- Command names
- File system names

There are restrictions on the number of bytes which can be used for these names.

It should be noted that a single UNIX system is able to handle such a Japanese dialog on one terminal, and other languages (e.g. German, French) on others.

## 7. FUTURE INTERNATIONAL INTERFACES

In the next ten years, when the problems of continuous voice recognition have been overcome, it is likely that voice will become an important user interface to computers. This will make it very much easier for users to communicate with computers in their own languages, for certain suitable applications. Computers will become part of our daily life, and it will be normal to tell the garage door to open, use our voice pattern as a security check, turn of the lights by voice, annotate and edit text by voice, etc. All of these applications will be internationalised for specific areas of the world.

Another interesting application is the building of automatic translation into interfaces to networked computers. We can look forward to the time when we speak in English to our computer asking it to buy stocks on the Tokyo Stock Exchange. The message, translated into an intermediate language from English, is sent to Tokyo, where it is translated into Japanese, and the stocks bought. A reverse process transmits a Japanese message to the purchaser which is translated to inform in voice or text in English that the transaction has taken place. Within our lifetime it is likely that such services will be provided, on an international basis, much as the telephone service is today. They will provide voice services coupled with fully integrated high-resolution interactive colour graphics to allow the user access to information services in any language. The ultimate aim is a telephone (or electronic mail) service in which a user of one language can communicate transparently with another person speaking a different language anywhere in the world.

# ワイン・リスト Katakana : Wine List

Kanji

ドイツ連邦共和国参議院議長・ラインラント・ファルツ州首相
ベルンハルト・フォーゲル来日記念ドイツワイン・レセプション

1. Rheinhessen
   1986er Rheinhessen Silvaner QbA, trocken } Romaji
   Weingut Stallmannshof
   ラインヘッセン・シルバーナー、Q.b.A. 辛口

   ラベル上のRSという文字はラインヘッセン・シルバーナー・ワインを意味し、このRSワインは、厳選されたシルバーナー種のみを使用しRS・ワイン醸造所同盟のワインケラーにおいて厳正な規制に基づき造られた辛口のワインです。

   輸入元: 雪印乳業(株) tel. 06-397-2078(大阪)/03-226-2420(東京)

2. Rheingau
   1986er Schloss Vollrads Riesling Q.b.A., halbtrocken
   Schloss Vollrads
   シュロス・フォルラーツ、リースリング、Q.b.A. 半辛口

   シュロス・フォルラーツはワイン生産地域のなかでも最高峰のひとつに数えられるラインガウで長い伝統を持つ名門の醸造家であり、リースリングの上品な酸味を生かした辛口の個性あるワインを生み出しています。

   輸入元: サントリー(株) tel: 06-346-1131(大阪)/03-470-1131(東京)

3. Württemberg
   1983er Stettener Heuchelberg Kerner Kabinett
   Württembergische Weingärtner Zentralgenossenschaft
   シュテッテナー・ホイヒェルベルク、ケルナー、カビネット

   ヴュルテムベルクはネッカー河とその支流に位置し、その作付面積のおよそ半分が赤ワイン用のぶどうで占められています。シュテッテナー村はヴュルテムベルク地域の西側に位置しています。このホイヒェルベルクはケルナー種で造られており、香りはケルナー種独特のフルーティーで甘い香りをかもし出します。

   輸入元: ヤマオカゾーン tel. 03-445-6853

   Hiragana Kanji Katakana Romaji

4. Baden
   1983er Achkarrener Schlossberg Ruländer Kabinett
   Winzergenossenschaft Achkarren
   アッハカーレナー・シュロスベルク、ルーレンダー、カビネット

   アッハカーレン村はバーデン地域のカイザーシュトゥール・トゥーニベルグ地区にあり品質の良いワインが産出されています。香りはルーレンダー独特のブーケをかもし出し、味は甘味の押さえられた厚みのあるしっかりしたワインとなっています。

   輸入元: ヤマオカゾーン tel. 03-445-6853

Example of Fou Japanese character Sets

Attachment 1

# Japanese Syllabary Chart

Hiragana / Katakana / Phonetic sound

| | K | S | t | n | h | m | Y | r | W | n |
|---|---|---|---|---|---|---|---|---|---|---|
| あ ア a | か カ ka | さ サ sa | た タ ta | な ナ na | は ハ ha | ま マ ma | や ヤ ya | ら ラ ra | わ ワ wa | ん ン n |
| い イ i | き キ ki | し シ shi | ち チ chi | に ニ ni | ひ ヒ hi | み ミ mi | | り リ ri | | |
| う ウ u | く ク ku | す ス su | つ ツ tsu | ぬ ヌ nu | ふ フ fu | む ム mu | ゆ ユ yu | る ル ru | | |
| え エ e | け ケ ke | せ セ se | て テ te | ね ネ ne | へ ヘ he | め メ me | | れ レ re | | |
| お オ o | こ コ ko | そ ソ so | と ト to | の ノ no | ほ ホ ho | も モ mo | よ ヨ yo | ろ ロ ro | を ヲ o | |

| G | Z | D | B | P |
|---|---|---|---|---|
| が ガ ga | ざ ザ za | だ ダ da | ば バ ba | ぱ パ pa |
| ぎ ギ gi | じ ジ ji | ぢ ヂ ji | び ビ bi | ぴ ピ pi |
| ぐ グ gu | ず ズ zu | づ ヅ zu | ぶ ブ bu | ぷ プ pu |
| げ ゲ ge | ぜ ゼ ze | で デ de | べ ベ be | ぺ ペ pe |
| ご ゴ go | ぞ ゾ zo | ど ド do | ぼ ボ bo | ぽ ポ po |

| | | | | | |
|---|---|---|---|---|---|
| きゃ キャ kya | ぎゃ ギャ gya | しゃ シャ sha | じゃ ジャ ja | ちゃ チャ cha | ぢゃ ヂャ ja |
| きゅ キュ kyu | ぎゅ ギュ gyu | しゅ シュ shu | じゅ ジュ ju | ちゅ チュ chu | ぢゅ ヂュ ju |
| きょ キョ kyo | ぎょ ギョ gyo | しょ ショ sho | じょ ジョ jo | ちょ チョ cho | ぢょ ヂョ jo |

| | | | | | |
|---|---|---|---|---|---|
| にゃ ニャ nya | ひゃ ヒャ hya | びゃ ビャ bya | ぴゃ ピャ pya | みゃ ミャ mya | りゃ リャ rya |
| にゅ ニュ nyu | ひゅ ヒュ hyu | びゅ ビュ byu | ぴゅ ピュ pyu | みゅ ミュ myu | りゅ リュ ryu |
| にょ ニョ nyo | ひょ ヒョ hyo | びょ ビョ byo | ぴょ ピョ pyo | みょ ミョ myo | りょ リョ ryo |

1) For aa add あ
2) ii add い
3) uu add う
4) ee add い    Exceptions おねえさん
5) oo add う    "    おおきい
ふおり . と

# Index